BOUNDARIES OF FREEDOM

BOUNDARIES OF FREEDOM

The Quantum Proposal
of Divine Sovereignty and Human Responsibility

LEE THAI, MD

Foreword by Gerry Breshears

RESOURCE *Publications* · Eugene, Oregon

BOUNDARIES OF FREEDOM
The Quantum Proposal of Divine Sovereignty and Human Responsibility

Resource Publications
An Imprint of Wipf and Stock Publishers
199 W. 8th Ave., Suite 3
Eugene, OR 97401

www.wipfandstock.com

PAPERBACK ISBN: 978-1-5326-5836-5
HARDCOVER ISBN: 978-1-5326-5837-2
EBOOK ISBN: 978-1-5326-5838-9

Manufactured in the U.S.A.   01/09/19

Contents

Foreword

DOES GOD ORDAIN TERRORIST attacks? Does He predetermine thousands of deaths from tsunamis? How about child abuse and pregnancies from rapes? Does our loving Lord *sovereignly* decree these horrendous evils or are they the results of Man's *free will*?

On a more personal level, why was my friend brutally murdered during a robbery? Was that the Lord's foreordained plan for his life or was it just the consequence of the robber's evil choice? Why did I have melanoma? Was that God's doing or was it the by-product of too much sun in my New Mexico childhood? We have all struggled with these questions. They have plagued fellow sufferers since the dawn of Christianity.

In the first section of the book, Lee Thai, a graduate of Western Seminary where I am a professor of theology, shows that the answers given over the centuries (Calvinism, Arminianism, Molinism, and Open Theism) are ultimately not successful. Using extensive quotes from well-known scholars, he treats the various theological systems with sensitivity and fairness. The tone is irenic as this is an in-house conversation among brothers and sisters in Christ.

In the next section, Thai uses his combined training in science and theology to propose a better resolution to the dilemma of God's sovereignty and Man's free will. This proposal with ten concise tenets, can be summarized as "Man has freedom of choice within God's sovereign boundaries." Thai carefully demonstrates that the standard claim that God only gives Man *one* option, either by foreknowledge or decree, is logically fallacious. As clearly stated in the Scriptures, Adam was given two options by God (i.e., obey or disobey), and was not limited to the one and only path of disobedience.

Thai's proposal is then applied to ten thorny theological problems, most notably the question, "Who is responsible for evil in this world? God or Man?" He thoughtfully supports his argument with numerous

Scriptures from both the Old and the New Testaments. Difficult problems, such as "Was Judas preordained to be lost?" and "Was Jesus deceitful in offering the kingdom to Israel without any possibility of giving?" resolve as we recognize that we indeed have God-given choices within His sovereign boundaries.

Why is it important for us to move toward resolution of the problem of free will and sovereignty? If whatever happens is permitted or decreed by "God's will," then it surely seems to mandate fatalism. If the balance is toward free choice, then it sure seems that God's plan is held captive to our sinful choices. However, if we are given real choices within God's preset confines, we can seek the Lord's advice to choose the best possible alternative. We are not "doomed" to the one and only path foreknown or foreordained by Him. Thus, prayer does change the outcome as we are able to select His recommended option among the various God-given alternatives. We can make wise choices within His blessable options in choosing the most suitable career. We can pray for His help in trials and temptations.

Why does God not prevent these challenges from coming into our lives (e.g., my melanoma)? Thai suggests that God can use evil in our lives for the purpose of edification (e.g., Job), discipline (e.g., Israel), deterrence (e.g., Paul's thorn in the flesh), or rehabilitation (e.g., Peter's denials). As we go through trials, we can trust that God is loving enough and powerful enough to do good no matter how horrific the evil.

In the last section, Thai gives us twelve practical principles we can use in our everyday lives. While we have freedom to choose within God's boundaries, we need to understand that obedience leads to blessings and disobedience leads to discipline. Therefore, we commit ourselves to follow wisely and obediently, to let "thy will be done on earth as it is in heaven."

This groundbreaking work addresses a conundrum that has plagued the Church for centuries. Thai explains deep theological issues in lay terms; so, it is accessible to regular church people as well as being thought-provoking to more academically-focused Christians. Anyone who wants to find God's best option among His given alternatives will do well to read and ponder.

Lee Thai has done some wonderfully creative work here building from the quantum physics model into a way to connect God's omniscience/sovereignty and human choice. It will be especially helpful to those with a bit of a scientific bent. One thing I really like is that his proposal incorporates the "Calminian" idea that God has His way of doing different things with different people. Because Thai bypasses some of the endless wrangling with this age-old problem (dare I call it a foolish controversy in many cases?), he does the Church a great service by helping people come to where they can trust the God of the Bible in the face of terrible disappointments in life and horrible results of disobedience.

Gerry Breshears, PhD
Professor of Theology
Western Seminary, Portland

Preface

Dear Readers,

The problem of God's sovereignty/man's free will and the related problem of evil have troubled me since my early days as a Christian. How could a good and loving God decree (Calvinism) or permit (Arminianism) all the unspeakable evils in this world (e.g., the Holocaust)? Who is responsible for the mass murders, child abuses, and pregnancies from rape that we hear about every day? The sovereign Lord or men with free will? Did God foreordain the Columbine High School shooting and the 2017 Las Vegas massacre? Or were they the results of men exercising their freedom to commit horrendous evils?

Although I was a full-time physician, I decided to go to seminary (part-time over eight years) to get some resolutions for my nagging questions. Little did I realize that none of my professors knew the answers either! The quandary of God's sovereignty and Man's free will has plagued Christendom for almost two thousand years. The proposed solutions (Calvinism, Arminianism, Molinism, and Open Theism) caused further dissensions in the Church rather than helped unite the body of believers.

With a background in science, I have endeavored to look at the problem from a different perspective. Was the conundrum a result of Man's faulty reasoning? Were there any fallacies in the claim that God decreed or permitted the evils we experience in this world?

This book is the result of a painstaking research spanning over a decade. If you ever wonder whether God preordained our horrendous pains and sufferings, whether He will change His mind in response to our desperate prayers, or whether we are doomed to whatever fate He predetermined for us, the Quantum Proposal will supply the needed answers using Scriptures from both the Old and New Testaments.

In science, any new proposal needs to be peer-reviewed prior to publication, especially concerning a problem that has eluded the best efforts of scholars for centuries. In that spirit, Dr. Randal Roberts, the president of Western Seminary, Dr. Gerry Breshears, Professor of Theology at Western, and Dr. John DelHousaye of Phoenix Seminary were kind enough to review the manuscript and give me their endorsements. I would like to thank them for their advice and support. Vickie, my wife of thirty-four years, and my two (engineer) children, Daniel and Joshua have provided me with valuable help and feedback. Thank you!

Finally, I would like to dedicate this book to you, my readers, with the hope that we may all "grow in the grace and knowledge of our Lord and Savior Jesus Christ. To Him be the glory, both now and to the day of eternity. Amen." (2 Peter 3:18).

PART ONE

Classical Understanding

Chapter 1

Definitions

THERE ARE AS MANY definitions of sovereignty as there are definitions of love. Some statements about love are whimsical ("Love at first sight is cured by a second look").[1] Others reveal a deeper truth (love is "either a horrible disease or a blessing").[2] Likewise, "sovereignty" means different things to different people. Is sovereignty "a word that is used often but it has really no specific meaning"?[3] Is sovereignty something to be feared? "In the absence of justice, what is sovereignty but organized robbery?"[4] Is God's sovereignty so fragile that "all human kingship risks a denial of the sovereignty of God"?[5] Unless we agree on the definitions, we may be talking to each other at cross-purposes!

DEFINITION OF GOD'S SOVEREIGNTY.

Instead of conjuring up my own interpretation and unfairly advancing my proposal, I have chosen to combine the explanations of five theologians into a "master" statement of God's sovereignty. However, when we discuss the various theological schools (e.g., Calvinism, Arminianism), we will use their specific definitions.

---

1. https://holidappy.com/greeting-cards/Top-10-Best-Funny-Love-Quotes

2. https://thoughtcatalog.com/marisa-donnelly/2016/04/36-definitions-of-love-according-to-urban-dictionary/

3. Zbigniew Brzezinski. www.brainyquote.com/topics/sovereignty

4. Augustine. www.brainyquote.com/topics/sovereignty

5. Peter Hollingworth. www.brainyquote.com/topics/sovereignty

Dr. Norman Geisler stated: "Sovereignty is God's control over his creation, dealing with his governance over it."[6] Dr. Charles Ryrie wrote: "The word means principal, chief, supreme. It speaks first of position (God is the chief being in the universe), then of power (God is supreme in power in the universe) . . . Ultimately, God is in control of all things, though he may choose to let certain events happen according to natural laws which he has ordained."[7] Dr. R. C. Sproul said: "Sovereignty is a natural attribute of the creator. God owns what he makes, and he rules what he owns."[8] Dr. J. I. Packer explained: "Divine sovereignty is a vast subject: it embraces everything that comes into the biblical picture of God as Lord and King in his world, the one who 'worketh all things after the counsel of his own will' (Eph 1:11), directing every process and ordering every event for the fulfilling of his own eternal plan."[9] The scholar Arthur W. Pink affirmed: "To say that God is sovereign is to declare that he is the Almighty, the possessor of all power in heaven and earth, so that none can defeat his counsels, thwart his purpose, or resist his will."[10] A "master" definition of God's sovereignty can be as follows:

> *God's sovereignty is God's control over all things, directing every process and ordering every event for the fulfilling of his sovereign will, though he may choose to let certain events happen according to natural laws which he has ordained. God owns what he makes, and he rules what he owns. No one can defeat his counsels, thwart his purpose, or resist his will.*

We can condense this explanation into a logical proposition and then illustrate it with a diagram. After all, "a picture is worth a thousand words."[11]

ILLUSTRATION OF GOD'S SOVEREIGNTY.

Since God is sovereign, today or in the past or timelessly, he foreknows/decrees that I will go to the gym tomorrow. "A" stands for "I will go to the

6. Geisler, *Systematic Theology, Vol. 2*, 536.

7. Ryrie, *Basic Theology*, 43.

8. Sproul, *Now, That's a Good Question!* 26.

9. Packer, *Evangelism and the Sovereignty of God*, 13–14.

10. Pink, *The Sovereignty of God*, 15.

11. "Use a picture, it's worth a thousand words." in "Speakers Give Sound Advice." Syracuse Post Standard, page 18. March 28, 1911.

gym tomorrow." "B" stands for "I will stay home and not go to the gym tomorrow." God's sovereignty can be represented by the proposition: A is true, and B is false.

Path A (go to the gym)

However, *if* God decrees that I will stay home tomorrow, the diagram will change to: path A is false, non-existent, and not possible while path B is true, real, and fixed.

Path B (stay home, not go to the gym)

God's sovereignty can be visualized as a fixed, decreed, and foreknown path from all eternity. *The future will be whatever God had decided.* This interpretation of God's sovereignty immediately raises difficult questions. Was the September 11 terrorist attack foreordained by the omniscient Lord? Did he sovereignly decree that my two-year-old boy would have heart trouble? Why did he allow a drunk driver to hurt my loved ones? We will address these questions later in the book.

A STORY OF GOD'S SOVEREIGNTY.

I was born in South Vietnam and raised as a Buddhist. My family and I often went to pagodas to beg favors from the deities (Buddhism is not a monotheistic religion). We also worshiped our ancestors as they surely would want to help their descendants "live long and prosper." Furthermore, to hedge our bets, we occasionally visited Hindu temples with their cornucopia of gods and goddesses to keep everyone happy. After all, hell hath no fury like a goddess scorned!

In 1972, at the age of seventeen, I went to America to pursue my college studies. Sadly, South Vietnam fell to the communists in April 1975. My dad passed away during the debacle (my mom died when I was young). Overnight, I became an orphan without a country and with no source of income. Alone and despondent, I sat in the dormitory over Christmas, starving since the cafeteria was closed and my bank account was empty. My desperate cries to the gods went unanswered. The thought of jumping out of the window to end the misery crossed my mind. While I was mulling the decision, an American friend came by and kindly invited me to his home. Hearing about the lavish holiday spreads, my gurgling stomach overruled my morbid brain, causing my spindly legs to hustle me to the benefactor's car. After many sumptuous meals, my friend asked if I would like to read the Bible. Sure, why not? What had my gods done to help me? I learned that Jesus, the only true God, promised to love and care for me in this life and the one to come. With my friend's blessing, I became a Christian in January 1976.

In all honesty, had my dad been alive, I would not have changed religion. That was a clan decision in Vietnam, not an individual choice. "Family conversion," reflecting an Eastern culture, was the norm in the New Testament (e.g., the Philippian jailer "and all his family" were converted in Acts 16:33). Looking back, I am still amazed by God's omniscience and omnipotence. The compassionate Lord called a destitute kid across a vast ocean, saved him from certain death, and appointed him to eternal life! However, was I predestined to salvation by the sovereign God or did I exercise my "free will" to accept Christ? What exactly is "free will"?

DEFINITION OF MAN'S FREE WILL.

As with "sovereignty," there are many definitions of "free will." Is free will somewhat of an illusion? "No one has free will until they are an adult, and by then the choices that were made for them, have already set them on a course that gives limited freedom in the choices to be made."[12] Or is Man's free will absolute? "Zeus himself cannot get the better of my free will."[13] Setting aside these musings, I have used the statements of five philosophers to craft a working definition of free will.

Thomas Hobbes said: "A free agent is he that can do if he will, and forbear if he will; and that liberty is the absence of external impediments."[14] David Hume defined free will as the "power of acting or not acting, according to the determinations of the will."[15] Peter Voss, a philosopher and entrepreneur, wrote: "Free will means that we are self-determined, not (ultimately) subject to forces outside of our control—it means, we could have done otherwise."[16] Dr. Robert Kane stated: "We view ourselves as agents with free will from a personal standpoint, we think of ourselves as capable of influencing the world in various ways. Open alternatives seem to lie before us. We reason or deliberate among them and choose."[17] Dr. Randolph Clarke asserted: "I shall say that when an agent acts freely (or with free will), she is able to do other than what she does then."[18] Combining these explanations, we can define Man's free will as follows:

> Free will means that we are self-determined free agents, not (ultimately) subject to forces outside of our control and to external impediments. Open alternatives seem to lie before us. We reason or deliberate among them and choose according to the determinations of our will. We are able to do other than what we do.

Let us condense this definition into a logical proposition and visualize it in a diagram. This will help us see the conundrum that has plagued Christianity for centuries.

12. www.goodreads.com/quotes/385604-no-one-has-free-will-until-they-are-an-adult

13. www.goodreads.com/quotes/472663-you-may-fetter-my-leg-but-zeus-himself-cannot-get

14. Hobbes, *Of Liberty and Necessity*, 35.

15. Hume, *An Enquiry Concerning Human Understanding*, 53.

16. Voss, "The Nature of Free Will," lines 46–47.

17. Kane, "Introduction," 4–5.

18. Clarke, *Libertarian Accounts of Free Will*, 3.

ILLUSTRATION OF MAN'S FREE WILL.

Since I have free will, I can decide to go to the gym (A), or I can decide to stay home and not go to the gym (B). *Both* choices are possible for me to decide tomorrow. Man's free will can be represented by the proposition: it is possible that A is true, and it is possible that B is true.

Path A   **Path B**

Man has alternative possibilities. He has free will to choose either path A or path B. Thus, it is *possible* that A is true, and it is *possible* that B is true ("possible" is indicated by broken lines).

A STORY OF MAN'S FREE WILL.

After my conversion, my friend (being a good Baptist) wanted me to be baptized. However, for me, going to church ranked right next to having my impacted molars extracted without anesthetics! I exercised my free will and flatly refused. All I wanted from God was help with food and lodgings. Since my friend was leaving for Africa as a missionary, he introduced me to another Christian who would help me "grow in the Lord." We met every morning for Bible study, which I was quite willing to do as I wanted to learn more about my new religion. Eventually, I realized the need to be identified with God's people and gladly joined a line of new converts into the "dunk tank"! Did I voluntarily follow this course of action or was it predetermined? Was I free or was I a robot fulfilling some foreordained plan? Is there a conflict between God's sovereignty and Man's free will? To that problem we now turn.

Chapter 2

The conflict between God's sovereignty and Man's free will

To DECIDE WHETHER THERE is a conflict, we need to evaluate the definitions and their logical propositions. We also want to visualize the problem by comparing the diagrams of God's sovereignty and Man's free will. If they match, there is no real controversy. If they don't, we have a problem that needs to be resolved.

CONFLICT IN THE DEFINITIONS.

God's sovereignty is God's control over all things, directing every process and ordering every event for the fulfilling of his sovereign will, though he may choose to let certain events happen according to natural laws which he has ordained. God owns what he makes, and he rules what he owns. No one can defeat his counsels, thwart his purpose, or resist his will.

Free will means that we are self-determined free agents, not (ultimately) subject to forces outside of our control and to external impediments. Open alternatives seem to lie before us. We reason or deliberate among them and choose according to the determinations of our will. We are able to do other than what we do.

It is obvious that if God is in control over all things, Man is subject to outside forces and external impediments. If God directs every process and orders every event, Man cannot deliberate and choose among alternative possibilities. If no one can resist God's will, Man cannot do other than what he does.

CONFLICT IN THE PROPOSITIONS.

God's sovereignty: A is true, and B is false (statement 1).
Man's free will: It is possible that A is true, and it is possible that B is true (statement 2).

Statement 1 contradicts statement 2. "B is false" contradicts "It is possible that B is true." If statement 1 is true (God is sovereign), then statement 2 (Man has free will) must be false and vice versa. In a nutshell, that is the conflict between God's sovereignty and Man's free will.

CONFLICT ILLUSTRATED IN DIAGRAM FORMS.

Path A   Path B
It is possible that A is true, and it is possible that B is true
Man's free will

Path A
A is true, and B is false
God's sovereignty

God's sovereignty and Man's free will (as defined) are not compatible in the classical understanding of the problem. The conflict (as illustrated by the dissimilar diagrams) is real and needs to be resolved.

Imagine yourself standing in your beautifully renovated kitchen. Thrilled by the wonderful outcome, you spontaneously choose to finger drum on the quartz countertop to whatever tune your heart desires. Would you not say that you have complete free will? What if I tell you that God foreordained your "random" actions in eternity past and that you are just *performing according to his decreed scenario*? Would you believe me? This conundrum brings up many theological problems that have plagued the church over the centuries. In the next chapter, we will take a closer look at ten major issues.

Chapter 3

The theological problems

Many theological problems arise from the dilemma of God's sovereignty and Man's free will. We will limit our discussion to the most prominent ten.

THE PROBLEM OF GOD'S SOVEREIGNTY AND MAN'S RESPONSIBILITY.

"I am God, and there is no one like me, declaring the end from the beginning, and from ancient times things which have not been done, saying, 'My purpose will be established, and I will accomplish all my good pleasure'" (Isa 46:9–10). "But our God is in the heavens; he does whatever he pleases," (Ps 115:3) "according to his purpose who works all things after the counsel of his will" (Eph 1:11). "So then he has mercy on whom he desires, and he hardens whom he desires. You will say to me then, 'Why does he still find fault? For who resists his will?'" (Rom 9:18–19). We gather from these verses that the Lord is sovereign, "declaring the end from the beginning," accomplishing his "purpose" and "good pleasure." "He does whatever he pleases" and no one "resists his will." If God is in full control, whatever happens, happens only according to his will and purpose. Should Man be held responsible if he has no say in the matter?

"For we must all appear before the judgment seat of Christ, so that each one may be recompensed for his deeds in the body, according to what he has done, whether good or bad" (2 Cor 5:10). "For the Son of Man is going to come in the glory of his Father with his angels and will then repay every man according to his deeds" (Matt 16:27). Thus, Man is held responsible and will be judged "according to his deeds," even though God sovereignly predetermines all outcomes!

THE PROBLEM OF PREDESTINATION/ FOREORDINATION.

"By predestination we mean the eternal decree of God, by which he determined with himself whatever he wished to happen with regard to every man."[1] Foreordination is the doctrine "that God has foreordained every event throughout eternity (including the final salvation of mankind)."[2] Foreordination is broader than predestination for it includes other pre-ordained events not related to man's destiny (e.g., the creation of stars in distant galaxies).

"'I will have mercy on whom I have mercy, and I will have compassion on whom I have compassion.' So then it does not depend on the man who wills or the man who runs, but on God who has mercy" (Rom 9:15–16). "You did not choose me, but I chose you" (John 15:16). From these verses, we learn that predestination/foreordination is the sole choice of God and "does not depend on the man who wills or the man who runs."

Some questions illustrate the problem of predestination/foreordination and Man's free will:

1. If God is sovereign and decrees that I will be condemned (i.e., I am predestined for reprobation[3] and not elected for salvation), why am I blamed for my damnation? Where is my free will in the matter?

2. Since God is infallible, when he foreknows a future event, he cannot be wrong. Therefore, that future circumstance must happen. If he is omniscient and already knows that I will be condemned (even before I was born), that event is unchangeable. Am I not therefore "doomed" to perdition? Do I really have any free will to decide otherwise?

---

1. Calvin, *Institutes*, 3.21.5.

2. http://www.the freedictionary.com/foreordination

3. "The doctrine of predestination to damnation is called the doctrine of reprobation." Ligonier Ministries, "The Doctrine of Reprobation," lines 6–7. www.ligonier.org/learn/devotionals/the-doctrine-of-reprobation/. Though he subscribed to it, Calvin called the decree of reprobation, "decretum horribile" (a dreadful decree). Calvin, *Institutes*, 3.23.7.

3. Why do I need to evangelize or support missions if God already foreknew/decreed who will be saved? Does Man have any choice in the matter of salvation?

4. Why did God bless Abraham so abundantly when he had already decreed that the patriarch would give up his only son Isaac as a sacrifice? Did Abraham have any other choice but to fulfill what God had foreordained? Did he deserve to receive the blessings?

5. What did the heroes of the "Hall of Faith" (Heb 11) do to merit special mentions if God had already predestined their outcomes? Did they have any other option but to do whatever the Lord had decreed for them?

6. Are pregnancies from rapes "something that God intended to happen"?[4] Did he really foreordain that evil outcome?

Many similar questions can be raised on this issue of God's predestination/foreordination and Man's free will.

THE PROBLEM OF GENUINENESS IN THE OFFER OF SALVATION TO ALL.

"For God so loved the world, that he gave his only begotten son, that whoever believes in him shall not perish, but have eternal life" (John 3:16). "For the grace of God has appeared, bringing salvation to all men" (Titus 2:11). "This is good and acceptable in the sight of God our savior, who desires all men to be saved" (1 Tim 2:3–4). From these verses, we gather that God wants to save all, that Christ can bring salvation to everyone, and that eternal life is given to "whoever" believes. Therefore, anyone can choose to accept the universal offer of salvation by believing in Jesus.

However, Romans 11:7 states: "What Israel is seeking, it has not obtained, but those who were chosen obtained it, and the rest were hardened." "Those who are outside get everything in parables, so that while seeing, they may see and not perceive, and while hearing, they may hear and not understand, otherwise they might return and be forgiven" (Mark 4:11–12). "For certain persons have crept in unnoticed, those who were

---

4. In a 2012 debate with a Democratic Party rival and a Libertarian Party candidate for one of Indiana's U.S. Senate seats, the Republican nominee suggested that "pregnancies resulting from rape" were intended by God. Madison, "Richard Mourdock," lines 6–7.

long beforehand marked out for this condemnation" (Jude 1:4). So, on the one hand, God offers salvation to everyone, and on the other hand, he hardens (blinds, deafens) some so that they may not "return and be forgiven." Some are "marked out" long beforehand for condemnation. Can the Lord be "deceitful"? Does he proclaim a "universal" offer of salvation while (secretly) restricting it to the chosen few?

A related question sometimes raised is: "Did Christ die for all or did he die only for the elect?"[5] Did Christ die for Judas the traitor? Why would he do so if Judas had already been condemned according to the Scriptures (John 17:12)? Did Jesus give Judas and the non-elect (e.g., my parents who never heard about Christ as far as I know) a genuine offer of salvation?

THE PROBLEM OF EVIL.

If God foreknows/decrees any and every event, is he the author of evil? "I am the Lord, and there is no other, the one forming light and creating darkness, causing well-being and creating calamity; I am the Lord who does all these (Isa 45:6–7). "Calamity" is the Hebrew "ra" also used in Genesis 2:9 to denote the tree of the knowledge of good and evil (ra). The meanings for "ra" include: bad, evil, wicked, adversity, calamity, and wrong.[6] Yet, James 1:13 states: "Let no one say when he is tempted, 'I am being tempted by God'; for God cannot be tempted by evil, and he himself does not tempt anyone." This conflict between God's absolute sovereignty and the presence of "horrendous evils"[7] in the world (e.g., the Holocaust) is a quandary that has yet to be resolved.

The Westminster Confession of Faith stated: "God from all eternity did by the most wise and holy counsel of his own will, freely and unchangeably ordain whatsoever comes to pass; yet so as thereby neither is God the author of sin; nor is violence offered to the will of the creatures, nor is the liberty or contingency of second causes taken away, but rather established."[8]

5. The problem of unlimited versus limited atonement.

6. http://biblehub.com/hebrew/7451.htm

7. The term "horrendous evils" was coined by Marilyn McCord Adams in *Horrendous Evils and the Goodness of God.*

8. Westminster Confession of Faith chapter III. http://www.reformed.org/documents/wcf_with_proofs/

Dr. R. C. Sproul said: "Adam and Eve were not created fallen. They had no sin nature. They were good creatures with a free will. Yet they chose to sin. Why? I don't know. Nor have I found anyone yet who does know. In spite of this excruciating problem we still must affirm that God is not the author of sin."[9]

Dr. Erwin Lutzer wrote: "Both Calvinists and Arminians teach that God does not and cannot do evil. Calvinists say that God nonetheless ordains it through secondary causes. Arminians say God only permits it. Nonetheless, his permission necessarily means that he bore ultimate responsibility for it. After all, he could have chosen 'not to permit it.'"[10]

Why did the Lord permit Adam to sin? Why did he put Man to the test? Obviously, he knew that Adam would surely fail. The Fall would entail countless miseries for billions and billions of Adam's descendants and necessitate the atoning death of God's son, Jesus, on the cross. Was that what the Lord had in mind all along, Adam's creation and fall requiring Christ's atoning sacrifice? How could these events be aspects of God's "love"? Could this be the "best possible" way for the Lord to accomplish his ultimate purpose?[11]

Furthermore, why did he blame Adam? Was the Fall not preordained by God? Did Adam have the free will not to sin? Were the gruesome evils of this world (e.g., Rwanda's genocide) the actions of men (thus making them responsible) or were they foreordained (thus making God responsible)?

THE PROBLEM OF MAN'S DEPRAVITY.

"Therefore, just as through one man sin entered into the world, and death through sin, and so death spread to all men, because all sinned" (Rom 5:12). "Among them we too all formerly lived in the lusts of our flesh, indulging the desires of the flesh and of the mind, and were by nature children of wrath" (Eph 2:3). "Perhaps God may grant them repentance leading to the knowledge of the truth, and they may come to their senses and escape from the snare of the devil, having been held captive by him

---

9. Sproul, *Chosen by God*, 20.

10. Lutzer, *The Doctrines That Divide*, 209–10.

11. "This is not the best of all possible worlds, it is the best of all possible ways (i.e., a necessary way) to achieve the best of all possible worlds." Geisler and Corduan, *Philosophy of Religion*, 313.

to do his will" (2 Tim 2:25–26). From these verses, we gather that, after the Fall, men are "by nature children of wrath," totally depraved,[12] and held captive by the devil to do his will. Enslaved men are not able to come to Christ unless God grants them the right. Does the sovereign Lord provide that saving grace to all depraved men? And if he does not, what are his reasons? Furthermore, if Man is totally depraved and unable to do what is good, how can he be held responsible for his sins? Was (the depraved) Hitler responsible for the Holocaust or was it God's doing?

THE PROBLEM OF THE PERSEVERANCE OF THE SAINTS/LOSS OF SALVATION.

If God foreknows that a certain man will not persevere (e.g., loss of salvation or never saved in the first place), does he have the freedom to do otherwise? If the Lord decrees that all believers will persevere, can they behave differently? Do our actions on earth have an impact on our eternal destiny (e.g., entrance to heaven, eternal rewards)? Is our final condition already foreknown/decreed by God and therefore unchangeable? Consider the case of Demas, Paul's fellow worker. "For Demas, having loved this present world, has deserted me and gone to Thessalonica" (2 Tim 4:10). Demas apparently changed his mind and left Paul for the love of this world. Did Demas act freely or was that desertion decreed by the Lord and therefore inevitable no matter what Demas wanted?

THE PROBLEM OF PRAYER.

If God foreknows/decrees that some events will take place, they will certainly happen. Why do we bother to exercise our "free will" and pray when the outcome is unalterable? "Where are we to buy bread, so that these may eat? This he was saying to test him, for he himself knew what he was intending to do (John 6:5–6). "Declaring the end from the beginning and from ancient times things which have not been done, saying, 'My purpose will be established, and I will accomplish all my good

---

12. Total depravity means that every man is "morally corrupt, enslaved to sin and . . . utterly unable to choose to follow God or choose to turn to Christ in faith for salvation." It "does not mean, however, that people are as bad as possible." www.theopedia.com/total-depravity

pleasure'" (Isa 46:10). These verses seem to indicate that God's plans are preordained and immutable.

However, there are instances where prayers appear to change the final outcomes. God told King Hezekiah: "'Set your house in order, for you shall die and not live.' Then he turned his face to the wall and prayed to the Lord saying, 'Remember now, O Lord, I beseech you, how I have walked before you in truth and with a whole heart and have done what is good in your sight'" (2 Kgs 20:1–3). God quickly answered: "I have heard your prayer, I have seen your tears; behold, I will heal you . . . I will add fifteen years to your life" (2 Kgs 20:5–6). Did Hezekiah's petition change the course of events or was the solemn declaration of his death only a "test" since the Lord intended, in eternity past, to let him live? Is prayer a free will choice/request between options or just a "rubber stamp" of God's predetermined will? Are the prayers for my child to be healed making any difference if the Lord already foreordained the day of his death (Ps 139:16)?

THE PROBLEM OF GOD'S IMMUTABILITY (DOES GOD EVER CHANGE HIS MIND?).

This is related to the previous issue about prayer. Does God ever change his mind in response to human actions? "Also, the Glory of Israel will not lie or change his mind" (1 Sam 15:29). "God is not Man, that he should lie, or a son of man, that he should change his mind" (Num 23:19 ESV). "Change mind" is the Hebrew "nacham" meaning "to be sorry, to suffer grief, to console oneself, to repent of."[13] We gather from these verses that the Lord never changes his mind, never repents of what he has done.[14] After all, since he is omnipotent, omniscient, and infallible, why would he need to do so?

However, in some instances, it appeared that God changed his mind. For example, Moses interceded for the Israelites after they worshiped the golden calf in the desert. "Why should the Egyptians speak, saying, 'With evil intent he brought them out to kill them in the mountains and to destroy them from the face of the earth?' Turn from your burning anger

13. http://biblehub.com/hebrew/5162.htm

14. "But whoever repents of what he has done, has a changeable will . . . I answer that the will of God is entirely unchangeable . . . These words of the Lord are to be understood metaphorically, and according to the likeness of our nature." Aquinas, *Summa Theologica*, 1.19.7. See Gen 6:6–7 and 1 Sam 15:11.

and change your mind (nacham) about doing harm to your people . . . So, the Lord changed his mind (nacham) about the harm which he said he would do to his people" (Exod 32:12–14). When Exodus 32:14 stated that God "changed his mind," was that just a figure of speech (e.g., an anthropomorphism attributing human actions to deity)? Was that only a "test" to see what Moses would do? Did the Lord ever intend to punish Israel for worshiping the golden calf? Did he "entice" Moses to plead for Israel so that he could void the announced punishment without "losing face"? Does God *ever* change his mind about a terminal cancer diagnosis and let a person live longer? Is there any hope for a miracle?

THE PROBLEM OF FREE WILL CHOICE IN SERVING GOD.

Do humans have a free will to serve or not to serve God? Are we compelled to serve him if we have been "chosen" and "elected" by him (without our input)? "You did not choose me, but I chose you and appointed you that you would go and bear fruit" (John 15:16). "Peter, an apostle of Jesus Christ, to those . . . who are chosen according to the foreknowledge of God the Father, by the sanctifying work of the Spirit, to obey Jesus Christ and be sprinkled with his blood" (1 Pet 1:1–2). From these verses, we learn that the "chosen according to the foreknowledge of God" will "obey Jesus Christ," "be sprinkled with his blood," and "bear fruit."

However, there are other passages that seem to indicate that serving God is a choice. "If it is disagreeable in your sight to serve the Lord, choose for yourselves today whom you will serve" (Josh 24:15). "How long will you hesitate between two opinions? If the Lord is God, follow him; but if Baal, follow him" (1 Kgs 18:21). Does the Lord want us to voluntarily serve him? Do we have any option other than the outcome that he already decreed? How can the two views be reconciled?

THE PROBLEM OF JESUS' OFFER OF THE KINGDOM TO ISRAEL.

"Jesus was going through all the cities and villages, teaching in their synagogues and proclaiming the gospel of the kingdom" (Matt 9:35). "Therefore, I say to you, the kingdom of God will be taken away from you and given to a people, producing the fruit of it" (Matt 21:43). From these verses, we learn that Jesus came to genuinely offer the kingdom to Israel. The invitation was only rescinded and given to the Gentiles after Israel rejected the Messiah.

However, other passages seem to indicate that Jesus' rejection by Israel was foreordained and therefore inevitable. "This man, delivered over by the predetermined plan and foreknowledge of God, you nailed to a cross by the hands of godless men and put him to death" (Acts 2:23). "There were gathered together against your holy servant Jesus, whom you anointed, both Herod and Pontius Pilate, along with the Gentiles and the peoples of Israel, to do whatever your hand and your purpose predestined to occur" (Acts 4:27–28). If the Lord had decreed that the Gentiles would receive the prize, was Jesus' offer of the kingdom to Israel genuine? How could the offer be "taken away" and "given to a people producing the fruit of it" when Israel was *never* predestined to receive it in the first place?

THE TEN THEOLOGICAL PROBLEMS.

In summary, we have at least ten major theological problems arising from the conflict between God's sovereignty and Man's free will. In the following chapters, we will consider the standard solutions, namely Calvinism, Arminianism, Molinism, and Open Theism. We will discuss the various attempts to solve the logical dilemma and address the theological issues raised. For the sake of simplicity, we will "suppose that the concept of free will is very closely connected to the concept of moral responsibility."[15]

---

15. O'Connor, "Free Will," lines 6–7. Free will and moral responsibility are complex topics under debate. See Kane, *The Oxford Handbook of Free Will*. Also see Haji and Caouette, *Free Will and Moral Responsibility*.

Chapter 4

Calvinism as a solution

How does Calvinism handle the conundrum of God's sovereignty and Man's free will? I will start by presenting the major tenets of the system. I will then explain the various solutions adopted by Calvinist scholars. Finally, I will address the ten theological problems raised.

THE TENETS OF CALVINISM.

The standard acronym for Calvinism is TULIP.

Total depravity: "The effect of the Fall upon man is that sin has extended to every part of his personality—his thinking, his emotions, and his will."[1]

Unconditional election: "God chose those whom he was pleased to bring to a knowledge of himself, not based upon any merit shown by the object of his grace and not based upon his looking forward to discover who would 'accept' the offer of the gospel. God has elected, based solely upon the counsel of his own will some for glory and others for damnation."[2]

Limited atonement: "Christ died to atone for specific sins of specific sinners." "He did not atone for all men, because obviously all men are not saved."[3]

1. Barlow, "Calvinism," lines 24–25.
2. Barlow, "Calvinism," lines 32–35.
3. Barlow, "Calvinism," lines 52–54.

Irresistible grace: "The result of God's irresistible grace is the certain response by the elect to the inward call of the Holy Spirit."[4]

Perseverance of the saints: "A doctrine which states that the saints (those whom God has saved) will remain in God's hand until they are glorified and brought to abide with him in heaven."[5]

With the tenets in place, let us consider the proposed solutions to the quandary.

THE CALVINIST SOLUTIONS.

John Calvin said: "But now, removing from God all proximate causation of the act, I at the same time remove from him all guilt and leave Man alone liable. It is therefore wicked and calumnious to say that I make the Fall of Man one of the works of God. But how it was ordained by the foreknowledge and decree of God what Man's future was without God being implicated as associate in the fault as the author or approver of transgression, is clearly a secret so much excelling the insight of the human mind, that I am not ashamed to confess ignorance."[6]

As Calvin called the quandary a "secret so much excelling the insight of the human mind," he did not solve the logical dilemma of God's sovereignty and Man's free will.[7] Calvinist scholars like Berkhof,[8] Grudem,[9] Erickson,[10] Geisler,[11] and Carson[12] agree that the problem is a

4. Barlow, "Calvinism," line 57.

5. Barlow, "Calvinism," lines 64–65.

6. Calvin, *Concerning the Eternal Predestination of God*, 123–24.

7. Hunt, *Calvin's Dilemma*.

8. Berkhof, *Systematic Theology*, 175. "The problem of God's relation to sin remains a mystery."

9. Grudem, *Systematic Theology*, 330. "We have to come to the point where we confess that we do not understand how it is that God can ordain that we carry out evil deeds and yet hold us accountable for them and not be blamed himself."

10. Erickson, *Christian Theology*, footnote 12, 359. "In the final analysis, the exact relationship between divine sovereignty and human freedom is necessarily a mystery."

11. Geisler, "God Knows All Things," 78. "Now that we have described what is meant by the mystery of human free will and divine determinism, just why is it a mystery? Or, to put it another way, why is it that we cannot know how the two fit together? Why cannot we know *how* God determines free actions without violating their freedom? I would suggest that the reason we cannot know how is because there is no 'how' to be known."

12. Carson, *How Long*, 201. "The mystery of providence defies our attempt to tame

"mystery." Of course, a "mystery" is not really a solution. However, there are many "mysteries/paradoxes" in Christianity (e.g., the doctrine of the Trinity). Should we just accept this conundrum as "God's mystery" or should we attempt to cut this "Gordian knot," using the mind that the Lord has given us and the help of the Holy Spirit?

In an attempt to resolve the dilemma, Dr. John Feinberg defines free will as: "If the act is according to the agent's desires, then even though the act is causally determined, it is free, and the agent is morally responsible."[13] In other words, if I follow my desire to smoke cigarettes (without any outside pressure and against the Surgeon General's warnings), I make a free will choice and am morally responsible for my action. Where does that desire (and act) to smoke come from? It is "causally determined" by the Lord.

Returning to the workout example, God "causally determined" that I will go the gym tomorrow (path A is true). Thus, I will "freely" choose to exercise tomorrow, following my "God-caused" desire. So, if we redefine free will like Dr. Feinberg (i.e., a soft determinism[14] or compatibilism[15] approach), the propositions will change to the following:

God's sovereignty: A is true, and B is false, "causally determined" by God (statement 1).

Man's free will: A is true, and B is false, "freely" chosen, following a "God-caused" desire (statement 2).

---

it by reason."

13. Feinberg, "God Ordains All Things," 37. Jonathan Edwards said: "If the acts of the will are excited by motives, those motives are the causes of those acts of the will; which makes the acts of the will necessary; as effects necessarily follow the efficiency of the cause." Edwards, *The Works of President Edwards*, 115.

14. "A soft determinist believes both that determinism is true, and that man has free will." Cahn, *A New Introduction to Philosophy*, 44. Determinism: all events are determined by previous causes.

15. Compatibilism: free will is compatible with determinism. More in-depth discussions can be found in Peterson and Williams, *Why I Am Not an Arminian*, 136–61, and Walls and Dongell, *Why I Am Not a Calvinist*, 98–110.

Statement 1 agrees with statement 2.

Path A
A is true, and B is false
Man's free will
"Freely" chosen following a "God-caused" desire

Path A
A is true, and B is false
God's sovereignty
"Causally determined" by God

If we adopt Dr. Feinberg's definition of free will, the logical dilemma is seemingly "solved" (as shown by the identical diagrams). However, would that approach resolve the theological problems raised previously?

THE THEOLOGICAL PROBLEMS.

The problem of God's sovereignty and Man's responsibility.

If God had "causally determined" for me to have the desire to smoke and I "freely" followed my God-caused desire and subsequently died of lung cancer at thirty, the age that the Lord had foreordained for me, should I be held responsible? Could I successfully resist my God-caused desire? If I could, would that not ruin his omnipotence? If I could not resist, was I not "coerced" into smoking? Where did that destructive desire come from? Did I ask for it? Who inserted it in my genetic makeup? Who put me in a family of smokers? And who decided that I would die at thirty? How could I be held responsible for decisions over which I had no control? "Shall not the judge of all the earth deal justly?" (Gen 18:25). Did I really have any "free" will if God had "causally determined" *every event in my life*?

Furthermore, does Man always act according to his desires? What if he has conflicting desires? "I do not understand what I do. For what I want to do I do not do, but what I hate I do" (Rom 7:15 NIV). Did the Lord foreordain Paul to sin by giving him *irresistible* sinful desires? Who was responsible for the sin, Paul or God?

The problem of predestination/foreordination.

If God had "causally determined" all the events in my life (including my salvation or perdition), could I have done otherwise? After all, who could resist his will? Did he foreordain pregnancies from rapes by giving men irresistible evil desires to violate women and by causing the eggs to be present at that *exact* time? If so, wasn't he responsible for what happened?

The problem of genuineness in the offer of salvation to all.

If God had "causally determined" that I would die before I could hear the gospel, was the universal offer of salvation a genuine offer for me? If he had foreordained that some would be lost, could it be otherwise? Is the offer of salvation given to all or only to some?

The problem of evil.

If God had "causally determined" that I would die painfully of lung cancer at a young age due to my God-caused desire to smoke, how was he not responsible for that evil? Did he decree "ethnic cleansings," rapes, and child abuses by giving some men irresistible evil desires that they had to follow? Did he foreordain the Holocaust to bring about some "ultimate good"? What could be the "ultimate good" that would outweigh all the horrendous evils in the world over the centuries?[16]

If God had decreed that Adam and Eve would fall by "freely" following their God-caused desires, how was he not the author of evil in this fallen world? How could he hold them responsible for their sins? Furthermore, if he could "causally determine" that Adam and Eve would fail "freely," what prevented him from "causally determining" that they would *not* fail "freely"? Would that not be better? After all, isn't that what will happen in the new heaven and the new earth (free will and no sin)? Should the Lord have created that world instead? Did he make a mistake in creating this realm? Dr. Millard Erickson, a Calvinist theologian, said: "A total solution to the problem of evil is beyond human ability."[17]

The problem of Man's depravity.

If God had "causally determined" that I would be so depraved as to smoke myself to death, would I have the free will to do otherwise? Furthermore, if he had decreed that I would be totally depraved (with inherited guilt and inherited sin nature), how could I be held responsible for my sins?

---

16. Dr. Alvin Plantinga proposed the "greater good" of Christ's incarnation and atonement. See Alvin Plantinga, "Supralapsarianism," 363–89. However, Dr. Kevin Diller observed: "Perhaps it is the incarnation alone which wins for us the great enhancements in the intimacy of our relationship with God . . . But the incarnation alone does not require suffering and evil, so neither then is evil required for enhancing the intimacy of human relationship with God." Diller, "Are Sin and Evil Necessary," 403.

17. Erickson, *Christian Theology,* 423.

The problem of the perseverance of the saints/loss of salvation.

Let us say that I was a Christian at the age of ten. If God had "causally determined" for me to smoke from the age of twenty until my death at thirty and, because of my addiction, desert[18] my faith, would I have the free will to decide otherwise? If he had foreordained that I would not persevere, could I do differently? How could I be held responsible for my perdition?

The problem of prayer.

If God had "causally determined" for me to smoke and die, would any of my prayers to be delivered from the evil of smoking make a difference? What was the point of praying if he had already foreordained the unalterable outcome?

The problem of God's immutability
(does God ever change his mind?).

If God had "causally determined" for me to die at thirty, would he ever change his mind and let me live longer? If he should choose to give me a reprieve, would that not ruin his omniscience? If he had irrevocably sentenced me to an early death, why should I even bother to repent (i.e., quit smoking)? If I told my students at the beginning of the semester that I had preordained their grades (i.e., their final grades had already been entered by the registrar and could not be changed), would they come to class or study for the exams?

The problem of free will choice in serving God.

Do I have the free will to quit serving God at any time (like Demas)? Is my "free will" real or just empty words since I cannot do other than what he has "causally determined" for me in eternity past?

The problem of Jesus' offer of the kingdom to Israel.

If God had "causally determined" that Israel would reject the Messiah, was the offer of the kingdom to the Jews a genuine offer? Was there *any* possibility that they would accept the invitation? Was Israel responsible

18. A "loss" of salvation or never a "true" Christian.

for Christ's rejection and crucifixion since it only followed its "God-caused" selfish desire? After all, who could resist God's will?

Also, could Jesus be "deceitful" in offering the kingdom to the Jewish nation? Did he not know that God had already decreed that the prize would be given to the Gentiles at Israel's expense? Why did the Lord send Christ *exclusively* to the Jews when he had foreordained that they would reject the proposal? Should Jesus not waste his time with Israel and just go to the Gentiles instead?

Furthermore, if God could "causally determine" that the Israelites would "freely" reject Jesus, what prevented him from "causally determining" that they would "freely" accept Jesus? Would that not be better?[19]

CALVINISM AS A SOLUTION.

In my opinion, the "causally determined" approach does not solve all the theological problems raised.[20] So, we are left with Calvin's "secret[21] so much excelling the insight of the human mind." The dilemma of God's sovereignty and Man's free will stays unresolved. Let us consider the Arminian solution. Will we be more successful there?

---

19. Christ could still die for our sins on the cross. He could have been crucified by the Romans without any Jewish involvement if Israel had accepted Jesus as the Messiah. This scenario will be discussed later in the book.

20. Critiques of Feinberg's position can be found in Norman Geisler's, Bruce Reichenbach's, and Clark Pinnock's responses in Basinger and Basinger, *Predestination and Free Will*, 45–60. "Causal determinism threatens both our control over our actions and volitions, and our ability to originate those same actions and volitions." Timpe, "Free Will," section 4c.

21. "The standard appeal to paradox is nothing less than the affirmation that a logical reconciliation of the sovereignty/freedom tension is impossible . . . the appeal to paradox is probably a failure." Ciocchi, "Reconciling Divine Sovereignty and Human Freedom," 399. Dr. Randy Alcorn stated: "I doubt anyone this side of heaven will ever manage to fully 'explain' how God's sovereignty and human choice fully fit together." Alcorn, *hand in Hand*, 173. Pastor Scott Christensen wrote: "Thus, we can say that God is the ultimate cause of evil in the sense that it conforms to his immutable active decree . . . This is a difficult pill to swallow, and most Calvinists admit that we run into mystery at this juncture." Christensen, *What About Free Will?* 250.

Chapter 5

Arminianism as a solution

As CALVINISM DERIVES ITS title from John Calvin, Arminianism is named after Jacob Arminius (1560–1609 AD), an adopted orphan who later became a famous theologian in the Netherlands. The five points of Calvinism were crafted at the Synod of Dort (1618–1619 AD) to counter the five major tenets of Arminianism.

THE TENETS OF ARMINIANISM.

Arminianism can be summarized by the FACTS acronym.[1]

Freed by grace (to believe): "God's saving grace is resistible, which is to say that he dispenses his calling, drawing, and convicting grace (which would bring us to salvation if responded to with faith) in such a way that we may reject it. Those who hear the gospel may either accept it by grace or reject it to their own eternal destruction."[2]

Atonement for all: "While God has provided for the salvation of all people by Christ's sacrificial and substitutionary death for all, the benefits of Christ's death are received by grace through faith and are only effective for those who believe."[3]

---

1. Abasciano and Glynn, "An Outline of the FACTS of Arminianism," line 1. Another acronym for Arminianism is DAISY. See https://theologyawareness.wordpress.com/2017/06/09/arminianism-daisy-daisy/

2. Abasciano and Glynn, "An Outline of the FACTS of Arminianism," lines 40–43.

3. Abasciano and Glynn, "An Outline of the FACTS of Arminianism," lines 32–34.

Conditional election: "God individually chose each believer based upon his foreknowledge of each one's faith and so predestined each to eternal life."[4]

Total depravity: "Total depravity does not mean that human beings are as bad as they could be, but that sin impacts every part of a person's being and that people now have a sinful nature with a natural inclination toward sin, making every human being fundamentally corrupt at heart."[5]

Security in Christ: "God protects our faith relationship with him from any outside force irresistibly snatching us away from Christ or our faith, and he preserves us in salvation as long as we trust in Christ."[6]

How does Arminianism solve the dilemma of God's sovereignty and Man's free will using these five tenets?

THE ARMINIAN SOLUTION.

The Arminian scholar Jack Cottrell defined free will "as the ability to freely choose between good and evil, the choice being actually determined by the will of man and not by the will of God."[7] He defined God's sovereignty as "God's decree is all-inclusive . . . God knows the free acts of men even before the world was created . . . God's knowledge is then completely independent and absolutely all-inclusive. The free will of Man does not alter this one bit. God is still no less than absolutely sovereign."[8] Furthermore, the Lord's foreknowledge does not *cause* the future event.[9]

4. Abasciano and Glynn, "An Outline of the FACTS of Arminianism," lines 56–58.

5. Abasciano and Glynn, "An Outline of the FACTS of Arminianism," lines 20–22.

6. Abasciano and Glynn, "An Outline of the FACTS of Arminianism," lines 70–72.

7. Cottrell, "Sovereignty and Free Will," lines 24–25.

8. Cottrell, "Sovereignty and Free Will," lines 27, 204–207.

9. "My certainty as to what would happen has in no way affected the reality of the events . . . his (God's) foreknowledge no more affects the contingency of the events than does my after-the-fact knowledge of a past event." Cottrell, *What the Bible Says about God the Creator*, 288. While it is true that God's foreknowledge does not *cause* the event, does God's foreknowledge affect/restrict Man's free will? It surely does *if God is infallible*! For example, I flip a coin and you and I must guess whether it is going to be "heads or tails." Now, if I flip the coin a million times and my predictions are *infallibly* correct, would you not say that I am somehow cheating (e.g., I use a coin with two "heads"; thus, only my choice of "heads" is possible)? Thus, God's *infallible* foreknowledge *does* affect/restrict Man's freedom. Now, it is true that my *fallible* foreknowledge would not affect your freedom. For example, I (in Phoenix) somehow "foreknow" that you (in Florida) will go to the gym tomorrow. Now, my "foreknowledge" does *not* impact/cause your decision in any way. You do not even know that I

Using these Arminian definitions, how can God's sovereignty and Man's free will be stated in propositional form?

God knew "even before the world was created" that I would go to the gym tomorrow (path A is true). God's decree included that known fact. God's sovereignty (in the Arminian understanding) can be represented by the statement: A is true, and B is false.

Man has "the ability to freely choose." I will be able to choose to go to the gym or stay home and not go to the gym tomorrow. Man's free will (in the Arminian understanding) can be represented by the statement: it is possible that A is true, and it is possible that B is true.

Putting the two statements together:

God's sovereignty: A is true, and B is false (statement 1).

Man's free will: It is possible that A is true, and it is possible that B is true (statement 2).

Statement 1 contradicts statement 2.

Path A   Path B
It is possible that A is true, and it is possible that B is true
Man's free will

made a prediction. However, logic dictates that I will *have to be wrong* some of the time in my "foreknowledge/prediction" for you to have complete free will. Your free will and my *infallible* foreknowledge are contradictory. Either you are wrong (you do not have free will) or I am wrong (I do not have infallible foreknowledge). Both of us cannot be right at the same time, thus the dilemma of God's sovereignty/infallible foreknowledge and Man's free will. "The claim is not that foreknowledge causes anything, but only that if someone such as God knows what will happen with absolute certainty, it cannot happen otherwise." Olson, *Arminian Theology*, 194–95.

Path A
A is true, and B is false
God's foreknowledge/sovereignty

The dissimilar diagrams illustrate the unresolved conflict of God's sovereignty and Man's free will. Thus, the controversy is not settled by the Arminian solution. Furthermore, does Arminianism solve our theological problems?

THE THEOLOGICAL PROBLEMS.

The problem of God's sovereignty and Man's responsibility.

If God knew, "even before the world was created," my free will choice to smoke and die of cancer at the age of thirty, why did he not do something to prevent that disaster?[10] Is he not omnipotent? Does he not care?

10. Jack Cottrell said: "God's foreknowledge also enables him to plan his own responses to and uses of human choices even before they are made." Cottrell, "The Nature of the Divine Sovereignty," 112. According to David Hunt, God can use his foreknowledge to get a "providential edge," raising the odds "that he will get the outcome he desires." Hunt, "The Simple-Foreknowledge View," 98. However, Open Theists maintain that simple foreknowledge does not give God much (if any) providential control over future events to accomplish his purposes. According to John Sanders, there are two types of simple foreknowledge. The first is Complete Simple Foreknowledge (CSF) defined as "even though he knows things will occur in sequence, God does not acquire the knowledge in sequence. God simply sees the whole at once." The second is Incremental Simple Foreknowledge (ISF) when God "timelessly accesses the future in *sequence or incrementally.*" Sanders argued that neither CSF nor ISF gave God much providential control over events. Sanders, "Why Simple Foreknowledge," 26–40. William Hasker concurred: "According to CSF, God 'sees' the entire future all at once, in a single glance as it were, *including* God's own future actions *and the reasons for which God will perform those actions* . . . At this point, there is no 'determining' left to

If an adult sees a child cross a busy freeway and knows with absolute certainty that it will result in death, should the all-powerful adult not do the right thing and save the child? After all, does the Bible not teach that "knowledge/foreknowledge" also entails responsibility (Luke 12:47–48, Rom 1:20)? And if God cannot (or will not) do something to protect the child, is he truly omnipotent and omnibenevolent (all-good)? Would the child not rather lose his "free will," have the Lord intervene and live rather than insist on his "free will" and die?

Thus, how could Man be held totally responsible for the Fall? Was God not partially responsible since he foreknew the disaster and did nothing to prevent it? Furthermore, why did he choose to create *this world* knowing that it would spawn horrendous evils?[11]

The problem of predestination/foreordination.

If God foreknew my free will choice to smoke and die unsaved and yet chose to include these "foreknown/unchangeable" facts in his "all-inclusive decree," how was he not responsible for the evil outcome? After all, he could have chosen not to give me the desire to smoke. He could have decided not to create me. Since there could not be a different outcome from the one written in stone in God's decree, was I not "doomed" to do whatever he had already foreknown? Should I even bother to quit smoking if I knew that "whatever will be, will be"[12] and could not be changed? Did God foreknow the genocides, child abuses, and pregnancies from rapes? Did he do anything to prevent them? How could he allow all these disasters and claim to be a loving Lord?

---

be done!" Hasker, "Why Simple Foreknowledge," 539.

11. Some Arminians appeal to the concept of simple foreknowledge to resolve the problem of God "foreknowing yet allowing" evils or "foreknowing yet creating" a world with evil. "What if God knew what humanity would do only after he made a decision to create us? This could be understood as a logical order, not by necessity a temporal one, since God is everlasting. What if after God decided to create us, he was unwilling or unable to take back that decision?" Jackson, "An Explanation of Simple Foreknowledge," lines 27–30. If this is correct, God would be somewhat "reckless" in his creative activity, unwittingly spawning "monsters" (i.e., evils) and lacking the power (or will) to put the "genie" back inside the bottle.

12. "Fatalism is the doctrine that whatever will be will be." Helm, "An Augustinian–Calvinist Response," 117.

The problem of genuineness in the offer of salvation to all.

If God foreknew that I would die before I could hear the gospel, was the universal offer of salvation a genuine offer for me? Should I be held responsible for my perdition? Furthermore, if Christ died for all, why did he blind and deafen some on purpose? How could he proclaim that "God so loved *the world*" when he had already foreknown/decreed some to be "vessels of wrath prepared for destruction"?

The problem of evil.

If God foreknew my evil choice to smoke myself to death and did nothing, how was he not responsible (at least partially) for that evil? If he foreknew that Adam would sin, and evil would enter the world and he chose to create the world and Adam anyway, how was he not the author of evil? Does the end (e.g., some "ultimate good") justify the means (e.g., the Holocaust)? And what can be the "good" for billions of Adam's descendants whose final destiny is the eternal lake of fire? Furthermore, can the omnipotent Lord create a world without sin? And if that cannot be done, would it not be better not to create than to create an evil world? After all, I and many others would prefer not to be born/created than to be condemned to hell eternally! Dr. Jack Cottrell said: "We do not claim to have solved all the problems relating to the presence of evil in the world."[13]

The problem of Man's depravity.

If God foreknew my depraved choice to smoke and die unsaved, could I do otherwise? Furthermore, if he knew that Man would be totally depraved, and he chose to create the world anyway, how could Man be held responsible for his sins and depravity?

The problem of the perseverance of the saints/loss of salvation.

If God infallibly foreknew my choice to smoke and, as a result, abandon my faith, would I have the option to decide otherwise? If he knew that some would (or would not) persevere, would that not be an unchangeable event? Where is free will in the matter?

13. Cottrell, *What the Bible Says about God the Ruler*, 404.

The problem of prayer.

If God foreknew my choice to smoke and die, would any of my fervent prayers to be delivered from the evil of smoking make a difference? What would be the point of praying if nothing could be changed?

The problem of God's immutability
(does God ever change his mind?).

If God infallibly foreknew my death at thirty, would he ever change his mind and let me live longer? Would I even bother to reform if I knew that my repentance would not change anything in God's foreknown/decreed plans for me?

The problem of free will choice in serving God.

If God foreknew all my decisions and included them in his fixed decree, do I have the free will to quit (or not quit) serving him? Is free will compatible with infallible foreknowledge?

The problem of Jesus' offer of the kingdom to Israel.

If God had foreknown Israel's decision to reject the Messiah and had included that fact in his decree, would Israel have any other choice but to do what had been decreed? Was Jesus' offer to the Jews genuine since he foreknew that the kingdom would not be given to them? Could he be "deceitful" in dangling the prize in front of the Israelites? And what was the point of going to the Jews exclusively when he knew that they would never accept his invitation? Should he just go to the Gentiles instead? Furthermore, why did the Lord choose to create a world where Christ would be rejected when he could have made the universe where Messiah would be accepted?

ARMINIANISM AS A SOLUTION.

In my opinion, Arminianism does not resolve the logical dilemma or the theological problems raised by the conflict between God's sovereignty and Man's free will.[14] Arminius said: "The mode in which He (God) knows certainly future contingencies, and especially those which appertain to creatures of free will, and which He has decreed to permit, not Himself to do—this I do not comprehend."[15] Dr. Roger Olson, an Arminian scholar, stated: "The upshot is that classical Arminianism may involve a paradox: God's exhaustive and infallible foreknowledge (simple foreknowledge) together with libertarian free will."[16] Will the Molinist solution be more successful in resolving the dilemma?

14. Critiques of the Arminian position (David Hunt's) can be found in Greg Boyd's, William Lane Craig's, and Paul Helm's responses in Beilby and Eddy, *Divine Foreknowledge,* 104–18. Other critiques of the Arminian position (Bruce Reichenbach's) can be found in John Feinberg's, Norman Geisler's, and Clark Pinnock's responses in Basinger and Basinger, *Predestination & Free will,* 125–40.

15. Arminius, *The Works of Arminius,* 64. David Hunt concurred with Arminius: "The fact is that I'm not at all sure *how* God knows the future." Hunt, "The Simple Foreknowledge View," 67.

16. Olson, *Arminian Theology,* 198–99.

Chapter 6

Molinism as a solution

MOLINISM WAS NAMED AFTER Luis de Molina (1535–1600 AD), a Spanish Jesuit priest who advocated a strong belief in Man's free will. Like Calvinism and Arminianism, Molinism can be summarized in five tenets.

THE TENETS OF MOLINISM.

The ROSES acronym has been proposed by Molinists.[1]

Radical depravity: "Every aspect of our being is affected by the Fall and renders us incapable of saving ourselves or even wanting to be saved."[2]

Overcoming grace: "It is God's persistent beckoning that overcomes our wicked obstinacy."[3]

Sovereign election: Molinism "affirms that God desires the salvation of all yet accentuates that our salvation is not based on us choosing God but on God choosing us."[4]

Eternal life: "Believers enjoy a transformed life that is preserved, and we are given a faith which will remain."[5]

Singular redemption: "Christ died sufficiently for every person, although efficiently only for those who believe."[6]

1. Keathley, *Salvation and Sovereignty*, 3–4.

2. Keathley, *Salvation and Sovereignty*, 3.

3. Keathley, *Salvation and Sovereignty*, 4.

4. Keathley, *Salvation and Sovereignty*, 4.

5. Keathley, *Salvation and Sovereignty*, 4.

6. Keathley, *Salvation and Sovereignty*, 4.

Molinism proposes that God has three distinct types of knowledge. Natural knowledge is God's knowledge "of what *could* be"[7] (knowledge of all *logically possible* worlds, e.g., a world with Martians). Middle knowledge is God's "counterfactual knowledge of what *would* be."[8] For example, God knew what would have happened had Zedekiah obeyed and surrendered to the Babylonians in Jeremiah 38:17–18. God, using his middle knowledge, knew all the feasible[9] worlds that would accomplish his will. Finally, free knowledge is God's "knowledge of what *will* be"[10] (knowledge of the *actual* world that God created out of all the feasible worlds that would accomplish his will).[11]

"The following is a synopsis of the *logical order* postulated in Molinism:

God's knowledge of all possible and necessary truths (natural knowledge).

God's knowledge of all feasible worlds (middle knowledge).

Divine decree to create his selected world.

God's foreknowledge set through his selected decree (free knowledge)."[12]

Molinism is more of a philosophical construct[13] than a theological system as the theory of "middle knowledge" is not addressed in the Scriptures. How does Molinism resolve the problem of God's sovereignty and Man's free will?

---

7. Craig, "The Middle-Knowledge View," 121.

8. Craig, "The Middle-Knowledge View," 121.

9. There are some logically possible worlds that are not feasible for God to create due to Man's free will. For example, the worlds where Judas *stays loyal* to Christ when offered thirty pieces of silver (or more) are *not* feasible for God to create since Judas *always* freely betrays Christ when offered that amount of money (or more). However, all the worlds with thirty pieces of silver or more and *a traitor Judas* are feasible for God to create.

10. Craig, "The Middle-Knowledge View," 121.

11. God chose to create the feasible world of "thirty pieces of silver for traitor Judas" out of a multitude of other feasible options (e.g., forty, fifty, sixty pieces of silver for traitor Judas) that would accomplish God's will (the betrayal of the Messiah by Judas).

12. http://www.theopedia.com/molinism

13. "Dr. Craig's analysis (Molinism) is simply the inevitable manifestation of an approach to thinking about the providence of God that privileges philosophical speculation over the careful examination of what God has revealed in his Word." Helseth, "Response," 104.

THE MOLINIST SOLUTION.

Luis de Molina affirmed: "All things without exception are individually subject to God's will and providence."[14] Dr. Kenneth Keathley, a Molinist scholar, stated: "From the infinite set of possible worlds that could happen (God's natural knowledge), there is an infinite subset of feasible worlds which would accomplish his will (God's middle knowledge). God freely chooses one of the feasible worlds, and he perfectly knows what will happen in this actual world (God's free knowledge). In the Molinist model, God sovereignly controls all things, yet humans possess real freedom for which they must give an account."[15] Dr. William Lane Craig wrote, God "is dealt a hand of cards having all true counterfactuals of creaturely freedom printed on them . . . God must now play with the hand he has been dealt."[16]

In other words, God cannot create any world he desires. There are some (logically) *possible* worlds/scenarios that are *not feasible* for him to actualize. For example, there was no feasible world for him to create (i.e., card for him to play) where Judas, when offered thirty pieces of silver, would *freely* choose to be loyal to Christ. If Judas was offered that amount, he would *always* betray Christ.[17] However, the Lord could create one of the worlds where Judas remained loyal freely when offered less than *thirty pieces of silver*.[18] He could also actualize a world without Judas.

Using these Molinist interpretations, how can God's sovereignty and Man's free will be stated in propositional form? "God sovereignly controls all things," "freely chooses one of the feasible worlds," and "perfectly knows what will happen in this actual world" (e.g., that I will go

14. Molina, *On Divine Foreknowledge, Part IV of the Concordia*, 4.53.3.17.

15. Keathley, *Salvation and Sovereignty*, 18.

16. Craig, "A Molinist View," 38.

17. "The problem is that it can be argued that middle knowledge is inconsistent with libertarian free will . . . Libertarian free will requires that there be a possible world in which Judas refrains, so that it follows that the concept of divine middle knowledge contradicts the very account of freedom it was devised to support." Ciocchi, "Reconciling Divine Sovereignty and Human Freedom," 405–406. While there is a (logically) *possible* world in which Judas refrains under identical circumstances, such a world is *not feasible* for God to create since Judas *always* freely betray Christ when he is offered thirty pieces of silver. See Craig, *A Molinist View*, 37–38. Ciocchi's argument can be amended to read: "Libertarian free will requires that there be a *feasible* world in which Judas refrains."

18. For the sake of discussion, we can assume that the amount of thirty pieces of silver was the tipping point for Judas to betray Christ.

to the gym tomorrow, path A is true). God's sovereignty (in the Molinist understanding) can be represented by the statement: in this actualized/created world, A is true, and B is false. "Humans possess real freedom," but God chooses to actualize/create only "one of the feasible worlds" (i.e., the one where I will go to the gym tomorrow). Man's free will (in the Molinist understanding) can be represented by the statement: in this actualized/created world, A is true, and B is false.

So, if we redefine God's sovereignty and Man's free will like the Molinist scholars, the propositions will change to the following:

God's sovereignty: In this actualized/created world, A is true, and B is false (statement 1).

Man's free will: In this actualized/created world, A is true, and B is false (statement 2).

Statement 1 agrees with statement 2.

Path A
A is true, and B is false
Man's "free will" in this actualized world

Path A
A is true, and B is false
God's sovereignty in this actualized world

If one adopts the Molinist definitions of God's sovereignty and Man's free will, the logical dilemma is seemingly "solved" (as the diagrams are identical). However, is Molinism the answer to our ten theological problems?

THE THEOLOGICAL PROBLEMS.

The problem of God's sovereignty and Man's responsibility.

If God freely chooses to actualize/create "one of the feasible worlds" out of "an infinite subset of feasible worlds," he is in total control of any and every outcome. "He perfectly knows what will happen in this actual world." Thus, everything is *fixed and unchangeable* in this created universe. Would it be sensible to tell Man that he has free will choices, but his choices are *in some other worlds that are never actualized?*

Using his "middle knowledge," the Lord knows that a certain person put in a specific situation will "freely" do a certain action. He then creates that person and that precise situation. If that inevitably *guarantees* the action, in what way is the person "free"? For example, the challenges of the hostile Jews would *always* cause Peter to deny Christ. Dr. Craig stated: "There is a possible world in which Peter freely affirms Christ in precisely the same circumstances in which he in fact denied him; but given the counterfactual truth that if Peter were in precisely those circumstances he would freely deny Christ, then the possible world in which Peter freely affirms Christ in those circumstances is not feasible for God."[19] Thus, there was *no feasible world* for the Lord to create where Peter would freely stay loyal to Christ under the same circumstances. The events would have to change (e.g., no challenges from the Jews) to get a different outcome (e.g., Peter remained loyal). Was Peter free then to deny Christ or not if the underlying circumstances were fixed? Was he not "doomed" to the one outcome actualized by God?

How could Adam be held responsible if the Lord created a specific scenario (e.g., a garden with a forbidden fruit and a serpent tempter) guaranteeing that Adam would sin? Once the circumstances had been fixed, the Fall was the foregone conclusion! Also, God appeared to be "stacking the deck" against Adam, manipulating the situation in such a way that Adam could do nothing else but fail. Furthermore, if this created

19. Craig, "A Molinist View," 38.

world had been the Lord's choice among a *multitude* of other options, why did he blame Adam for the Fall? After all, Adam had no say in the decision-making process!

The problem of predestination/foreordination.

If God chose to create the world where I would be lost, how was he not responsible for my perdition? Why did he actualize this option with so few people saved when he could have created any universe he wanted (or none at all for that matter)?

Furthermore, how could a loving Lord choose to actualize a scenario with the Holocaust, innocent children abused, and pregnancies from rapes when he could have chosen to immediately create a "new heaven and a new earth, where righteousness dwells" (2 Pet 3:13 NIV)? How could this fallen realm be the "best possible"[20] or best feasible world for God to create? Why did the loving creator beget this cesspool of horrendous moral (e.g., the Las Vegas massacre) and natural (e.g., Hurricane Katrina) evils?

The problem of genuineness in the offer of salvation to all.

God "perfectly knows what will happen in this actual world." He knows who will be saved and who will be lost. Therefore, is the universal offer of salvation, as announced in this world, a genuine offer to all men? Should Christ not forthrightly declare that salvation was reserved for the few and that he did not choose to rescue everyone?

The problem of evil.

If God freely chose to actualize this wicked world, how was he not the author of evil? After all, he could have chosen to create a different world without sin! And if that could not be done, would it not be better not to create than to create a world with unspeakable evils (e.g., Cambodia's killing fields)?

"It would be better for him (Judas) if he had not been born" (Matt 26:24 NIV). If so, why was he created? Would it be righteous and loving to "use" him for evil in Christ's betrayal, and then condemn him for

---

20. The German philosopher Gottfried Leibniz thought that our world is "the best of all possible worlds" that God could create. Leibniz, *Leibniz Selections*, 345–55.

eternity? Dr. Kenneth Keathley, a Molinist advocate, acknowledged: "The mystery of evil remains."[21]

The problem of Man's depravity.

If God "sovereignly controls all things" including the fact of Man's depravity, does Man have the free will to be otherwise? Furthermore, if the Lord chooses to actualize/create *the world* where Man is totally depraved, how can Man be held responsible for his sins?

The problem of the perseverance of the saints/loss of salvation.

If God directs every event, does Man have the free will to be faithful or not? If circumstances in this created world are preordained/fixed, why does the Lord reward some more than others? After all, they are only "acting out" the scenario that God actualized. Why does he blame me if his chosen "master plan" guarantees that I will not persevere?

The problem of prayer.

Why should we pray if the outcome was already predetermined by God? Why should we ask for a different ending if he only created *the one* scenario that could not be changed?

The problem of God's immutability (does God ever change his mind?).

Since the events are unalterable in this actualized world, how can God ever change his mind in response to my actions (rebellion or repentance)? After all, once a scenario had been created with its fixed events, how could it be modified? What would be the point of repentance then?

The problem of free will choice in serving God.

Since everything is fixed in this actualized world, does Man have free will to serve or not serve God? Does Man have free will at all if the Lord created the circumstances guaranteeing that Man would do a certain action?

21. Keathley, *Salvation and Sovereignty*, 13.

The problem of Jesus' offer of the kingdom to Israel.

The Jews were "doomed" to reject Christ once the Lord had chosen to actualize *this* scenario. Thus, who was responsible for the crucifixion? Israel or God? After all, God could have decided to create the world where the Israelites would welcome their king! Furthermore, in this actualized world, was Christ "deceitful" in offering the kingdom with no possibility of giving?

MOLINISM AS A SOLUTION.

In my opinion, Molinism does not resolve all the theological problems raised by the conflict between God's sovereignty and Man's free will.[22] Let us consider Open Theism, the latest proposed solution to the quandary.

---

22. Critiques of the Molinism position (William Lane Craig's) can be found in Greg Boyd's, David Hunt's, and Paul Helm's responses in Beilby and Eddy, *Divine Foreknowledge*, 144–59. Critiques of William Lane Craig's position can also be found in Paul Helseth's, Ron Highfield's, and Greg Boyd's responses in Gundry and Jowers, *Four Views on Divine Providence*, 101–39. Other critiques of William Lane Craig's position can be found in Phillip Cary's, William Hasker's, Thomas Jay Oord's, and Stephen Wykstra's responses in Meister and Dew, *God and the Problem of Evil*, 131–42, 151–84.

Chapter 7

Open Theism as a solution

OPEN THEISM IS A recently promoted theory (1980)[1] addressing the dilemma of God's sovereignty and Man's free will. It has created a significant amount of controversy due to the claim that "God limits his knowledge" and is not omniscient in the classical sense. "Free actions (of men) are not entities which can be known ahead of time."[2] What are the teachings of Open Theism?

THE TENETS OF OPEN THEISM.

The eight points of Open Theism are encapsulated in the acronym DAFFODIL.[3]

Deliberate Depravity: Humans deliberately choose to sin.

All-Encompassing Invitation: The salvation offer is given to all.

Freedom of God: God is free. In love, he allows others to be free to have a free loving relationship with him.

Freedom of Man: Man is genuinely free to make his own decisions.

Openness of God's Character: God is "open" to what man may decide. The future is not set.

Determination of God's Ultimate Will: God is resourceful and will fulfill his promises.

Infinite Atonement: Christ's death atones for all sins.

---

1. Rice, *The Openness of God*. Open Theism may have its roots in the fourth century. See Jowers, "Open Theism."

2. Pinnock, "God limits his knowledge," 157.

3. Rogers, "Calvinism, Arminianism, and Open Theism," line 116.

Loving Relationship: God's central attribute is love.

Using these eight basic tenets, how does Open Theism address the problem?

THE OPEN THEISM SOLUTION.

Dr. John Sanders, an Open Theism scholar, stated: "Because the future exists as possibilities of what might happen, God possesses what is called dynamic omniscience in which God has exhaustive knowledge of the past and the present and understands 'the future' as what might happen. Divine omniscience is dynamic in that God constantly acquires knowledge of which possible future actions creatures select to actualize. The so-called 'future' does not exist as a reality and since God knows reality as it is, the future is not known."[4] Dr. Greg Boyd, a prominent Open Theism apologist, said: "Open Theists believe God created humans and angels with free will and that these agents are empowered to have 'say so' in what comes to pass. In Open Theism, therefore, what people decide to do genuinely affects God and affects what comes to pass."[5] Using these Open Theism explanations, how can God's sovereignty and Man's free will be stated in propositional form?

Since "the future is not known," even by God, everything is theoretically possible. Tomorrow, I can decide to go to the gym (path A) or I can decide to stay home and not go to the gym (path B). Tomorrow, God will acquire "knowledge of which possible future actions creatures select to actualize." Thus, God's sovereignty (in the Open Theism understanding) can be represented by the statement: it is possible that A is true, and it is possible that B is true. Since Man has free will and is "empowered to have 'say so' in what comes to pass," everything is possible for Man to decide. Man's free will (in the Open Theism understanding) can be represented by the statement: it is possible that A is true, and it is possible that B is true.

So, if we redefine God's sovereignty and Man's free will like the Open Theism scholars, the propositions will change to the following:

God's sovereignty: It is possible that A is true, and it is possible that B is true (statement 1).

4. Sanders, "The Key Ideas of Openness Theology," lines 9–13.
5. Boyd, "Five Ways the Bible Supports Open Theism," lines 4–6.

Man's free will: It is possible that A is true, and it is possible that B is true (statement 2).

Statement 1 agrees with statement 2.

Path A   Path B
It is possible that A is true, and it is possible that B is true
Man's free will

Path A   Path B
It is possible that A is true, and it is possible that B is true
God's sovereignty

If one adopts the Open Theism definitions of God's sovereignty and Man's free will, the logical dilemma is seemingly "solved" (as illustrated by the identical diagrams). However, can Open Theism untangle our ten theological problems?

THE THEOLOGICAL PROBLEMS.

The problem of God's sovereignty and Man's responsibility.

"I am God, and there is no one like me, declaring the end from the beginning, and from ancient times things which have not been done" (Isa 46:9–10). The omniscient Lord knows and declares "the end from the beginning." How can he do so if "the future is not known"? "And I will make you (Abraham) a great nation" (Gen 12:2). The omnipotent Lord gave an ironclad promise to Abraham to make of him "a great nation." How does one reconcile this declaration with the Open Theism proposal that "the future is not known" and not predetermined? Can God's solemn promise to Abraham be subject to Man's "say so"?

If some parts of the future are "open" (undetermined) and other parts of the future "closed" (fixed), how can one decide which is which since both are future events? For example, is the date of Christ's second coming fixed or undetermined? "But of that day and hour no one knows, not even the angels of heaven, nor the Son, but the Father alone" (Matt 24:36). Does the Father know the day and the hour or is that future event "open"?

Is the day of my death fixed or undetermined? "In your book were all written the days that were ordained for me" (Ps 139:16). Is my future really "open" when the Lord already ordained the number of my days? After all, if he already decreed the day of my funeral, it appears to me that my future destiny is very much closed (the end) *no matter what I do*!

"But our God is in the heavens; he does whatever he pleases" (Ps 115:3). "So then he has mercy on whom he desires, and he hardens whom he desires . . . Or does not the potter have a right over the clay, to make from the same lump one vessel for honorable use and another for common use?" (Rom 9:18–21). How does one reconcile these teachings with the Open Theism proposal that Man is "empowered to have 'say so' in what comes to pass"? What "say so" does Man have when the Lord "does whatever he pleases"? Does the clay have any "say so" in what the potter decides to make?

The problem of predestination/foreordination.

"'The older will serve the younger.' Just as it is written, 'Jacob I loved, but Esau I hated.' . . . So then it does not depend on the man who wills or the man who runs, but on God who has mercy" (Rom 9:12–16). How does one reconcile this teaching with the Open Theism proposal that "the future is not known" and predetermined? Were there any possibilities that the outcome would be "Esau I loved, but Jacob I hated," and "the younger will serve the older"? Were Esau and Jacob "empowered to have 'say so' in what came to pass"? Did the outcome "depend on the man who wills or the man who runs" or on God alone?

"You did not choose me, but I chose you, and appointed you that you would go and bear fruit" (John 15:16). "For those whom he foreknew, he also predestined to become conformed to the image of his son, so that he would be the firstborn among many brethren; and these whom he predestined, he also called; and these whom he called, he also justified; and these whom he justified, he also glorified" (Rom 8:29–30). The sovereign, omnipotent, and omniscient Lord "foreknew," "chose," "predestined," "called," "justified," and "glorified." How does one reconcile this teaching with the Open Theism proposal that "the future is not known" and predetermined? Do those who are "predestined to become conformed to the image of his son" have any "'say so' in what comes to pass?" Do those who are chosen and appointed to "go and bear fruit" have any "say so" in their future? Can they do otherwise and prove God wrong?

The problem of genuineness in the offer of salvation to all.

"What then? What Israel is seeking, it has not obtained, but those who were chosen obtained it, and the rest were hardened" (Rom 11:7). "Those who are outside get everything in parables, so that while seeing, they may see and not perceive, and while hearing, they may hear and not understand, otherwise they might return and be forgiven" (Mark 4:11–12). The sovereign Lord chose some for salvation and "hardened" others so that they might not "return and be forgiven." How does one reconcile this teaching with the Open Theism proposal that the future "is not known" and predetermined? Do those who are "hardened" have any "say so" in what comes to pass? Are there "possible future actions creatures select to actualize" that would allow them to "return and be forgiven" despite God's declaration? Is God's universal invitation a genuine offer if he makes some "blind and deaf" to the gospel message?

"What if God, although willing to demonstrate his wrath and to make his power known, endured with much patience vessels of wrath prepared for destruction?" (Rom 9:22). "They stumble because they disobey the word, as they were destined to do (1 Pet 2:8 ESV). Some "vessels of wrath," were "prepared for destruction" and "they were destined" to stumble. How does one reconcile these teachings with the Open Theism proposal that the future "is not known"? Does anyone have any "say so" about salvation or perdition? Is there any possibility that the "vessels of wrath prepared for destruction" will not come to their doom?

The problem of evil.

Dr. Greg Boyd said concerning the problem of evil: "The open view, I submit, allows us to say consistently, in unequivocal terms, that the ultimate source of all evil is found in the will of free agents rather than in God."[6] However, did God not put Adam to the test in the Garden of Eden? Adam did not choose to be tempted, did he? According to Open Theism, the Lord might not know for sure what Adam and Eve would do. Nevertheless, he obviously understood that there was a possibility that Adam and Eve would fall and bring evil into the world. Would loving parents put their children through that kind of test? And if they did, and their children failed the test and died, would the adults (i.e., God) be *totally blameless* in the matter?

Dr. John Sanders stated: "But in making creatures who should love him but may oppose him, God places the risk out in the open. Yet there is no reason to expect anything except love in return," but then "the unexpected happens."[7] If I planted a poisonous tree in my backyard, and I left my children unsupervised, if they ate from the tree and died, could I claim that "the unexpected happened" and that I bore no responsibility whatsoever for my son and daughter's deaths?

Even if God did not know beforehand what Adam and Eve would do, could the omnipresent Lord not intervene and rescue Eve when she was tempted and about to fall? And if he chose not to interfere, either with Eve or with Adam later, how could he not be (at least) partially responsible for their fall? Furthermore, he appeared to be "stacking the deck" against Adam. Who put the forbidden fruit in Eden? Who allowed the serpent tempter to roam the garden? Who was conveniently absent (or pretended to be absent since he was omnipresent) when Adam and Eve needed him the most? Thus, was God totally blameless in the matter of Adam's temptation and fall?

6. Boyd, *God of the Possible*, 102.

7. Sanders, *The God Who Risks*, 44.

"I form the light and create darkness, I bring prosperity and create disaster (Isa 45:7 NIV). "If a calamity occurs in a city has not the Lord done it?" (Amos 3:6). According to these verses, did God not take *some responsibility* for the evil in the world? Dr. Greg Boyd said: "I do not want to claim that the open view entirely solves the problem of evil."[8] Dr. William Hasker stated: "The fact is that very often we *just do not know* why certain sorts of evil are permitted by God; that this is so can be a test of faith— sometimes a severe test of faith—for a believer (italics in original)."[9] Dr. Thomas Jay Oord commented: "All of this means that Hasker eventually appeals to mystery."[10]

The problem of Man's depravity.

"As it is written, 'There is none righteous, not even one; there is none who understands, there is none who seeks for God'" (Rom 3:10–11). "Perhaps God may grant them repentance leading to the knowledge of the truth, and they may come to their senses and escape from the snare of the devil, having been held captive by him to do his will" (2 Tim 2:25–26).

How do we reconcile these teachings with the Open Theism assertions that humans are "empowered to have 'say so'"? What "say so" can unrighteous, depraved men have as the devil's captives? "For this reason, I have said to you, that no one can come to me unless it has been granted him from the Father" (John 6:65). "Among them we too all formerly lived in the lusts of our flesh, indulging the desires of the flesh and of the mind, and were by nature children of wrath" (Eph 2:3). If men are "by nature children of wrath" and unable to come to Christ, how can they be free to affect "what comes to pass"?

The problem of the perseverance of the saints/loss of salvation.

"This is the will of him who sent me, that of all that he has given me I lose nothing but raise it up on the last day" (John 6:39). "You, who are protected by the power of God through faith for a salvation ready to be revealed in the last time" (1 Pet 1:4–5). We learn from these verses that Christians "are protected by the power of God." None of those "given" to Christ can be lost. How do we reconcile these teachings with the Open

8. Boyd, *God of the Possible*, 99.

9. Hasker, "An Open Theist View," 76.

10. Oord, "The Essential Kenosis Response," 164.

Theism proposal that "the future is not known" and that "what people decide to do genuinely affects God and affects what comes to pass"?

The problem of prayer.

The Open Theism theologian Clark Pinnock said that prayer "is an activity that brings new possibilities into existence for God and us."[11] "You scrutinize my path and my lying down and are intimately acquainted with all my ways. Even before there is a word on my tongue, behold, O Lord, you know it all" (Ps 139:3–4). "Likewise, the Spirit helps us in our weakness. For we do not know what to pray for as we ought, but the Spirit himself intercedes for us with groanings too deep for words" (Rom 8:26 ESV). From these verses, we learn that our Father knows *all* our prayers "even before there is a word on" our tongue. Furthermore, the Holy Spirit must help us and intercede for us since "we do not know what to pray for as we ought." How do we reconcile these teachings with the Open Theism proposal that our prayer "brings new possibilities into existence for God and us"? What are the "new possibilities" that can come "into existence" in the mind of the omniscient Lord who is "intimately acquainted" with all our ways and our prayers?

"This is the confidence which we have before him, that, if we ask anything according to his will, he hears us. And if we know that he hears us in whatever we ask, we know that we have the requests which we have asked from him" (1 John 5:14–15). "Therefore, I say to you, all things for which you pray and ask, believe that you have received them, and they will be granted you" (Mark 11:24). If the Lord does not know and does not control the future, how can we have confidence that his solemn promises to answer our prayers will be fulfilled? Dr. Eleonore Stump wondered: "Could one trust such a God with one's child, one's life?"[12]

Dr. Greg Boyd said: "God promises his ultimate purpose for creation and humanity will not be thwarted. So, even if I couldn't explain how that is true, I have warrant for simply trusting that it is true . . . we can think of free will as a degree of 'say so' that God gives agents to affect what comes to pass. By definition, every degree of 'say so' that God gives away is a degree of 'say so' that God himself no longer possesses. To this degree, God *can't guarantee that he will get all that he wants* (italics mine)."[13] Is

11. Pinnock, *Most Moved Mover*, 46.

12. Stump, "Review of Peter Van Inwagen, God, Knowledge, and Mystery," 466.

13. Boyd, "Ask an Open Theist," lines 332–39.

that statement compatible with: "I am God, and there is no one like me, declaring the end from the beginning, and from ancient times things which have not been done, saying, 'my purpose will be established, and I will accomplish all my good pleasure'" (Isa 46:9–10)?

The problem of God's immutability (does God ever change his mind?).

Dr. Greg Boyd stated: "I therefore conclude that when the Bible says God changes his mind (which it does 39 times), it quite literally describes God changing his plans in response to changing circumstances in history. And this implies that the future is partly open."[14]

"Also the Glory of Israel will not lie or change his mind; for he is not a man that he should change his mind" (1 Sam 15:29). "God is not Man, that he should lie, or a son of Man, that he should change his mind" (Num 23:19 ESV). We gather from these verses that the Lord never changes his mind. His purpose is unchangeable. How does one reconcile this teaching with the Open Theism assertion that he changes his mind thirty-nine times in the Bible?

Concerning Hezekiah who was granted a reprieve from death (2 Kings 20, 2 Chronicles 32, and Isaiah 38, major texts used by Open Theism proponents to show that the Lord changed his mind), Dr. Bruce Ware remarked: "God granted to Hezekiah fifteen years of extended life—not two, not twenty, and certainly not 'we'll both see how long you live,' but fifteen years exactly. Does it not seem a bit odd that this favorite text of open theists, which purportedly demonstrates that God does not know the future and so changes his mind when Hezekiah prays, also shows that God knows precisely and exactly how much longer Hezekiah will live? On openness grounds, how could God know this? Over a fifteen-year time span, the contingencies are staggering!"[15]

Concerning Moses' intercession for Israel after the worship of the golden calf (Exodus 32, another major text used by Open Theists), Dr. William Barrick commented: "God revealed that even Moses' prayer could not remove the irrevocable sentence of death that the people had incurred . . . Was his statement to Moses an unalterable decree or a mere

14. Boyd, "Isn't God Changing His Mind," lines 29–31.
15. Ware, *God's Lesser Glory*, 97.

threat? It was obviously a decree (cf. Ps 95:8–11). The punishment was inevitable, even if it were temporarily delayed."[16] Did the Israelites escape their deserved penalty? Did they live to enter the Promised Land? Did the Lord change his mind about Israel's capital punishment for rebellion?

The problem of free will choice in serving God.

"You did not choose me, but I chose you and appointed you that you would go and bear fruit, and that your fruit would remain" (John 15:16). "Peter, an apostle of Jesus Christ, to those . . . who are chosen according to the foreknowledge of God the Father" (1 Pet 1:1–2). From these verses, we learn that the "chosen according to the foreknowledge of God" will *definitely* serve him and "bear fruit." How do we reconcile this teaching with the Open Theism assertion that men "are empowered to have 'say so' in what comes to pass"?

The problem of Jesus' offer of the kingdom to Israel.

"So you are to know and discern that from the issuing of a decree to restore and rebuild Jerusalem until Messiah the Prince there will be seven weeks and sixty-two weeks" (Dan 9:25). After extensive research of the date of the issue "of a decree to restore and rebuild Jerusalem" and precise calculations of the solar days involved in the prophecy of the "seven weeks and sixty-two weeks," Dr. Harold Hoehner concluded: "Nisan 444 BC marks the terminus a quo of the seventy weeks of Dan 9:24–27"[17] and "the terminus ad quem of the sixty-ninth week was on the day of Christ's triumphal entry on March 30, AD 33."[18] How do we reconcile the precise time frame prophesied in Daniel 9 with the Open Theism proposal that "the so-called 'future' does not exist as a reality and since God knows reality as it is, the future is not known"?

"This man, delivered over by the predetermined plan and foreknowledge of God, you nailed to a cross by the hands of godless men and put him to death" (Acts 2:23). "For truly in this city there were gathered together against your holy servant Jesus, whom you anointed, both Herod

---

16. Barrick, "The Openness of God," 164. The Lord's punishment was delayed until the event of the twelve spies (Num 14). God's pronouncement in Exodus 32:10 (i.e., "destroy them") was fulfilled in Numbers 14:29. The delay was about one year. https://aschmann.net/BibleChronology/The_Exodus.htm

17. Hoehner, *Chronological Aspects*, 128.

18. Hoehner, *Chronological Aspects*, 139.

and Pontius Pilate, along with the Gentiles and the peoples of Israel, to do whatever your hand and your purpose predestined to occur" (Acts 4:27–28). These verses seem to indicate that Jesus' rejection and crucifixion were predetermined and therefore inevitable. How do we reconcile this teaching with the Open Theism proposal that the future is "open"?

OPEN THEISM AS A SOLUTION.

Open Theism, in my opinion, does not resolve all the theological problems raised by the conflict between God's sovereignty and Man's free will.[19] We have now covered all the standard answers to the problem (i.e., Calvinism, Arminianism, Molinism, and Open Theism). Unfortunately, the solution to the conundrum is still elusive. Should we resign ourselves to call the question a "mystery"[20] or is there a way to resolve the enigma? Were there any fallacies in reasoning that led us down the wrong paths for almost two thousand years? Did we overlook some errors in logic resulting in faulty conclusions?

19. Critiques of the Open Theism position (Greg Boyd's) can be found in David Hunt's, William Lane Craig's, and Paul Helm's responses in Beilby and Eddy, *Divine Foreknowledge,* 48–64. Other critiques of the Open Theism position (Greg Boyd's) can also be found in Paul Helseth's, William Lane Craig's, and Ron Highfield's responses in Gundry and Jowers, *Four Views on Divine Providence,* 209–42. Critiques of the Open Theism position (Clark Pinnock's) can be found in John Feinberg's, Norman Geisler's, and Bruce Reichenbach's responses in Basinger and Basinger, *Predestination & Free will,* 163–77. Critiques of the Open Theism position (William Hasker's) can be found in Phillip Cary's, William Lane Craig's, Thomas Jay Oord's, and Stephen Wykstra's responses in Meister and Dew, *God and the Problem of Evil,* 131–50, 163–84.

20. "It is important, however, not to invoke 'mystery' prematurely. We must go as far as we can with our human reasoning and understanding before we label something a mystery." Erickson, *Christian Theology,* footnote 12, 359.

Chapter 8

Fallacies in human reasoning

CALVINISM ASSERTS THAT GOD foreordained whatever comes to pass, the *only* decreed path of history (e.g., the Fall and evil in the world). Arminianism and Molinism affirm that God infallibly foreknew the *one* path/world with all its events (e.g., Adam's disobedience). If so, how can Man be held responsible if he is given no other choice but to do whatever the Lord foreknew/foreordained? Is this problem a "mystery/paradox" or is it the result of Man's faulty reasoning?

MAN'S INCORRECT REASONING.

1. Adam is given two options: A (obedience) and B (disobedience).
2. God commands Adam to choose option A.
3. Adam chooses option B.
4. Adam reasons that since B is true, A must be false.
5. Adam reasons that God foreknew/foreordained that B is true, and A is false.
6. Adam reasons that B has always been true, and A has always been false.

7. Adam reasons therefore that he is only given one option, B (thus, he has no free will choice and is not responsible for the Fall and evil in the world. Evil is God's problem).[1]

Statement (7) contradicts statement (1), i.e., one option versus two options. What are the fallacies in Man's argument?

Fallacy #1.

In statement (4), option B being true/chosen does not *necessarily* make option A false/not chosen since A and B are not *necessarily* mutually exclusive. For example, I have the options of steak (A) and lobster (B) at a restaurant. Option B being chosen (I order lobster) makes "B is not chosen" (I do not order lobster) false. It does *not* make "option A is chosen" (I order steak) false. After all, I can order steak *and* lobster (both A and B are chosen/true). The point is that B being true/chosen does not *necessarily* make A false/not chosen.[2] Man, due to his limited point of view, *assumes wrongly* that his options A and B are *always* mutually exclusive. In quantum physics, light can be perceived as a wave (A) *and* a particle (B) at the same time.[3] Both options A and B are simultaneously true and are not mutually exclusive.[4]

Furthermore, Adam's decision to take the path of disobedience does not make the *paths themselves* real/true or unreal/false. Paths/options

1. The argument that God's infallible belief/foreknowledge of the one and only option negates Man's free will is detailed in Zagzebski, "Foreknowledge and Free Will," section 1.

2. It is important to differentiate choices from options. There are four possible choices with the two options A and B. The possible permutations/choices are: A-B (A and not B), AB (both A and B), -AB (B and not A), -A-B (neither A nor B). If the options A and B are mutually exclusive, then we are left with three choices: A-B, -AB and -A-B (after removing choice AB). Option B being true means that we must further remove the choices (A-B) and (-A-B), leaving -AB as the only remaining choice (i.e., option B is chosen, and option A is not chosen. This does *not* mean that option A is non-existent). However, if the options A and B are *not* mutually exclusive, we will have four possible choices. Thus, B being true/chosen does not mean that A is *necessarily* false/not chosen since AB and -AB are both possible choices (after removing A-B and -A-B since B is chosen). Since Man assumes wrongly that options A and B are *always* mutually exclusive, he fallaciously concludes that B being chosen/true *necessarily* means that A is not chosen/false.

3. Gray, "Einstein Was Right!" line 1.

4. In Quantum Mechanics, "the potential outcome states integrated in the pure state are not necessarily mutually exclusive." Epperson, "The Common Sense of Quantum Theory," 219.

A and B are real/true independently of anyone's decision to take or not take them. "Adam chooses option B" does *not* make option A (the path of obedience created and commanded by God) unreal/non-existent. In the analogy of the homeowner who has the option to enter her house through the front door (door A) or the back door (door B), the fact that she chooses to enter through the back door does not make the front door unreal/non-existent.

In summary, the fact that I choose B does not *necessarily* mean that "I choose A" is false (e.g., steak *and* lobster). Furthermore, the fact that I choose B does *not* mean that option A is non-existent/unreal (e.g., front door). Therefore, statement (4) is incorrect.

Fallacy #2.

Statement (4) is incorrect. However, even if it is correct, statements (5) and (6) do not *necessarily* follow from statement (4). Just because Adam believes that "B is true, and A is false" does not *necessarily* mean that option B has always been true (or timelessly true) and option A has always been false (or timelessly false) from God's point of view. Man commits the fallacy of *assuming* that God's perception is identical to Man's perception.

In the light analogy, "Adam perceives light as a particle" does not *necessarily* mean that "Adam perceives light as a wave" is impossible (i.e., timelessly, always false from God's point of view) or that light is always a particle and never a wave. In the swan (white and black) analogy, "Adam sees a white swan" does not *necessarily* mean that "Adam sees a black swan" is impossible (i.e., timelessly, always false from God's point of view) or that swans are always white and never black.

Therefore, due to these fallacies, Adam's conclusion in statement (7) that he was only given *one* option by God is erroneous.

THE CORRECT REASONING.

1. Adam is given two options: A (obedience) and B (disobedience).

2. God commands Adam to choose option A.

3. Adam chooses option B.

4. Adam is given two options and goes against God's command. Therefore, Adam is responsible for the Fall and evil in the world.

The Christian apologist David Hunt stated: "If God foreknows that Adam will sin, then Adam will sin—that's beyond dispute."[5] (i.e., path A obedience was impossible from all eternity). However, in the correct point of view (God's), both paths A and B were true and real (not mutually exclusive) even though Adam could only experience one or the other (mutually exclusive from Adam's point of view). Adam's decision to choose B did not make option A false, unreal, impossible, non-existent, or fake (nor did it make option B fixed, inevitable, immutable, or the only possible event).

For example, does the fact of the Holocaust mean that it was fixed, inevitable, foreknown, and decreed by God as the only possible option, thus making the Lord responsible for the horrendous evils? Does the rich young ruler's decision not to follow Christ (Matt 19:16–30) mean that the event was fixed, foreknown, and decreed by God as the only possible option, and that the option to follow Christ was false, non-existent, or fake, thus making Christ's offer "insincere"?

From Man's point of view, most (but not all) of his options are *mutually exclusive*. Therefore, Man reasons that if B is true, A must be false. The problem is that Man is *limited* to an existence in one place at one time, making most of his options mutually exclusive. His mistake is that he *projects* his finite viewpoint onto God, fallaciously reasoning that the omnipresent, omnipotent, and omniscient Lord perceives things the same limited way as Man.

From God's point of view, the options he creates are real and are *not* mutually exclusive. If A and B are mutually exclusive, then *only one* option can be true. Since the Lord is omniscient, he would know which one is true and which one is false. There would only be *one* true/real option due to God's infallible foreknowledge.

Thus, when God says there are options for Man, there must be real, *non-mutually-exclusive* alternatives. Since the Lord cannot lie,[6] the options he offers must be actual. In Adam's case, God *commanded* option A. Adam obeyed the Lord and took option A until the creation and fall of Eve. Option A was real and available. Since Adam subsequently chose option B, option B was also real and available. Both options A and B were available to Adam.

---

5. Hunt, "The Simple-Foreknowledge View," 75.

6. Num 23:19, 1 Sam 15:29, Heb 6:18, Titus 1:2.

Consequently, statement (1), "There are two options, A and B," is correct and statement (7), "There is only one option," is incorrect. God cannot be "insincere," claiming to offer two (or more) options[7] when there is only one. The Lord is righteous, omnipresent, omnipotent, and omniscient. From his point of view, both options A and B (or even more options) that he creates are *real /true at all times*, no matter what Man perceives/experiences.

Man is not *necessarily* limited to only one option due to God's sovereignty and foreknowledge.[8] Man is mistaken in asserting that the Lord foreordained him to carry out evil deeds (God's one and only decreed plan). He misjudges in affirming that the Lord foreknew yet permitted his evil actions (the one and only foreknown path). He errs in claiming that God selected *the* scenario of the Fall and the subsequent evils (the one and only actualized world). He falls short in limiting God's omniscience (i.e., men's free will actions cannot be known by the Lord ahead of time).

In summary, the quandary of God's sovereignty/Man's free will and the related problem of evil are the results of Man's faulty reasoning. Man fallaciously projects his limited perception onto the omnipotent, omnipresent, and omniscient Lord. The "mysteries" are resolved when God's Word is taken at face value. Man has real options and is responsible for his choices, decisions, and actions, whether good or evil. Since the classical solutions (Calvinism, Arminianism, Molinism, and Open Theism) to the problem of God's sovereignty and Man's free will have been found wanting, let us consider a new solution, the "Quantum Proposal," an approach that incorporates non-mutually-exclusive choices, and avoids the previous fallacies in human reasoning.

---

7. There are many examples of God offering options to men: Israel was offered at least three choices (Josh 24:15); Cain was given two options (Gen 4:7); Israel had two choices, the way of life and the way of death (Deut 28); the Jews could follow God or Baal (1 Kgs 18:21); Zedekiah was given the options to surrender or fight (Jer 38:17–18); Christ gave the people the choices to build on rock or sand (Matt 7:24–28).

8. This is not to say that God *always* offers men options. For example, John the Baptist had no alternative but to be Christ's forerunner (even from his mother's womb, Luke 1:14–17).

PART TWO

The Quantum Proposal

Chapter 9

The Quantum Proposal as a Solution

THE QUANTUM PROPOSAL DIFFERS from the previous solutions by asserting the absolute omnipotence, unlimited omniscience, and infinite omnipresence of the sovereign Lord. It also affirms that God, in his wisdom, may give Man some choices within his foreordained/decreed boundaries. Man is not *necessarily* "doomed" to the *one and only* option created by God. The ten tenets of the Quantum Proposal are as follows.

THE TENETS OF THE QUANTUM PROPOSAL.

Tenet #1: Man does not have total free will.

For example, I do not have the free will choice to be seven feet tall (I am only five feet four inches on a good day!). Paul did not have the free will choice to refuse God's call (Acts 9:15). Job did not have the free will choice not to suffer (Job 1). John the Baptist did not have the free will choice not to be the forerunner of the Messiah (Luke 1:17). God is the sovereign Lord over Man.

Tenet #2: Man has a certain amount of free will given to him by God.

For example, I was given a limited free will to marry whomever I wanted. Non-believers have no free will ("having been held captive by him to do his will" 2 Tim 2:26), unless given some by the Lord in his mercy. Believers have some limited free will ("For you were called to freedom, brethren; only do not turn your freedom into an opportunity for the flesh" Gal 5:13). The rich young ruler was free to follow Christ or not (Matt 19:21–22). Israel was offered the free will choice to worship God, the gods of their ancestors, or the gods of the Amorites (Josh 24:15). The Lord sovereignly gives Man some real, non-mutually-exclusive options (e.g., Israel could choose to worship the gods of their ancestors *and* the gods of the Amorites).

Tenet #3: Man's limited free will does not extend to the events already decreed by God.

My limited free will choices cannot change the outcomes already decreed by the Lord. For example, the second coming of Christ was decreed and fixed (Acts 1:11). The resurrection of the dead in Christ was decreed and fixed (1 Thess 4:16). A judgment after death was decreed and fixed (Heb 9:27). Therefore, whether I decide to marry Susan or Jane, Christ will still return at the appointed time and I will still be resurrected and judged after my death. God sovereignly decreed some fixed events in my life to accomplish his purpose.

Tenet #4: God sovereignly predestines Man.

"For those whom he foreknew, he also predestined (Proorizo) to become conformed to the image of his son, so that he would be the firstborn among many brethren; and these whom he predestined (Proorizo), he also called; and these whom he called, he also justified; and these whom he justified, he also glorified" (Rom 8:29–30). "4309.[1] Proorizo: (from 4253 / *pro*, 'before' and 3724 / *horizo*, 'establish boundaries, limits')— properly, *pre-horizon*, pre-determine limits (boundaries), predestine."[2] God sovereignly sets predetermined boundaries for Man (i.e., limits for Man's free will and choices). Proorizo does not *necessarily* mean *only one* fixed path. The Lord may give Man some alternative options within his foreordained confines (e.g., serve God or money, Luke 16:13).

---

1. These numbers are used in *Strong's Concordance* to reference Greek and Hebrew words.

2. http://biblehub.com/greek/4309.htm

Tenet #5: God's sovereignty and omniscience include the knowledge of all alternative scenarios.

For example, God knew what would have happened had I married Susan rather than Jane. In an alternative scenario, Saul went to Keilah and captured David (1 Sam 23:10–11). In an alternative scenario, Zedekiah's sons were not killed by the Babylonians (Jer 38:17–18). The alternative scenarios/options were forever known/created by the omnipotent, omniscient, and sovereign Lord.

Tenet #6: The alternative scenarios incorporate all the events already decreed by God.

For example, both alternative scenarios (me/Susan or me/Jane) included Christ's return at God's appointed time. Judah would still be taken by Babylon (decreed in 2 Kgs 20:16–18) even if Zedekiah's sons survived. David would still become king (decreed in 1 Sam 16) even if he was captured by Saul at Keilah.

Tenet #7: God's sovereignty may entail his advice on the better path among his given options.

For example, I could seek God's advice through prayer to determine the better choice for a mate (Susan or Jane?). God warned Jehoshaphat not to go with Ahab to battle (2 Chr 18). He advised David to leave Keilah (1 Sam 23). He counseled Zedekiah to surrender to the Babylonians (Jer 38:17–18).

Tenet #8: God sovereignly allows Man to make some free will decisions within the boundaries set by God.

For example, I could propose to either Susan or Jane (the only two available options in God's boundaries). Peter was free to go anywhere he wanted after he was delivered from jail by the angel (Acts 12). The rich young ruler had two options: sell his possessions and follow Christ or not sell his possessions and not follow Christ. The Lord set the boundaries and did not give a third option: follow Christ but not sell his possessions.

Tenet #9: Once Man has made a free will choice, the range of
possibilities within God's sovereign boundaries disappears.

For example, once I had chosen to marry Jane, the option to wed Susan
lapsed. Once Zedekiah had elected not to submit to the Babylonians, the
choice to surrender vanished. Once Jehoshaphat had opted to ally himself with Ahab, the alternative to turn down the alliance slipped away.
Once the rich young ruler had decided not to sell his possessions, the
opportunity to follow Christ disappeared.

Tenet #10: After making some free will choices, Man may be
allowed to make some future free will choices within God's
predetermined boundaries (i.e., mistakes may not be final).

For example, if I made the choice to use illicit drugs, God may give me
a future free will choice to join a drug treatment program. Pursued by
Saul, David foolishly decided to seek refuge in Gath, the hometown of
Goliath (1 Sam 21). The Lord mercifully allowed David to escape (1 Sam
22:1). Subsequently given another free will decision, David *again* foolishly chose to go back to Gath (1 Sam 27). God *again* had to rescue the
future king, this time from having to fight for the Philistines against the
Jews. This alliance with the enemy would forever ruin David's chances of
becoming Israel's monarch (1 Sam 29). Due to his solemn promise to David (1 Sam 16), the Lord set some boundaries that limited Man's free will.
David could not be killed by anyone (despite his poor decisions). David
had to become king (despite his questionable choices). The sovereign
Lord, in his mercy, may give us opportunities to remedy our mistakes.

Does the Quantum Proposal with its ten tenets solve the quandary
that has plagued the church for centuries? Can it successfully resolve the
logical dilemma?

THE QUANTUM PROPOSAL AS A SOLUTION.

Using the tenets of the Quantum Proposal, how can God's sovereignty
and Man's free will be stated in propositional form? The Lord in his
sovereignty allows Man some options within his predetermined boundaries (e.g., A: go to the gym tomorrow or B: stay home, and not go to
the gym tomorrow). As a human being limited in time and space, I can
only choose one option or the other. However, both options are real/true,

available, and created by the Lord. God's sovereignty can be represented by the statement: A is true, and B is true within God's boundaries. Since Man has a limited degree of free will within God's predetermined confines, he can choose to take either option A or option B. Man's free will can be represented by the statement: it is possible that A is true, and it is possible that B is true within God's boundaries. If we adopt the Quantum Proposal, the propositions will change to the following:

God's sovereignty: A is true, and B is true within God's boundaries (statement 1).

Man's free will: It is possible that A is true, and it is possible that B is true within God's boundaries (statement 2).

Statement 1 agrees with statement 2. "It is possible that A is true" agrees with "A is true." "It is possible that B is true" agrees with "B is true."

Path A   Path B
It is possible that A is true, and it is possible that B is true
Man's free will
"Possible" illustrated by broken lines

Path A   Path B
A is true, and B is true
God's sovereignty
"True/real" illustrated by solid lines

In the Quantum Proposal of God's sovereignty and Man's free will, the logical dilemma is seemingly "solved" (the diagrams are similar). However, does that approach resolve the ten theological problems raised?

Chapter 10

The problem of God's sovereignty and Man's responsibility

IF GOD IS SOVEREIGN over his creation, does Man have free will? Can Man be responsible for his actions if God predetermined all outcomes?

THE QUANTUM PROPOSAL AS A SOLUTION.

The Quantum Proposal asserts that God is Lord of all and "does whatever he pleases." However, in his sovereignty and for his glory, he allows Man a limited degree of free will to make some choices within his predetermined boundaries.[1] In love, he also points Man to the best path among the given options. Man can then make his decision and must bear full responsibility for his action, especially if he ignores God's advice.

For example, when Cain was angry about the offerings, God gave him two choices within God's preset confines. "If you do what is right, will you not be accepted? But if you do not do what is right, sin is crouching at your door; it desires to have you, but you must rule over it" (Gen 4:7 NIV). The Lord's acceptance would have been available had Cain chosen to reconsider his ways. God would have "accepted" (i.e., "exalt, dignify, uplift" from the Hebrew "seeth"[2]) him (e.g., as the *firstborn* son of Adam). In his mercy, the Lord also gave Cain a glimpse of the other possible path. Sin, like a hungry man-eater in wait, was crouching at the door, desiring to devour Cain. "Your adversary, the devil, prowls around

---

1. God also gave free will to demons and good angels (2 Pet 2:4, Jude 1:6, Ps 103:20).

2. http://biblehub.com/hebrew/7613.htm

69

like a roaring lion, seeking someone to devour" (1 Pet 5:8). Despite the warning, Cain embraced the destructive option and was therefore totally responsible for his action. Obviously, once Cain had made his decision, the better alternative disappeared. The Lord, in his sovereignty, did not give Cain other choices (e.g., "accept" Cain even if he does not do what is right, remove the enemy who is "crouching" at the door, or actively help Cain "rule over" his enemy).

The sovereign Lord gave Zedekiah two options within his predetermined boundaries in Jeremiah 38. The king could submit to the Babylonians or fight them. In his mercy, God even let Zedekiah glimpse into the future with a "sneak peek" of the two paths. "If you will indeed go out to the officers of the king of Babylon, then you will live, this city will not be burned with fire, and you and your household will survive. But if you will not go out to the officers of the king of Babylon, then this city will be given over to the hand of the Chaldeans; and they will burn it with fire, and you yourself will not escape from their hand" (Jer 38:17–18). Zedekiah was free to choose between the two options. He foolishly ignored God's advice, refused to surrender, and suffered the consequences of his action. Once he had made his choice, the better scenario vanished. God did not give Zedekiah other alternatives: a victory in battle, a miracle causing the Babylonians to withdraw, or a total annihilation of the Babylonian army by an angel.

The sovereign Lord gave Jehoshaphat two choices: he could go with Ahab to battle or he could decline the offer. In his mercy, God even let Jehoshaphat glimpse into the future. "I saw all Israel scattered on the mountains, like sheep which have no shepherd; and the Lord said, 'These have no master. Let each of them return to his house in peace'" (2 Chr 18:16). Jehoshaphat was then given total freedom to decide. To his detriment, he selected the destructive path and was held accountable for his action. Once Jehoshaphat had made his decision, the better choice disappeared. The Lord did not give Jehoshaphat other options: go with Ahab and succeed, have a good excuse for not going (e.g., illness), or have a miraculous victory without going to war.

The Quantum Proposal resolves the dilemma of God's sovereignty and Man's responsibility by giving Man limited free will choices within God's preset confines. Man can choose to obey and glorify the Lord voluntarily out of love and gratitude. Man can also decide to disobey God and insist on his own designs. In either case, Man will have to bear full responsibility for his decisions whether good or evil. Man is the origina-tor[3] of his actions and is therefore the appropriate recipient of any moral praise and blame.[4] By setting boundaries and creating some limited op-tions, the Lord asserts his sovereignty over all creation. Through love, God endeavors to protect and guide Man, allowing him to grow to his greatest potential as a free will being.

A STORY OF GOD'S SOVEREIGNTY AND MAN'S RESPONSIBILITY.

As a self-employed anesthesiologist, I had to drive from hospital to hospital to handle various operations. One day, I was running very late, causing the whole surgical team (and the distraught patient) to anxiously await my arrival. Oh no! A stop sign before I can make a left turn! Should I do a California stop[5] (no disrespect to California) or should I obey the rules? What would Jesus do? Nah! I don't see any car coming (nor do I see any "black and white cruiser" lurking in the bushes). It is perfectly safe to proceed. Full speed ahead! Screeeeech! Bang! I was T-boned by a hu-mongous pickup truck that appeared from nowhere! Please find another anesthesiologist for the much-delayed surgery! A "Godfather offer"[6] was promptly issued to attend a "snorrendously" educative meeting on the fine art of "defensive driving." Did God get a chuckle from the incident? Did he try to repress the "I told you so! Choose but choose wisely"? Yes, Lord! My fault! I am sorry! However, was I foreordained ("doomed") to wreck my car? To that question, we will now turn!

---

3. "Yet it is plausible (Kane 1996) that the core metaphysical feature of freedom is being the ultimate source, or originator, of one's choices, and that being able to do otherwise is closely connected to this feature." O'Connor, "Free Will," section 4.4.

4. "An agent is morally responsible for an event or state of affairs only if she is the appropriate recipient of moral praise or moral blame for that event or state of affairs (an agent can thus be morally responsible even if no one, including herself, actually does blame or praise her for her actions)." Timpe, "Free Will," section 1.

5. A "California" stop is a "rolling" stop.

6. A "Godfather offer" is an offer that one cannot refuse.

Chapter 11

The problem of predestination/ foreordination and Man's free will

"'I will have mercy on whom I have mercy, and I will have compassion on whom I have compassion.' So then it does not depend on the man who wills or the man who runs, but on God who has mercy" (Rom 9:15–16). Some questions illustrate the conundrum of God's predestation/fore-ordination of all events and Man's free will. How does the Quantum Proposal resolve these issues?

IF GOD IS SOVEREIGN AND DECREES THAT I WILL BE CONDEMNED (NOT ELECTED FOR SALVATION), WHY AM I BLAMED FOR MY PERDITION? WHERE IS MY FREE WILL IN THE MATTER?

The Quantum Proposal affirms that Man does not have total free will. "On the contrary, who are you, O man, who answers back to God? The thing molded will not say to the molder 'Why did you make me like this,' will it?" (Rom 9:20). All men, prior to accepting Christ, are "held captive by him (the devil) to do his will" (2 Tim 2:26). Captive men have no free will of their own. However, in his mercy, the sovereign Lord may allow *some to have the free will choice* to follow him (e.g., the rich young ruler). If Man chooses to reject Christ's offer of salvation, Man will be held responsible for that decision. In God's sovereignty, the option to refuse is not accorded to some (e.g., Paul in Acts 9, John the Baptist in Luke 1).

Furthermore, whether men are given an opportunity to hear the gospel or not, they are still held responsible[1] for their actions as they can perceive the Lord through creation (i.e., general revelation). "For since the creation of the world, his invisible attributes, his eternal power and divine nature, have been clearly seen, being understood through what has been made, so that they are without excuse" (Rom 1:20).[2]

SINCE GOD IS OMNISCIENT AND ALREADY KNOWS THAT I WILL BE CONDEMNED, THAT EVENT IS UNCHANGEABLE. WHY THEN AM I BLAMED FOR MY PERDITION?

The Quantum Proposal suggests that predestination (Proorizo) does not necessarily mean only *one* predetermined/foreknown path. For example, God gave the Israelites two options: follow him or not. He took great care to give them a "sneak peek" of the *two* foreknown paths in Deuteronomy 11, the path of blessing/salvation (rain, wine, oil, and cattle) and the path of disobedience (drought and death). They could have chosen the way of blessing but instead decided to forsake him. Furthermore, he gave them many opportunities to repent and be saved but they stubbornly refused. Therefore, he rightfully held them responsible for their decision. They were not "doomed" to disobedience and destruction by his predestination and foreknowledge.

In the Quantum Proposal, the Lord sovereignly gives Man some free will choices within his predetermined/foreknown boundaries. Man is free to adopt the recommended option or not (e.g., obey the stop sign, become a Christian). No one is "doomed" to have an accident or reject Christ. Of course, once Man has made his selection, the alternative path disappears.

---

1. Dr. Keathley explained the difference between two kinds of freedom. "Freedom of responsibility is the ability to be the originator of a decision, choice, or action . . . Freedom of integrity is the ability to act in a way that is consistent with what a person knows to be the right thing to do . . . A person can have enough freedom to be responsible yet lack (or lose) the freedom of integrity . . . (people) in Rom 7:13–25 . . . heroin addicts, compulsive gamblers." Keathley, *Salvation and Sovereignty*, 77–78.

2. I assume this would apply to my parents since they never heard the gospel as far as I know.

WHY DO I NEED TO EVANGELIZE OR SUPPORT MISSIONS IF GOD ALREADY FOREKNEW/DECREED WHO WILL (OR WILL NOT) BE SAVED? WHERE IS MAN'S FREE WILL IN THE MATTER?

In the Quantum Proposal, God sometimes allows Man to make some free will decisions concerning eternal salvation or other matters. For example, the rich young ruler was given a free will choice to follow Christ or not. In Luke 9:59–60, we read: "And he said to another, 'Follow me.' But he said, 'Lord, permit me first to go and bury my father.' But he said to him, 'Allow the dead to bury their own dead; but as for you, go and proclaim everywhere the kingdom of God.'" The unknown man was given some options: follow Christ or take care of his father. We do not know which decision the man made. Since we are not told who is given a free will choice concerning salvation, evangelism and missions are expressions of our love and concern for the lost. We may be God's chosen instruments (ambassadors, 2 Cor 5:20), providing people opportunities to be saved for "how shall they hear without a preacher?" (Rom 10:14).

WHY DID GOD BLESS ABRAHAM SO ABUNDANTLY WHEN GOD HAD ALREADY FOREKNOWN/ FOREORDAINED THAT ABRAHAM WOULD GIVE UP ISAAC AS A SACRIFICE? DID ABRAHAM HAVE ANY OTHER CHOICE BUT TO DO WHAT GOD HAD DECREED?

In Genesis 17:19, God promised Abraham that he would make an "everlasting covenant" with Isaac and his descendants. When the Lord demanded Isaac's sacrifice, Abraham had two choices: obey or rebel. Faced with the decision, "Abraham reasoned that God could even raise the dead, and so in a manner of speaking he did receive Isaac back from death" (Heb 11:19 NIV).

The word "reasoned" is the Greek "logizomai, (the root of the English terms 'logic, logical')— properly, compute, 'take into account'; reckon (come to a 'bottom-line'), i.e., reason to a logical conclusion (decision)."[3] Abraham reasoned that God's promise was irrevocable and therefore, somehow, Isaac would have to live. Even if Isaac was offered as a sacrifice,

---

3. http://biblehub.com/greek/3049.htm

the Lord would raise him "back from death" to keep his word. So, after "taking into account" the advantages and disadvantages, Abraham logizomai "to a logical conclusion," came to a "bottom line" and decided to take the first option. And for that obedient choice, he was greatly blessed!

IN THE SAME VEIN, WHAT DID THE HEROES OF THE "HALL OF FAITH" (HEB 11) DO TO DESERVE SPECIAL MENTIONS IF GOD HAD ALREADY FOREORDAINED THEIR OUTCOMES? DID THEY HAVE ANY OTHER CHOICE BUT TO DO WHAT GOD HAD DECREED?

The Quantum Proposal holds that God sometimes allows Man to make some free will decisions. The Scriptures do not give all the details about the circumstances of the heroes/heroines of the Hall of Faith. However, we have some information about the decisions of some faithful men and women mentioned.

Noah.

Noah was told to build an ark and gather the needed animals. After receiving God's instructions, "thus Noah did; according to all that God had commanded him, so he did" (Gen 6:22). "By faith Noah, being warned by God about things not yet seen, in reverence prepared an ark for the salvation of his household, by which he condemned the world" (Heb 11:7).

The word "reverence" is the Greek "eulabeomai" meaning first, to act cautiously, circumspectly; second, to beware, to fear; third, to reverence, to stand in awe.[4] "This Noah condemned (the unbelieving sinful world of man) by his faith, namely, by the act, in that he set forth the culpability of its conduct by the contrast of his own conduct."[5] In "reverent fear," Noah "acted cautiously," chose the correct course of action and "did according to all that God had commanded him." But the disobedient "ancient world" chose the other path and ignored God's warning. "They were eating, they were drinking, they were marrying, they were being given in marriage, until the day that Noah entered the ark, and the flood came and destroyed them all" (Luke 17:27), "when the patience of God" was finally

---

4. http://biblehub.com/greek/2125.htm

5. Meyer's NT commentary. http://biblehub.com/commentaries/Heb/11-7.htm

exhausted. Noah made the right decision ("by which he condemned the world" that made the other choice) and was rightfully rewarded by God.

Abraham, Sarah, Isaac, and Jacob.

"By faith Abraham, when he was called, obeyed by going out to a place which he was to receive for an inheritance; and he went out, not knowing where he was going" (Heb 11:8). "All these (Abraham, Sarah, Isaac, and Jacob) died in faith, without receiving the promises, but having seen them and having welcomed them from a distance and having confessed that they were strangers and exiles on the earth" (Heb 11:13).

Abraham, Sarah, Isaac, and Jacob never actually owned/received the Promised Land. Day after day, they had a decision to make: "Should we stay in Canaan with all its difficulties or should we go back home to Mesopotamia?" "All their life long they would have been able to claim again their earlier fatherland, by returning whence they came."[6] "And indeed if they had been thinking of that country from which they went out, they would have had opportunity to return" (Heb 11:15). Yet, they made the correct, but more difficult, choice to stay as "strangers and exiles" in the land and were rightfully rewarded by God.

Joseph.

As Potiphar's slave in Egypt, Joseph was given a choice. "There is no one greater in this house than I, and he has withheld nothing from me except you, because you are his wife. How then could I do this great evil and sin against God?" (Gen 39:9). Joseph made the right decision by refusing Potiphar's wife. Therefore, he was greatly blessed by the Lord.

When Joseph was about to die, he had another choice to make: he could be embalmed in a lavish monument in Egypt; he could be entombed in Canaan immediately; or he could be buried later in the Promised Land with Israel's Exodus. "By faith Joseph, when he was dying, made mention of the Exodus of the sons of Israel, and gave orders concerning his bones" (Heb 11:22). Wisely, Joseph chose the best of the three available options. He decided to faithfully stay with Israel in Egypt until the day when they would all leave together in the promised Exodus. After all, he was the one responsible for bringing them into a foreign land. The embalmed body

6. Ellicott's Commentary for English Readers. http://biblehub.com/commentaries/Heb/11-15.htm

of Joseph was placed in a coffin and remained in Egypt for nearly four hundred years. "He *mentioned*, what he had never forgotten, the promise made to their fathers . . . so that even though dead he might leave Egypt and come into the Land of Promise. Those who are without faith, either take no care, or a vain and foolish concern about their bones."[7] "Now they buried the bones of Joseph, which the sons of Israel brought up from Egypt, at Shechem, in the piece of ground which Jacob had bought from the sons of Hamor the father of Shechem for one hundred pieces of money; and they became the inheritance of Joseph's sons" (Josh 24:32). Joseph made the right, but more difficult, choice[8] to remain in Egypt with the children of Israel until the Exodus and was therefore rewarded by God.

Amram, Jochebed, and Moses.

"By faith Moses, when he was born, was hidden for three months by his parents, because they saw he was a beautiful child; and they were not afraid of the king's edict" (Heb 11:23). Moses' parents (Amram and Jochebed) had some decisions to make. They could obey the king and kill Moses, or they could disobey and let Moses live. But would it be possible to hide Moses forever from Pharaoh's men? Thankfully, they came up with a clever solution (have Pharaoh's daughter adopt Moses and pay them to care for the baby). For making the right choice, Amram and Jochebed were blessed by the Lord and included in the "Hall of Faith."

"By faith Moses, when he had grown up, refused to be called the son of Pharaoh's daughter, choosing rather to endure ill-treatment with the people of God than to enjoy the passing pleasures of sin, considering the reproach of Christ greater riches than the treasures of Egypt" (Heb 11:24–26). Moses was given many options. He could be an Egyptian, the

---

7. Bengel's Gnomen. http://biblehub.com/commentaries/Heb/11-22.htm

8. "Decent burial was regarded to be of great importance in ancient Israel, as in the rest of the ancient Near East. Not only the Egyptians . . . but also the peoples of Mesopotamia dreaded above all else the thought of lying unburied. One of the most frequently employed curses found in Mesopotamian texts is: 'May the earth not receive your corpses,' or the equivalent. In the same way one can measure the importance that Israelites attached to burial by the frequency with which the Bible refers to the fear of being left unburied." https://www.jewishvirtuallibrary.org/ancient-burial-practices. According to Josephus, Joseph's brothers were all buried with their ancestors in Canaan before the Exodus. "At length his brethren died, after they had lived happily in Egypt. Now the posterity and sons of these men, after some time, carried their bodies, and buried them at Hebron." Josephus, *Antiquities of the Jews*, 2.198. Thus, Joseph's decision not to be buried in Canaan at his death had to be very difficult.

son of Pharaoh's daughter, or an Israelite (God's covenant people). He could "enjoy the passing pleasures of sin," or "endure ill-treatment with the people of God." He could be rich with "the treasures of Egypt," or live with "the reproach of Christ." Moses made the correct, but more difficult, decision and was therefore blessed by the Lord.

Rahab.

Rahab had a choice to make. She could surrender to God or persist in rebellion. "By faith Rahab the harlot did not perish along with those who were disobedient, after she had welcomed the spies in peace" (Heb 11:31). The word "disobedient" is the Greek "apeitheo, literally, *refuse to be persuaded* (by the Lord)."[9] Rahab took risks (i.e., turn traitor and shelter the spies) and made the wise decision to switch allegiance. Therefore, she was included in the "Hall of Faith" and became a prominent member in the genealogy of Christ (one of only five women mentioned in Matthew 1). The people of Jericho who chose the other option were destroyed. They were fully responsible for their action as they knew that the Lord had given Israel the land and that "he is God in heaven above and on earth beneath" (Josh 2:11). Yet, they "refused to be persuaded" even after hearing about the miracle of the Red Sea and the destruction of Sihon and Og.

The Scriptures recorded many free will choices of the heroes/heroines of the "Hall of Faith." In trust and obedience, they made the correct decisions and were rightfully blessed by their Lord.

ARE PREGNANCIES FROM RAPES "SOMETHING THAT GOD INTENDED TO HAPPEN"? DID GOD REALLY FOREORDAIN THAT OUTCOME?

Who is responsible for a pregnancy from rape? Man or God? Did the Lord decree that outcome? In the account of David and Bathsheba, "David sent messengers and took her, and when she came to him, he lay with her . . . she sent and told David, and said, 'I am pregnant'" (2 Sam 11:4–5). Obviously, God did not want this outcome for he said through Nathan the prophet: "Why have you despised the word of the Lord by doing evil in his sight?" (2 Sam 12:9). Accepting full responsibility for his actions, David confessed: "I have sinned against the Lord" (2 Sam 12:13). Was

9. http://biblehub.com/greek/544.htm

the rape of Bathsheba and her pregnancy one of the possible scenarios within God's predetermined boundaries? One would have to say yes since that was what happened. Was that God's recommended choice (or foreordained/decreed path) for David? Forcefully no!

What was God's plan for David? "At the time when kings go out to battle, that David sent Joab and his servants with him and all Israel . . . But David stayed at Jerusalem" (2 Sam 11:1). In his sovereignty, the Lord gave David some free will choices: do his duty as king and lead the army to battle or neglect his duty and stay home. David chose the easier/safer option and reaped the destructive consequences for himself and for everyone else around him. Uriah, Bathsheba's husband, was murdered. Joab, David's general, became an accomplice in the assassination. Bathsheba's child died. David's son Amnon raped his half-sister Tamar. Absalom, Tamar's brother, killed Amnon in revenge. Absalom rebelled against David, resulting in civil war. Ahithophel, Absalom's counselor and Bathsheba's grandfather, hanged himself when Absalom rejected his advice to pursue David. Twenty thousand Israelites died in the rebellion. Absalom was killed . . . The prophecy of the Lord was fulfilled: "Now therefore, the sword shall never depart from your house, because you have despised me" (2 Sam 12:10). Probably, none of this would have happened had David chosen to do his duty. "But David tarried still at Jerusalem; which is observed for the sake of the following history; it would have been well for him if he had gone forth with the army himself, then the sin he fell into would have been prevented."[10]

Disobedience of God's command will always result in pain and suffering, not only for oneself but also for everyone around since no one ever lives in a vacuum. Pregnancy from rape may be a possible scenario within God's boundaries. However, that is never the Lord's will "for God cannot be tempted by evil, and he himself does not tempt anyone." Like David, men willfully choose to do their evil deeds and are therefore fully responsible for their actions.

In summary, the Quantum Proposal resolves the dilemma of God's predestination/foreordination and Man's free will by advocating that predestination (Proorizo) does not necessarily mean only one predetermined/foreknown path. Man is given free will to choose among various options within God's foreordained boundaries and is therefore held accountable for his deeds, whether good or evil.

10. Gill's Exposition of the Entire Bible. http://biblehub.com/commentaries/2_samuel/11–1.htm

A STORY OF GOD'S FOREORDINATION AND MAN'S FREE WILL.

With the imminent addition of a new family member, my pregnant wife and I decided to forgo the much-vaunted apartment lifestyle and join the American dream of home ownership. A friend highly recommended this "unbelievable" agent who would help us newbies snatch our dream residence.

Hey! Is this normal to drive up and down the streets looking for houses? Should we just view the ones that meet our criteria (e.g., no pool)? However, how could two "young apprentices" argue with "Master Yoda"? After a few punishing weeks of Jedi training, my wife and I finally begged for an MLS book[11] to do our own search. We found a good home and made an offer that was promptly rejected! Good bye, Master! We will go to the dark side and find us a new helper.

The house hunting with "Mary Poppins" was like a trip to Mickey's fairy land. Unfortunately, no suitable dwellings within our budget could be found. Should we go back to the previous home and raise the offer? Should we return to "Master Yoda" (so as not to deprive him of his commission) or should we stay with our beloved "Mary Poppins"? In God's sovereignty, the free will choice was ours. We reluctantly went back to the "Master," raised the offer, and were approved!

On escrow day, we eagerly went to sign the papers with a flourish and take possession of our first home when . . . "I am sorry! Master Yoda's sales contract was unclear, allowing the seller to demand an additional thousand dollars. No extra money, no home!" After a flurry of back-and-forth phone calls, Yoda finally agreed to pay the sum out of his share. After all, no sale meant no commission! All was well that ended well, thanks to our "unbelievable" agent!

When God offers us choices in house hunting, real estate agents, or other matters, are they legitimate options? Do we have real alternatives in our lives and our eternal destinies? Can everyone receive Christ's offer of salvation? Is that a genuine invitation to all?

---

11. Thirty years ago, houses for sale were listed in a huge Multiple Listing Services (MLS) book.

Chapter 12

The problem of genuineness in the offer of salvation to all

"FOR GOD SO LOVED the world, that he gave his only begotten son, that whoever believes in him shall not perish, but have eternal life" (John 3:16). "This is good and acceptable in the sight of God our Savior, who desires all men to be saved and to come to the knowledge of the truth" (1 Tim 2:3–4). From these verses, it appears that the offer of salvation is given to all.

However, we also read: "What if God, although willing to demonstrate his wrath and to make his power known, endured with much patience vessels of wrath prepared for destruction?" (Rom 9:22). Thus, is the offer of salvation a genuine universal invitation?

THE QUANTUM PROPOSAL AS A SOLUTION.

The Quantum Proposal affirms God's sovereignty in offering salvation to whomever he desires. "So then it does not depend on the man who wills or the man who runs, but on God who has mercy" (Rom 9:16). However, is salvation offered to all (e.g., Pharaoh, Judas) or only to some? Are lost sinners "doomed" to destruction by the Lord in eternity past (i.e., decreed for reprobation) or are their final outcomes the results of their own poor choices? What can we learn from the Scriptures?

Mark 4:11–12.

"To you has been given the mystery of the kingdom of God, but those who are outside get everything in parables, so that while seeing, they may see and not perceive, and while hearing, they may hear and not understand, otherwise they might return and be forgiven." Mark's quote from Isaiah 6:9 referred to God and rebellious Israel. "The sense is, because you have so long heard my words, and seen my works, to no purpose, and have hardened your hearts, and will not learn nor reform, I will punish you in your own way; your sin shall be your punishment. I will still continue my word and works to you, but will withdraw my Spirit, so that you shall be as unable, as now you are unwilling, to understand."[1] Jesus did *not* start his ministry by speaking in parables to Israel (e.g., no parables in the Sermon on the Mount). "But his direct teaching was met with scorn, unbelief, and hardness. From this time forward 'parables' entered largely into his recorded teaching and were at once attractive and penal."[2] In other words, after much rejection, Jesus probably decided to apply the principle, "Do not give what is holy to dogs, and do not throw your pearls before swine, or they will trample them under their feet, and turn and tear you to pieces" (Matt 7:6). Henceforth, he would only teach people who wanted to learn. As the detractors had made up their minds to oppose the Messiah, the Lord "gave them over to the stubbornness of their heart, to walk in their own devices" (Ps 81:12). And what was the reason for this drastic step? "My people did not listen to my voice, and Israel did not obey me" (Ps 81:11) and "did not recognize the time of your visitation" (Luke 19:44). Again, God did not act capriciously and unfairly with his people when he chose to speak to some of them in parables. A "decree of reprobation" cannot be derived from these verses.

Romans 9:22.

"What if God, although willing to demonstrate his wrath and to make his power known, endured with much patience vessels of wrath prepared for destruction?" The word "prepared" is the Greek "katartizo (from 2596 / *kata*, 'according to, *down*,' intensifying *artizo*, 'to adjust,' which is derived from 739 /*artios*, 'properly adjusted') – properly, *exactly* fit (adjust) to

---

1. Benson Commentary. http://biblehub.com/commentaries/Isa/6–9.htm

2. Cambridge Bible for Schools and Colleges. http://biblehub.com/commentaries/mark/4–12.htm

be in good *working order*, i.e., adjusted *exactly* 'down' to fully function."[3] Romans 9:22 does not suggest that the Lord prepared the vessels of wrath for destruction. "There is not the semblance of a declaration that 'God had prepared them or fitted them for destruction.' It is a simple declaration that they were in fact suited for it, without making an affirmation about the manner in which they became so."[4] A "decree of reprobation" dooming these "vessels of wrath" to perdition cannot be derived from this verse.

Romans 11:7.

"What then? What Israel is seeking, it has not obtained, but those who were chosen obtained it, and the rest were hardened." The word "hardened" is the Greek "poroo (from *poros*, a kind of marble) – properly, made of *stone*; (figuratively) *insensible*; dull, *unperceptive* as *a rock*; calloused (hardened); i.e., unresponsive (dense), completely lacking sensitivity or spiritual perception."[5] Romans 11:7 does not suggest that the Lord hardened the rest. "In regard to 'the election,' it is affirmed that it was of God; Rom 11:4. Of the remainder, the fact of their blindness is simply mentioned, without affirming anything of the cause."[6] A "decree of reprobation" *from God* dooming these people to eternal perdition cannot be derived from the verse.

1 Peter 2:8.

"'A stone of stumbling, and a rock of offense.' They stumble because they disobey the word, as they were destined to do" (1 Pet 2:8 ESV). The word "destined" is the Greek "tithemi" meaning "to place, lay, set."[7] Commentators are divided on the meaning of the verse.[8] If one accepts the interpretation that some are "destined" for condemnation by a decree of reprobation,[9] the Quantum Proposal suggests that the Lord is ultimately sovereign over his creation. However, we are then left with the dilemma

---

3. http://biblehub.com/greek/2675.htm

4. Barnes' Notes on the Bible. http://biblehub.com/commentaries/Rom/9–22.htm

5. http://biblehub.com/greek/4456.htm

6. Barnes' Notes on the Bible. http://biblehub.com/commentaries/Rom/11–7.htm

7. http://biblehub.com/greek/5087.htm

8. http://biblehub.com/commentaries/1_peter/2–8.htm

9. God rejected or "passed over" the reprobates in his eternal decree of election.

of God's offer of salvation to all and his actual decision/decree to not save some.

On the other hand, 1 Peter 2:8 can be interpreted differently. Because they disobeyed the word of God, they stumbled, "as they were destined to do." The passage does not say that those who stumbled were decreed to perdition. "What he really affirms is that it is part of God's appointed order that the disobedient should stumble."[10] "But that stumbling does not necessarily imply condemnation . . . The word, the preaching of Christ crucified, was to the Jews a stumbling-block (1 Cor 1:23). But not all stumbled that they might fall."[11] "I say then, they did not stumble so as to fall, did they? May it never be!" (Rom 11:11). Stumbling as the "destined" result of disobeying the Word does not *necessarily* mean to be "decreed for reprobation" and guaranteed to "fall" into perdition. Thus, a "decree of reprobation" from God dooming those who "stumble" cannot be derived from this verse.

Jude 1:4.

"For certain persons have crept in unnoticed, those who were long beforehand marked out for this condemnation, ungodly persons who turn the grace of our God into licentiousness and deny our only Master and Lord, Jesus Christ." The word "marked out" is the Greek "prographo" meaning "to write before (of time)" or "to depict or portray openly."[12]

Commentators are divided on the meaning of the verse.[13] If one accepts the interpretation that God had "long beforehand marked out" (i.e., written before time)[14] some for condemnation, the Quantum Proposal would advocate that the Lord is sovereign over his creatures. As captives doing the devil's will, fallen men have no free will of their own. Their destiny is already assured by their malevolent father. However, with this interpretation, we are left with the quandary of God's universal offer of salvation and his decision to reprobate some.

On the other hand, Jude 1:4 can be interpreted differently. "If they do not repent . . . their names were written in letters of light, and

10. Cambridge Bible for Schools and Colleges. http://biblehub.com/commentaries/1_peter/2-8.htm

11. Pulpit Commentary. http://biblehub.com/commentaries/1_peter/2-8.htm

12. http://biblehub.com/greek/4270.htm

13. http://biblehub.com/commentaries/jude/1-4.htm

14. This interpretation uses the first meaning of "prographo."

announced to the universe that they would be damned."[15] In other words, these *types* of "ungodly people" ("persons who turned the grace of our God into licentiousness and denied our only Master and Lord") had been "portrayed and depicted openly"[16] as deserving of this condemnation, the same punishment that was given to Israelites in the Exodus who did not believe, angels who abandoned their proper abode, and Sodom and Gomorrah. If this interpretation is correct, if the Lord did not "destine," "harden," "prepare," "mark out," or decree "the vessels of wrath" for destruction from all eternity past and wanted all to be saved, how did they end up in disaster?

The Quantum Proposal suggests that, when graciously provided by God with many warnings and opportunities to repent, the vessels of wrath stubbornly chose the destructive options despite God's counsel. This pattern of behavior led to the hardening of one's heart and a deepening scorn for the truth. This eventually resulted in the situation of "dogs and swine" that would trample pearls (God's calls to repentance) under feet and tear pearl givers (Christ and his disciples) into pieces. This interpretation of Jude 1:4 would explain the disastrous endings of some people as the result of their own actions.

The case of Tyre and Sidon.

In his omniscience, Jesus knew that "if the miracles had been performed in Tyre and Sidon which occurred in you (Chorazin and Bethsaida), they would have repented long ago, sitting in sackcloth and ashes" (Luke 10:13). The Gospels stated that Jesus did go to the two cities. However, the only recorded miracle that he performed there was the healing of the daughter of the Syrophoenician woman. The reason for this sparse ministry was that "I was sent only to the lost sheep of the house of Israel" (Matt 15:24). Some people from the cities made the choice to go to Galilee to hear Jesus preach, an arduous eighty to one hundred miles[17] round trip (Mark 3:8). However, most of the population did not have opportunities to hear the gospel.

Nevertheless, Tyre and Sidon were later blessed as the message spread from Jerusalem "to Judea and Samaria and and even to the remotest part of the earth" (Acts 1:8). "And after looking up the disciples, we

---

15. Barnes' Notes on the Bible. http://biblehub.com/commentaries/jude/1–4.htm

16. This interpretation uses the second meaning of "prographo."

17. Reed, *Archaeology and the Galilean Jesus*, 185.

stayed there (in Tyre) seven days" (Acts 21:4). "And the next day we put in at Sidon; and Julius treated Paul with consideration and allowed him to go to his friends and receive care" (Acts 27:3). Tyre and Sidon were included in the universal offer of salvation as shown by the presence of disciples in Tyre and Paul's friends in Sidon.

The case of Pharaoh.

Did God long ago decree to reprobate Pharaoh by "hardening" his heart or did Pharaoh condemn himself by following his stubborn heart? Was Pharaoh's heart already hard since he mercilessly oppressed the Israelites with forced labor?

In three instances in the Old Testament, Pharaoh hardened his own heart (Exod 8:15, 8:32, and 9:34). In five instances, Pharaoh's heart was hardened by an unknown source (Exod 7:13, 7:14, 7:22, 8:19, 9:7, and 9:35). There were nine verses where God was said to "harden" Pharaoh's heart.

The Hebrew word "chazak" is used in seven of the nine verses where God "hardened" Pharaoh's heart (Exod 4:21, 9:12, 10:20, 10:27, 11:10, 14:4, and 14:8). "When you go back to Egypt see that you perform before Pharaoh all the wonders which I have put in your power; but I will harden (chazak) his heart so that he will not let the people go" (Exod 4:21). "Chazak" means "to be or grow firm, or strong, strengthen."[18] According to Dr. E. W. Bullinger, "chazak" is an active verb "used by the Hebrews to express, not the doing of the thing, but the permission of the thing which the agent is said to do."[19]

The word "qashah" is used in one verse. "But I will harden (qashah) Pharaoh's heart that I may multiply my signs and my wonders in the land of Egypt" (Exod 7:3). The Hebrew "qashah" in Exodus 7:3 means "make hard, stiff, stubborn, figurative of obstinacy."[20] This is "a form of figurative speech, very closely associated with metaphor, known as 'metonymy,' where one name or word is employed for another . . . [a]n action is sometimes said to have been accomplished, when all that is meant by it is that an occasion was given."[21] "The divine message (God's message

---

18. http://biblehub.com/hebrew/2388.htm

19. Bullinger, *Figures of Speech*, 823.

20. http://biblehub.com/hebrew/7185.htm

21. Miller and Butt, "Who hardened Pharaoh's Heart?" lines 109–16. Also see Dungan, *Hermeneutics*, 287, and Bullinger, *Figures of Speech*, 570.

to Pharaoh through Moses) would be the occasion, not the cause of the king's impenitent obduracy."[22]

The word "kabad" is used in one verse. "Go to Pharaoh, for I have hardened (kabad) his heart and the heart of his servants, that I may perform these signs of mine among them" (Exod 10:1). The Hebrew "kabad" means to be heavy, weighty or burdensome. The meaning in Exodus 10:1 is "make heavy, dull, unresponsive, the ears."[23] "God suffered his (Pharaoh's) natural obstinacy to prevail."[24]

Thus, in the nine instances where God "hardened" Pharaoh's heart, we can understand that to mean that the Lord permitted (chazak) Pharaoh's heart to be hardened and provided the occasion (qashah) for him to be stubborn and obstinate. God also allowed Pharaoh to make his ears heavy, dull, and unresponsive (kabad).

In the New Testament, we read concerning Pharaoh: "For this very purpose I raised you up, to demonstrate my power in you, and that my name might be proclaimed throughout the whole earth." Romans 9:17 quoted Exodus 9:16, "But I have raised you up for this very purpose, that I might show you my power and that my name might be proclaimed in all the earth" (NIV). The word "raised up" in Exodus 9:16 is the Hebrew "amad" meaning "cause to stand firm, maintain (opposed to overthrow)."[25] The word "raised up" in Romans 9:17 is the Greek "'exegeiro' (from 1537 / ek, 'wholly out from,' intensifying 1453 /egeiro, 'raise') – properly, raise out completely, emphasizing its end-impact on the person God raises up."[26] God "raised Pharaoh up completely," "maintained" him (as opposed to overthrow him) and "caused him to stand firm" to show God's power in Egypt. "The Lord gave Pharaoh the strength of will necessary to go on opposing him, in accord with Pharaoh's most fundamental desires."[27] "The expression cannot mean, either that God had brought Pharaoh originally into existence for the sole purpose of destroying him, or that he had from

---

22. Jamieson-Fausset-Brown Bible Commentary. https://biblehub.com/commentaries/exodus/7-3.htm

23. http://biblehub.com/hebrew/3513.htm

24. Adam Clarke Commentary. https://www.studylight.org/commentary/exodus/10-1.html

25. http://biblehub.com/hebrew/5975.htm

26. http://biblehub.com/greek/1825.htm

27. Cox, "The Hardening of Pharaoh's heart," 311.

the first irresistibly incited him to obduracy in order to condemn him, and so destroy him."[28]

Romans 9:18 stated: "So then he has mercy on whom he desires, and he hardens whom he desires." The word "hardens" is the Greek "skleruno" meaning to make hard, to harden; metaphorically, to render obstinate, stubborn.[29] Commentators are almost unanimous on the matter.[30] God does not actively harden the hearts of men. Barnes' Notes on the Bible states: "The word 'hardeneth' means only to harden in the manner speci-fied in the case of Pharaoh. It does not mean to exert a positive influence, but to leave a sinner to his own course, and to place him in circumstances where the character will be more and more developed."[31]

Even if the "hardening" is due to God's active action, it does not follow that the primary (or only) purpose of God is to condemn some-one. The same heat that melts "vessels of gold" also hardens "vessels of clay." God's miracles in Egypt showed his great power to the Israelites, something they needed to see prior to following Moses into the wilder-ness. However, God's miracles/plagues also hardened the stubbornness of Pharaoh who, being worshiped as a god in Egypt, refused to bow down to another god.

Furthermore, the active "hardening" could be considered God's righteous judgment of Pharaoh and Egypt for enslaving and mistreat-ing their guests without a cause.[32] Out of fear and greed, the Egyptians falsely accused the Israelites of being potential traitors ("join themselves to those who hate us" Exod 1:10). Pharaoh "appointed taskmasters over them to afflict them with hard labor" (Exod 1:11). This pattern culmi-

---

28. Pulpit Commentary. http://biblehub.com/commentaries/Rom/9-17.htm

29. http://biblehub.com/greek/4645.htm

30. http://biblehub.com/commentaries/Rom/9-18.htm

31. Barnes' Notes on the Bible. http://biblehub.com/commentaries/Rom/9-18.htm

32. God told Abraham in Genesis 15:13–16 that his descendants would be enslaved for four hundred years and that God would "judge the nation whom they will serve." However, the name of the nation was not mentioned. "Had it been expressly revealed that the country that would afflict them was Egypt, the patriarchs might have been unwilling to go thither." Ellicott's Commentary for English Readers. http://biblehub. com/commentaries/genesis/15-14.htm. The enslavement of the Jews had been de-creed and was therefore inevitable. However, the Lord's judgment on the enslaving nation could be lenient or severe depending on the cruelty and stubbornness of its ruler. This prophecy could have served as a warning to Pharaoh to let Israel go quickly and "with many possessions." There was no mention of a "decree of reprobation" for Pharaoh in Genesis 15.

nated in a ruthless policy of genocide, the eradication of the Hebrew race by murdering all the baby boys (Exod 1:16). Seeing the sufferings of his innocent people, the Lord declared: "I will stretch out my hand and strike Egypt with all my miracles which I shall do in the midst of it" (Exod 3:20). If God "hardens whom he desires," whether *actively or passively*, he does not do so without righteous reasons (e.g., as a decreed punishment for misdeeds). Romans 9 does not advocate an arbitrary "decree of reprobation" for Pharaoh in eternity past.[33]

On the contrary, it is clear from the Scriptures that God gave Pharaoh many opportunities to choose a different course of action (e.g., warnings before the plagues, Exod 7:16, 8:2, 8:21, 9:2–3, 9:13–14, and 10:3–4). The Lord endeavored to convince Pharaoh to relent and allow Israel's peaceful exodus. In his mercy, God only slowly ratcheted up the punishments, at long last culminating in the deaths of every firstborn in Egypt. Sadly, Pharaoh persisted in his obstinacy, made his ears dull and unresponsive, and hardened his heart against God. For his well-deserved destruction, he only had himself to blame! If the Lord did not reprobate Pharaoh in eternity past, did he nevertheless reprobate Judas the traitor?

The case of Judas.

"Did I myself not choose you, the twelve, and yet one of you is a devil?" (John 6:70). We must assume that Judas was *not* an actual devil,[34] for if he was, he could not be offered salvation as Christ did not die for fallen angels (Heb 2:16).

Was the traitor predestined to eternal condemnation? Were there prophecies in the Old Testament or early in the New Testament stating that Judas would betray the Messiah (i.e., a literal fulfillment of prophecies pointing to his "decreed reprobation")? Or were the pronouncements in the Old Testament only loosely applied to the situations in the New

33. For a different interpretation of Romans 9, see Beale, "An Exegetical and Theological Consideration."

34. Angels can appear in human forms (Matt 28:2–3, Luke 24:4). Demons are also angels. "Depart from me, accursed ones, into the eternal fire which has been prepared for the devil and his angels" (Matt 25:41).

Testament as "typological or analogical fulfillments"[35] (e.g., the event or person in the New Testament is only *similar* to an event or person in the Old Testament)? Was Judas given warnings and free will choices during Christ's ministry? Did he stubbornly insist on choosing the destructive options or was he "doomed" to betray Christ by God's eternal foreknowledge/decree?

Scholars are divided on the issue. Dr. R. C. Sproul stated: "God's decree of reprobation, given in light of the Fall, is a decree to justice, not injustice."[36] Dr. Roger Barrier said: "No one is predestined to heaven or hell."[37]

A *chronological* search of the Scriptures will help answer the question about a decree of reprobation for Judas. Pronouncements from the Old Testament, especially those quoted in the New Testament, will be crucial, particularly so if they come from messianic passages. Statements made early in the New Testament, thus qualifying them as prophecies for later events, will also be important.

Judas was first mentioned when Jesus chose the twelve disciples including "Judas Iscariot, who became a traitor" (Luke 6:16). Obviously, Judas could have chosen not to accept Christ's offer. He could have stayed with the larger group of unnamed followers, or he could have gone home and made money to satisfy his greed. After all, following Jesus who "has nowhere to lay his head" (Luke 9:58) was probably not the best way to get rich! Nothing was said about a "decree of reprobation." Nothing was said about a betrayal or a betrayer *at the time*. The comments "who became a traitor" in Luke 6:16, "the one who betrayed him" in Matthew 10:4, and "who also betrayed him" in Mark 3:19 were *not contemporaneous*[38] with the described events and were not known at the time. The identity of the

---

35. According to Dr. Strauss, there are three types of prophecy fulfillments. 1. Literal fulfillment: The Old Testament prophecies are cited and uniquely fulfilled (e.g., Micah 5:2 prophesied Bethlehem as Messiah's birthplace, fulfilled in Matthew 2:5–6). 2. Typological fulfillment: An Old Testament event or person serves as a type or model of another event or person in the New Testament (e.g., the virgin in Isaiah 7:14 was a model of the virgin Mary in Matthew 1:23). 3. Analogical fulfillment: "This event parallels, or is similar to, what happened in the Old Testament." (e.g., weeping mothers in Jeremiah 31:15 are similar to weeping Bethlehem mothers in Matthew 2:17.) Strauss, *Four Portraits*, 246.

36. Sproul, "Double Predestination," line 216.

37. Barrier, "Did Judas Have a Choice," line 56.

38. The gospel writers commented on the events with the benefit of hindsight, the knowledge that Judas was the betrayer.

traitor was still in question at the Last Supper (John 13:25). Since the comments about Judas were neither made by Christ nor known by the disciples at the time of the events, they could not be prophecies of Judas' betrayal.

"There are some of you who do not believe. (For Jesus knew from the beginning who those were who did not believe, and who it was who would betray him)" (John 6:64 ESV). The commentators are divided[39] on whether Judas acted out of free will or was foreordained to betray Christ. John 6:64b was a non-contemporaneous comment (in parenthesis in the ESV translation) made by John. "This intimation (Jesus knew from the beginning . . . who it was who would betray him) is purely apologetic and intended to show that Jesus was not deceived in appointing Judas."[40] Christ neither prophesied the treachery nor spoke about a "decree of reprobation" for Judas in this passage.

"So Jesus said to the twelve, 'You do not want to go away also, do you?'" (John 6:67). Judas was given a free will choice and could have decided to leave Christ then and there. This pronouncement came early in Jesus' ministry. Nothing was said about a betrayer.

"'Have I not chosen you, the Twelve? Yet one of you is a devil!' (He meant Judas, the son of Simon Iscariot, who, though one of the Twelve, was later to betray him)" (John 6:70–71 NIV). Judas could have taken the declaration/warning to heart and changed his ways. Christ did not prophesy a betrayal. John 6:71 (in parenthesis in the NIV translation) was a non-contemporaneous comment. The fact that Jesus called Judas "a devil" does not necessarily indicate his decreed perdition since Jesus also called Peter, "Satan." John 6:70 ("one of you is a devil") and Matthew 16:23 (Jesus "said to Peter 'Get behind me, Satan'") could easily have pointed to Peter, rather than to Judas, as the "devil" among the twelve. As it was, Jesus did not reveal the identity of the culprit. Only much later (probably with the betrayal "kiss," Luke 22:47–48), did the disciples

---

39. http://biblehub.com/commentaries/john/6-64.htm

40. Expositor's Greek Testament. http://biblehub.com/commentaries/john/6-64.htm.

realize that Jesus meant Judas.[41] Thus, Judas was not "labeled" as a traitor and could have chosen to repent or leave.

"Judas Iscariot, one of his disciples, who was intending to betray him, said, 'Why was this perfume not sold for three hundred denarii and given to poor people?' Now he said this, not because he was concerned about the poor, but because he was a thief, and as he had the money box, he used to pilfer what was put into it. Therefore, Jesus said, 'Let her alone'" (John 12:4–7). Judas could have taken Jesus' rebuke to heart. This happened just before Jesus' triumphal entry into Jerusalem. Christ did not mention a betrayer, a betrayal, or a "decree of reprobation" for Judas. The statements "who was intending to betray him" and "he was a thief"[42] were non-contemporaneous comments. These facts were not known by the disciples at the time.

"And Satan entered into Judas who was called Iscariot, belonging to the number of the twelve. And he went away and discussed with the chief priests and officers how he might betray him to them" (Luke 22:3-4). "And they weighed out to him thirty pieces of silver" (Matt 26:15). Probably, the die was cast by this time, since Satan entered Judas. This happened very late in Jesus' ministry, after Jesus' triumphal entry into Jerusalem. Up to this point, no Old or New Testament prophecies were given or quoted to predict that Messiah would be betrayed. Nothing was said about a "decree of reprobation" for Judas.

"It is that the Scripture may be fulfilled, 'He who eats my bread has lifted up his heel against me'" (John 13:18, quoting Psalm 41:9). This happened during the Last Supper. A betrayer was *first* mentioned here by Christ *after* Satan had entered Judas. Psalm 41:9 referred to David and his false friend. Jesus applied it to himself but removed the words "in whom I trusted" as he never trusted Judas. Psalm 41:9 was *not* a prophecy about the Messiah in the original context. The quoted Old Testament Scripture did not appear until *after* Satan had entered Judas and made the betrayal inevitable. A much stronger case could have been made for a prophecy about the "decreed reprobation" of Judas had this pronouncement been

41. "And after the morsel, Satan then entered into him. Jesus therefore said to him (Judas), 'What you do, do quickly.' Now no one of those reclining at the table knew for what purpose he had said this to him" (John 13:27–28). "No man at the table knew— This shows that Jesus had signified to John only who it was that should betray him." Barnes' Notes on the Bible. http://biblehub.com/commentaries/john/13-28.htm

42. At the Last Supper, Judas was still in charge of the money box (John 13:29). The fact that he was a thief was probably not known even at that time.

conveyed in a clear messianic passage in the Old Testament (like Daniel 9) or, if not, then introduced at the very beginning of Jesus' ministry (e.g., at Jesus' baptism, thus qualifying it as a prophecy for later events) and had it involved a close friend whom Jesus actually trusted (e.g., Peter, James, or John). The quote was not a clear messianic prophecy, had a different context in the Old Testament, appeared very late in the New Testament, and was applied to a disciple whom Jesus never trusted. The "fulfillment" is more of a "typological or analogical" fulfillment rather than a literal fulfillment of a prophecy. Thus, it is difficult to make this passage a "decree of reprobation" for Judas.

"But behold, the hand of the one betraying me is with mine on the table. For indeed, the Son of Man is going as it has been determined; but woe to that man by whom he is betrayed!" (Luke 22:21–22). Messiah was to be "cut off and have nothing" as prophesied in Daniel 9:26. However, no mention was made there of a betrayal or a betrayer, *as would be expected of such a major event* in Christ's capture and death by crucifixion. A woe was pronounced on the traitor only at the Last Supper. An eternal "decree of reprobation" for Judas cannot be obtained from this verse.

"The Son of Man goes as it is written of him, but woe to that man by whom the Son of Man is betrayed! It would have been better for that man if he had not been born." (Matt 26:24 ESV). This happened during the Last Supper. There was no mention of an eternal "decree of reprobation" against Judas in this verse. Would the omnibenevolent Lord have decreed the creation of "traitor Judas" if it would have been better for him not to be born? Would it be just to create a person, so God could "use" him for his purpose (e.g., to betray Christ) and then reprobate him for eternity? Is it not more likely that the statement means, "it would have been better for that man if he had not been born" since he *unwisely chose the destructive path of betrayal?*

"So, when he had dipped the morsel, he took and gave it to Judas, the son of Simon Iscariot. After the morsel, Satan then entered into him" (John 13:26–27). This happened during the Last Supper. Satan entered Judas again. The betrayal was probably inevitable at this juncture.[43]

"While I was with them, I was keeping them in your name which you have given me; and I guarded them and not one of them perished but the son of perdition, so that the Scripture would be fulfilled" (John 17:12). This happened during the Last Supper. The Scripture mentioned

---

43. This did not necessarily mean that Judas was "doomed" and could not repent later (e.g., at the foot of the cross).

was probably Psalm 109:8, "Let his days be few; let another take his office."[44] The context in the Old Testament was about the fate of a wicked man. Nothing was said about a "decree of reprobation" for Judas in Psalm 109. He was called the "son of perdition" in John, probably because Satan (the "son of perdition" in 2 Thess 2:3 KJV) had already entered him.

"But Jesus said to him, 'Judas, are you betraying the Son of Man with a kiss?'" (Luke 22:48). This happened in the Garden of Gethsemane. A foreordained reprobation was not mentioned.

"Then when Judas, who had betrayed him, saw that he had been condemned, he felt remorse and returned the thirty pieces of silver to the chief priests and elders" (Matt 27:3). This happened after Christ's capture and condemnation.

"Then that which was spoken through Jeremiah the prophet was fulfilled: and they took the thirty pieces of silver, the price of the one whose price has been set by the sons of Israel; and they gave them for the potter's field, as the Lord directed me" (Matt 27:9–10, quoting Jer 32:6–11 and Zech 11:12–13). This happened after Christ's capture and condemnation. Zechariah 11 and Jeremiah 32 addressed God, Israel, and Jeremiah. Matthew applied the situation to Jesus. There are significant differences between the Old Testament settings and the New Testament application. In Zechariah 11, God (the Great Shepherd) asked for wages (i.e., a parting of ways) from his flock (Israel). However, if the nation was ungrateful about the Lord's loving care, God would declare, "Never mind!" about the payment. The paltry sum of thirty pieces of silver (the price of a slave, Exod 21:32) given by Israel for the Lord's wages was equated in the New Testament with the price of Messiah's blood. In the Old Testament, the money was thrown in contempt "to the potter in the house of the Lord." In the New Testament, the money was given back due to remorse and was used to buy a potter's field. The purchase of a field in the New Testament was equated with the purchase of a field in Jeremiah 32. Thus, the "fulfillment" was more "typological or analogical" than literal. Due to the significant differences between the Old Testament contexts and the New Testament situation, it is difficult to call the Old Testament passages, prophecies of Judas's "decree of reprobation."

"Brethren, the Scripture had to be fulfilled, which the Holy Spirit foretold by the mouth of David concerning Judas, who became a guide to those who arrested Jesus . . . For it is written in the book of Psalms, 'Let

44. Gill's Exposition of the Entire Bible http://biblehub.com/commentaries/john/17-12.htm

his homestead be made desolate, and let no one dwell in it'; and, 'Let another man take his office'" (Acts 1:16–20, quoting Ps 69:25 and Ps 109:8). This happened after Jesus' ascension. The Psalms addressed David and his enemies. Peter applied them to Judas. "It has been (a) matter of much debate, whether they do, in their original sense, refer to Judas or to the enemies of David. It is certain the sixty-ninth Psalm is not to be confined to Judas; for Paul (Rom 11:9–10) has quoted the 22d and 23d verses of it as applicable to the unbelieving Jews in general."[45] Thus, the "fulfillment" is more "typological or analogical" than literal.

In summary, the Old Testament passages were not literal messianic prophecies fulfilled in the New Testament. They were quoted very late in Christ's ministry after the betrayal had been inevitable. In the New Testament, Christ did not reveal Judas as the betrayer until after Satan had entered him. Thus, the concept of an eternal "decree of reprobation" for Judas cannot be supported from the Scriptures.

As we have seen, Judas had plenty of opportunities to change his mind. When asked by Christ to join the group of disciples, he could have refused. When given the choice to leave Christ, he could have done so. When warned about greed, he could have heeded the admonition and not covet the "thirty pieces of silver." Even at the Last Supper, honored by Christ as the special guest (Christ gave Judas the sop, John 13:26) and fairly warned about the betrayal, he could have changed his mind. "It is an ordinary Oriental custom for the host to offer such a tidbit to any favored guest; and we are rather entitled to see in the act the last appeal to Judas's better feeling."[46] At the garden of Gethsemane, when challenged about the perfidy of the betrayal kiss, he could have repented (like Peter after the denials). Finally, after returning the money, he could have gone to the foot of the cross and sought salvation at the last minute (like the thief on the cross). Instead, he chose to end his life. For making all these poor choices, Judas's penalty was fully deserved!

In the Quantum Proposal, was the betrayal of Christ by Judas one of the possible scenarios within God's predetermined boundaries? One would have to say yes since that was what happened. However, it might not be the only possible scenario. Could Christ have been crucified without a betrayer? Probably yes since there were no prophecies in the Old Testament or early in the New Testament about a betrayal. For example,

45. Benson Commentary. http://biblehub.com/commentaries/acts/1–16.htm

46. Expositor's Greek Testament. http://biblehub.com/commentaries/john/13–26. htm

in an alternative sequence of events, the High Priest could have sent men to spy on Christ's comings and goings. They could have found an opportune time to arrest him (e.g., in the middle of the night in the Garden of Gethsemane). No betrayer was required. Judas was not "doomed" to betray Christ but chose to do so freely. Thus, he had only himself to blame for his disastrous outcome!

THE GENUINE UNIVERSAL OFFER OF SALVATION.

The Quantum Proposal resolves the dilemma of the universal offer of salvation and the "vessels of wrath prepared for destruction" by advocating that the "vessels of wrath" (e.g., Pharaoh, Judas) are not doomed to perdition by God's eternal decree but by their stubborn decisions against God's counsel. The Lord, in his wisdom and mercy, allows Man to make some free will choices[47] concerning salvation within God's predetermined boundaries and therefore rightfully holds Man accountable for his actions. Thus, while no one is turned away, not everyone is saved. The Quantum Proposal supports the concept of unlimited atonement and the genuine offer of salvation to all people.

On the other hand, if one adopts the alternative interpretation, that God had "long beforehand marked out" some for condemnation, the Quantum Proposal would suggest that God could have mercy on whomever he desired (Rom 9:20–22). Free will options might not be offered by the sovereign Lord (e.g., Peter's death as a martyr was decreed and fixed, John 21:19). In this view, God elected some (e.g., John the Baptist and Paul), and reprobated others (e.g., Pharaoh and Judas). Christ only died for the elect (i.e., limited atonement). However, we are then left with the dilemma of God's *seeming* offer of salvation to all[48] and his decision/ decree to save some and not save others. The belief that the Lord predes-

47. Does God give all (or only some) men choices concerning salvation? It is difficult to be dogmatic on the matter. God did not give John the Baptist or Paul choices concerning their calling. Since God is sovereign over Man, he can act as he sees fit.

48. The concept of a universal offer of salvation is under debate. Dr. Berkhof (Reformed) stated: "It should also be noted that the doctrine that Christ died for the purpose of saving all men, logically leads to absolute universalism, that is, to the doctrine that all men are actually saved." Berkhof, *Systematic Theology*, 395. Dr. Grudem (Calvinist) said: "Christ died for particular people (specifically, those who would be saved and whom he came to redeem)." Grudem, *Systematic Theology*, 596.

tined some to evil was declared "anathema" by the Council of Orange in 529 AD. "We not only do not believe that any are foreordained to evil by the power of God, but even state with utter abhorrence that if there are those who want to believe so evil a thing, they are anathema."[49]

A STORY ABOUT CHRIST'S OFFER OF SALVATION.

When I was in college, at the beginning of the semester, my Christian friends and I would go up and down the hallways of the dormitories to invite anyone and everyone to our Bible studies. We believed that God "wants all men to be saved," and that no one is denied an opportunity to hear the message of redemption. Many declined the invitation. A few came and were blessed. Fast forward forty years! Although I am teaching at a Christian school, it is improbable that all my students are Christians. I am still endeavoring to spread the gospel for "he who turns a sinner from the error of his way will save his soul from death and will cover a multitude of sins" (Jas 5:20).

However, are sins the results of men's free will choices or is God "the author of evil" if he preordained Man's fall into iniquity? We will address this "problem of evil" in the next chapter.

---

49. The Canons of the Council of Orange: conclusion. www.monergism.com/theth-reshold/articles/onsite/councilorange.html. The Council of Orange is not considered equal to the seven ecumenical councils (e.g., the First Council of Nicaea in 325 AD).

Chapter 13

The problem of evil

"The problem of evil is the most serious problem in the world. It is also the one serious objection to the existence of God."[1] Dealing with this complex issue will require a whole book.[2] Thus, we will limit our discussion to the question: "If the sovereign Lord foreknows/decrees any and every event, is he the author of sin?" In other words, who is responsible for the horrendous evils on this earth? God or man?

THE PROBLEM.

"I am the Lord, and there is no other, the one forming light and creating darkness, causing well-being and creating calamity; I am the Lord who does all these (Isa 45:6–7). Yet, James 1:13 states: "Let no one say when he is tempted, 'I am being tempted by God'; for God cannot be tempted by evil, and he himself does not tempt anyone." The presence of unspeakable evil in a world created by a good God is a profound enigma.

Augustine (354–430 AD) wrote: "We must take heed lest someone should suppose that the sin would have to be imputed to God which is committed by free will . . . Now, should any man be for constraining us to examine into this profound mystery, why this person is so persuaded as to yield, and that person is not, there are only two things occurring to me, which I should like to advance as my answer: 'O the depth of the riches!' and 'Is there unrighteousness with God?' If the man is displeased

---

1. Kreeft, *The Problem of Evil*, lines 1–4
2. I am working on a book dealing exclusively with the problem of evil.

with such an answer, he must seek more learned disputants; but let him beware lest he find presumptuous ones."[3]

Martin Luther (1483–1546 AD) observed: "But why does he (God) not at the same time change the evil wills that he moves? This belongs to the secrets of his majesty, where his judgments are incomprehensible (Rom 11:33). It is not our business to ask this question, but to adore these mysteries."[4]

John Calvin (1509–1564 AD) said: "But how it was ordained by the foreknowledge and decree of God what Man's future was without God being implicated as associate in the fault as the author or approver of transgression, is clearly a secret so much excelling the insight of the human mind, that I am not ashamed to confess ignorance."[5]

Dr. Louis Berkhof (Reformed) agreed with Augustine, Luther, and Calvin: "The problem of God's relation to sin remains a mystery for us, which we are not able to solve."[6] Dr. Wayne Grudem (Calvinist) concurred: "We have to come to the point where we confess that we do not understand how it is that God can ordain that we carry out evil deeds and yet hold us accountable for them and not be blamed himself."[7] Dr. Millard Erickson (Baptist) acquiesced: "A total solution to the problem of evil is beyond human ability."[8] Dr. Jack Cottrell (Arminian) stated: "We do not claim to have solved all the problems relating to the presence of evil in the world."[9] Dr. Norman Geisler ("Calminian")[10] said: "The existence of evil and suffering is more of a mystery than a problem."[11] Dr. Kenneth Keathley (Molinist) acknowledged: "The mystery of evil remains."[12] Dr. Greg Boyd (Open Theist) opined: "I do not want to claim that the open view entirely solves the problem of evil."[13] The coexistence of God and evil has been a dilemma for the church since the dawn of Christianity. Can this quandary be resolved successfully?

3. Augustine, *Of the Spirit and the Letter,* lines 2–3, 19–22.

4. Luther, "On the Bondage of the Will," 236.

5. Calvin, *Concerning the Eternal Predestination of God,* 123–24.

6. Berkhof, *Systematic Theology,* 108.

7. Grudem, *Systematic Theology,* 330.

8. Erickson, *Christian Theology,* 423.

9. Cottrell, *What the Bible Says about God the Ruler,* 404.

10. Geisler, *Chosen but Free,* 185.

11. Geisler and Bocchino, *Unshakable Foundations,* 238.

12. Keathley, *Salvation and Sovereignty,* 13.

13. Boyd. *God of the Possible,* 99.

THE QUANTUM PROPOSAL AS A SOLUTION.

Why did God allow Man to disobey and sin? Why did he create Adam and then put him to the test? God's reasons were not addressed in the Scriptures. One could speculate that the Lord, for his ultimate glory, wanted to create a man with free will who could voluntarily obey and love him.[14] After all, a "no-choice" love or a "robotic" love is no love at all!

However, free will comes with the possibility of sin entering the world. As it is illogical to ask the omnipotent Lord to make a circle a square, it is likewise irrational to demand that God gives Man free will to obey or disobey and at the same time insist on precluding any possibility of disobedience. Dr. Alvin Plantinga said: "To create creatures capable of *moral good*, therefore, he must create creatures capable of moral evil; and he can't give these creatures the freedom to perform evil and at the same time prevent them from doing so (italics in original)."[15]

Thus, in accordance with his sovereign will and for his own reasons, God gave Adam two choices in the Garden of Eden: do not eat from the tree and live or eat and die. He did not provide the following alternatives: move to a different garden without the tree, get rid of the serpent, stay single (no Eve) . . . Adam's options were limited within God's strict boundaries.

The only thing that stood between Adam, Eve, and the tree was God's command. They, as free agents, had a choice to make and were responsible for their decision, especially if they disobeyed God's directive. In the Quantum Proposal, the Lord did not decree/ordain Adam's downfall. He intimately foreknew the two possible scenarios and let Adam freely select the alternative that he desired. Obviously, when Adam chose the forbidden path, the preferred option vanished. Likewise, Adam's descendants freely decided to sin and were fully responsible for the world's evils.

Nevertheless, in his mercy, God provides men with a redeemer in the path of disobedience. Thus, if they decide to select a destructive option, they may yet find a way of escape (1 Cor 10:13) by following the Messiah (i.e., the "narrow way" of Matthew 7:14). Mistakes, if made, are not necessarily final. Men are given opportunities to repent and return

---

14. God also created angels with the free will to obey or disobey (e.g., Michael the Archangel, Satan).

15. Plantinga, *God, Freedom, and Evil*, 30.

to the creator. However, they can also decide to persist in rebellion and commit unspeakable evils (i.e., the "broad way" of Matthew 7:13).

One must say that the atrocities in this fallen world (e.g., September 11 terrorist attack, genocides, child abuses, pregnancies from rape, drunk drivers maiming innocent people, school shootings . . .) are within God's predetermined boundaries as they do happen. However, in the Quantum Proposal, these paths are *never* God's recommended options as they go against his edicts in the Scriptures. For example, was the Holocaust a possible scenario within God's preset confines? One would have to say yes since it happened. Was that God's recommended choice among his given alternatives? The answer is *emphatically no* since genocide is against God's command ("You shall not murder" Exod 20:13)!

Furthermore, these destructive events, freely chosen by Man against the Lord's injunctions, should not be connected to God in any way (thus making him partially responsible) by claiming that they are within his "permissive" or "decreed" will. In the Quantum Proposal, these deleterious options are possible but are *always* against God's will as clearly declared in his Word! If Man, as a free agent, chooses to go against the Lord's command (a logical result of free will to obey or disobey, and *not* a "self-limitation" of God's omnipotence[16] or omniscience[17]), Man must bear full responsibility for his actions as the Lord always stands against the path of disobedience. God does not "endorse," "approve," "decree," "foreordain," "permit," or "choose to actualize" such a rebellious step! If Man insists on following a disastrous, insubordinate course of action, *he would have to do it over Christ's dead body*, which was exactly what Man did!

In the Quantum Proposal, the Lord, in his sovereignty, may choose to remedy Man's wicked actions and bring about what is good. For example, God rescued Joseph from slavery and allowed him to rule over Egypt (Gen 41). However, the sinful way was *never* the Lord's preferred option as the practice of kidnapping and selling people[18] was strictly forbidden and under penalty of death (Exod 21:16 and Deut 24:7). In God's economy, the end never justifies the means! The Lord does not need to use Man's wrongdoings to accomplish his plans. For example, in a possible scenario not involving misdeeds, Joseph voluntarily went to Egypt

16. Reichenbach, "God Limits His Power," 101–24.

17. Pinnock, "God Limits His Knowledge," 143–62.

18. While the context in Exodus 21:16 and Deuteronomy 24:7 addressed Israelites, 1 Timothy 1:10 considered kidnapping "contrary to sound teaching."

to trade goods. While there, he was asked to explain Pharaoh's dreams. As a reward, he was promoted to second ruler of Egypt. Joseph's kidnapping and enslavement by his brothers were *not* necessary for God to accomplish his plan to save many lives! God's work must be done God's way and that never includes Man choosing iniquity, even in order that good may come! "What shall we say then? Shall we continue in sin, that grace may abound?" (Rom 6:1 KJV). The righteous Lord does not "entice" Man to make sinful choices. For example, God did not have to "beguile" the Sabeans to kill Job's servants for the fire of God could and did accomplish the exact same thing (Job 1:15–16)! The Lord does not tempt or cause anyone to sin to fulfill his plan!

This is not to say that the Lord never uses "evil" as a tool in this fallen world with the ubiquitous presence of sin (Satan is the "god of this world," 2 Cor 4:4). The sovereign Lord may dispense "evil"[19] for the purpose of edification (e.g., Job 1–2), punishment for disobedience (e.g., loss of the Promised Land, 2 Chr 36:15–21), deterrence (e.g., Ananias and Sapphira, Acts 5:1–11), or rehabilitation (e.g., Peter's denials in Luke 22). Job needed to understand that God, as the creator, was not obligated to answer Job's questions. Israel had to learn that disobedience brings discipline. The church was taught the drastic consequences of lying to the Holy Spirit. Peter had to overcome his boastful pride. God never acts capriciously and without good reasons in using "evil." He may allow Satan to tempt his people. Nevertheless, God forthrightly *takes responsibility* for that course of action in this fallen world, declaring, "I am the Lord, and there is no other, the one forming light and creating darkness, causing well-being and creating calamity; I am the Lord who does all these (Isa 45:6–7). In this wicked realm, "evil" is a tool (but not the only one, consider love, mercy, grace) that God uses to train his children. "For those whom the Lord loves, he disciplines, and he scourges every son whom he receives" (Heb 12:6).

Furthermore, in the Quantum Proposal, Man does not have total free will to sin whenever and however he wants. He only has a few choices within God's narrow bounds. For example, in Job 1:12, God restricted the creature (in this case Satan) to "all that he (Job) has is in your power, only do not put forth your hand on him." In Job 2:6, the sovereign Lord expanded Satan's purview. "Behold, he is in your power, only spare his

---

19. Of course, "evil" intended for good purposes is not actually evil. Thus, God is not evil in using "evil" (e.g., cancer, financial difficulties) for the purpose of doing good.

life." Nevertheless, God was always in full control and only allowed the creature to have some limited options.

Enforcing strict boundaries concerning Man's free will,[20] the omnipotent Lord restrains sins and evil (while holding men responsible for their choices). "For the mystery of lawlessness is already at work; only he who now restrains will do so until he is taken out of the way" (2 Thess 2:7). In his wisdom, God sovereignly guides events of this age toward the fulfillment of prophecies and promises he has given to his people (e.g., the Messiah's return).

In our fallen world, moral evil[21] happens in three main ways (or a combination of these ways). First, we may bring evil upon ourselves by choosing an option not recommended by God (e.g., drug use). Second, evil may come upon us by the free will choices of those around us since no one lives in a vacuum (e.g., a drive-by shooting). In this situation, the Lord may shield us from some (or all) of the consequences (e.g., a minor injury from the gun shots). Finally, moral "evil"[22] may come as part of God's process of edification, discipline, deterrence, or rehabilitation. For example, financial problems can teach us dependence on God. A lawsuit can be a good deterrent against questionable deals in business. A jail sentence for cheating on taxes can be God's disciplinary and rehabilitative tool.[23]

Natural evil[24] (e.g., cancers, earthquakes, hurricanes) is also the result of the Fall, a direct consequence of Man's disobedience. "Cursed is the ground because of you" (Gen 3:17). "For the creation was subjected

20. God also restrained Satan and his demons.

21. "Moral evils are those evils that are in some sense the result of a person who is morally blameworthy of the resultant evil." Meister and Dew, 3. I interpret "a person" to mean a human being and not God. The Catholic Catechism, referring to the works of Augustine and Aquinas, states: "God is in no way, directly or indirectly, the cause of moral evil." Section 311. http://www.vatican.va/archive/ccc_css/archive/catechism/p1s2c1p4.htm

22. These events (e.g., financial problems) may be moral evils from our point of view but not from God's. Thus, I put "evil" in quotation marks.

23. This moral evil (i.e., jail time) is the result of a combination of our action (i.e., cheating on taxes) and God's action (discipline). While we are evil in defrauding the government, God is not evil in chastising us. God takes responsibility for decreeing our punishment, but he is not "morally blameworthy." After all, God commanded us not to cheat on taxes (Rom 13:7).

24. "Natural evil is evil that results from the operation of natural processes, in which case no human being can be held morally accountable for the resultant evil." Trakakis, "The Evidential Problem of Evil," section 1b.

to futility, not willingly, but because of him who subjected it, in hope that the creation itself also will be set free from its slavery to corruption into the freedom of the glory of the children of God. For we know that the whole creation groans and suffers the pains of childbirth together until now" (Rom 8:20–22). Like moral evil, natural evil happens in the same three ways (or a combination of these ways with moral evils).[25] Natural evils may happen to us as the result of our poor decisions (e.g., we knowingly buy a house in a flood plain resulting in a flooded residence after some heavy rains).[26] Natural evils can come from other people's sinful choices (e.g., we unknowingly work in an office building built cheaply to save money, resulting in injuries after an earthquake). Natural "evils"[27] can be part of God's process of edification (e.g., Job and the windstorm, Job 1:19), discipline (e.g., Miriam's leprosy, Num 12:10), deterrence (e.g., fire and brimstone on Sodom and Gomorrah, Gen 19:24), or rehabilitation (e.g., Jonah's rehabilitation by the storm and the whale, Jonah 1). Thus, when we encounter moral or natural evils, we need to prayerfully consider the reasons behind our trials and respond accordingly, knowing that our Lord is always good and forever on our side.

In summary, who is responsible for the Fall? Adam who chose to disobey! Who is responsible for the entrance of evil in this world? Adam who chose to disobey! Who is responsible for this fallen world's natural disasters? Adam who chose to disobey! Who are responsible for the atrocities in this wicked realm (e.g., rapes, genocides, child abuses)? The sons of Adam and daughters of Eve who choose to spurn God's commands!

Who is responsible for the "evils" in Job's trials and edification, for using Nebuchadnezzar to discipline Israel, for destroying Sodom and Gomorrah as a warning to all men, and for reproving Peter's pride? The sovereign Lord forthrightly takes responsibility for these actions (Isa 45:6–7). God's children need to remember that he uses "evil" as a tool

---

25. Dr. Feinberg subdivided natural evils into "attached" natural evils, "evils that result from specific acts of moral evil" (e.g., forest fires started by careless campers) and "unattached" natural evils, evils which "are not direct results of any specific act of moral evil" (e.g., lightning-caused forest fires). Feinberg, *The Many Faces of Evil*, 146.

26. We can say that this natural evil (i.e., flooded houses) is the result of a combination of natural evils (i.e., rains and floods) and moral evils (e.g., the developer's greed in building houses in flood plains *and* our poor choice in house buying).

27. Although God brings these natural "evils" in our lives and takes responsibility for them, he is not morally blameworthy for these events as he intends them for our good.

and that his Word is "profitable for teaching, for reproof, for correction, for training in righteousness" (2 Tim 3:16).

A STORY ON THE PROBLEM OF EVIL.

When our first-born son Dan was almost two years old, my wife and I fearfully noticed that he was not gaining weight and often had to squat down to rest at the playground. Soon after, we were told that he had a severe heart problem that would require major surgery. Why us, Lord? Have we not been faithful Christians? What did we do to deserve this? And why do you punish our innocent boy? We cried and begged God to deliver us from this evil. But it was not to be! Dan not only had a large hole in his heart but also had a deformed mitral valve. The surgeon said that he would do his best, but the prognosis was guarded. The day of the operation came much too quickly! We tearfully gave Dan to the nurses and entrusted his life to the Lord. As we were no better than our father Abraham, we had to be prepared to give our "Isaac" back to God. "The Lord gave, and the Lord has taken away. Blessed be the name of the Lord" (Job 1:21). Lord, though we do not understand, we submit and trust that you have our best interests at heart. "I also suffer these things, but I am not ashamed; for I know whom I have believed, and I am convinced that he is able to guard what I have entrusted to him until that day" (2 Tim 1:12). Father, please watch over our little boy! Please help the surgeon and the surgical staff! Please allow the surgery to be successful! Yet, not our will but your will be done!

The Lord was merciful, and Dan was restored to us in good health! Looking back on this excruciating encounter with natural evil, I believe that it was God's process of edification, teaching us to hold our blessings loosely as we are only stewards of God's gifts. Our children are not our own possessions! Furthermore, he who loves his children "more than me is not worthy of me" (Matt 10:37). May we be worthy of our names as Christ's followers! Let us not forget that we were saved when we were yet living in sin and by nature children of wrath! How depraved were we and were we responsible for our condition?

Chapter 14

The problem of Man's depravity

"AMONG THEM WE TOO all formerly lived in the lusts of our flesh, indulging the desires of the flesh and of the mind, and were by nature children of wrath, even as the rest" (Eph 2:3). If Man is totally depraved and a sinner by "nature," how can he be held responsible by God for his sins?

THE QUANTUM PROPOSAL AS A SOLUTION.

The Quantum Proposal supports the concept that the Lord, in his mercy, allows depraved men to make some free will choices concerning salvation (and other matters) within his predetermined boundaries. They are not doomed to perdition and sins by his eternal decree but by their free, willful, stubborn choices against his counsel. In his sovereignty, he gives them the freedom to spurn his advice, choose their own destinies, and take responsibility for their actions (e.g., the rich young ruler was free to serve money, or he could decide to follow Christ. Ahab and Jezebel were free to worship idols, or they could choose to repent and follow the true God).

On the other hand, if the view that depraved men are given no free will choice[1] is correct, the Quantum Proposal would advocate that God

---

1. By that I mean no libertarian free will. "Libertarian free will means that our choices are free from the determination or constraints of human nature and free from any predetermination by God. All 'free will theists' hold that libertarian freedom is essential for moral responsibility, for if our choice is determined or caused by anything, including our own desires, they reason, it cannot properly be called a free choice. Libertarian freedom is, therefore, the freedom to act contrary to one's nature, predisposition and greatest desires. Responsibility, in this view, always means that one could have done otherwise." https://www.theopedia.com/libertarian-free-will

is ultimately sovereign over his creation and can have mercy on whomever he desires. Escape from depravity and sin would be solely God's decision accomplished through unconditional election and irresistible grace. However, with this interpretation, we are left with the problem of totally depraved men (i.e., unable to help themselves) who are held responsible by the Lord for their degenerate actions.

A STORY OF MAN'S DEPRAVITY.

When I was a medical intern in Chicago, I often had to take the "L" (elevated train) to commute as I did not own a car. The train lines were connected by underground tunnels allowing passengers to transfer to various destinations in the metropolis. While the dimly lit passageways offered some shelter from the "shivering polar bear" weather of the Windy City, they were the perfect cesspools of man's depravity complete with Dante's sign, "All hope abandon, ye who enter here."[2] In 2017, the *Chicago Sun Times* bemoaned that "crime on the L, CTA (Chicago Transit Authority) buses is up; 90 percent of serious incidents go unsolved."[3]

One late night, I had to enter this subterranean den of thieves to catch a train. Sure enough, as I was hurrying through the dark and foul shaft, a menacing gang cornered me near the exit. One rascal grabbed my leg while the other bandits tried to take my wallet. To this day, I can't explain what happened next. They suddenly ran off and left me scared stiff but unharmed. No, I did not see any policeman or anyone else coming to my rescue! I could only assume that "greater is he who is in you than he who is in the world" (1 John 4:4). The gangbangers I encountered were mostly juveniles. Why did they adopt this life of crimes? According to the *Chicago Tribune,* "there are many reasons—including poverty and prejudice—that gangs exist. But recent research seems to point to broken homes and troubled families as root causes."[4] What future awaited these youngsters in this hopelessly destructive path? May God have mercy on these children born and raised in depravity! May the Lord grant them an opportunity to hear the gospel and receive eternal life!

2. Dante, *Divine Comedy.* www.bartleby.com/20/103.html

3. https://chicago.suntimes.com/politics/crime-on-cta-l-trains-buses-up-but-90-percent-of-serious-incidents-go-unsolved-the-watchdogs/

4. http://articles.chicagotribune.com/1996–12-24/features/9612240065_1_gang-members-kids-probation-officer

However, is our eternal destiny a decreed fact or does it depend on our free will? Is there any hope for these inner-city kids who have experienced nothing but debauchery and wanton violence? Can they be saved and persevere as Christians?

Chapter 15

The problem of the perseverance of the saints/loss of salvation

IF MAN'S ETERNAL DESTINY is foreknown/decreed by God, does he have the free will to do otherwise? How can Man be rewarded or blamed for persevering or not persevering?

THE QUANTUM PROPOSAL AS A SOLUTION.

If Man's eternal destiny is decreed and fixed, various difficult issues arise (e.g., God's fairness to "non-elected" ghetto kids, or God's use of "reprobated Judas" to betray Christ). Furthermore, the tendency to be lax about sin may prevail, as decried by Paul, "What shall we say then? Are we to continue in sin so that grace may increase? May it never be! How shall we who died to sin still live in it?" (Rom 6:1–2). The Quantum Proposal suggests that God may allow Man to choose among some options concerning his eternal destiny (e.g., Demas' lack of perseverance in 2 Tim 4:10, the "thief on the cross" receiving salvation at the last minute in Luke 23:42). However, the Lord can also assert his sovereignty and decree Man's final outcome (e.g., Peter's perseverance in the faith and martyred death, John 21:19). Since we are not privy to God's plans for everyone, it is difficult to be dogmatic concerning the doctrine of eternal security.[1]

---

1. The doctrine of eternal security is under debate. See Gundry and Pinson, *Four Views on Eternal Security*. Some Christians believe the concept of "once saved, always saved." Others assert that Christians may lose their salvation. Some others affirm that "backsliding Christians" were never "true" Christians in the first place.

For example, Zedekiah was offered many opportunities to surrender to the Babylonians. He was helped and counseled by the prophet Jeremiah who stayed with him through the long siege of Jerusalem by Nebuchadnezzar. However, despite the wealth of information provided in the Scriptures, it is impossible to determine with any certainty Zedekiah's spiritual state (i.e., Was he saved or not? And if he was saved, did he lose his salvation by disobeying God? Or was it "once saved, always saved"?). After all, despite his many poor decisions, he did twice rescue Jeremiah, first from a harsh jail and then from certain death in the bottom of a dry cistern (Jer 37:16–21, 38:6–11).

Since "the Lord knows those who are his" (2 Tim 2:19), we probably should wait and "not go on passing judgment before the time." We may need to leave the determination of other people's eternal destinies (or rewards) to God "who will both bring to light the things hidden in the darkness and disclose the motives of men's hearts" (1 Cor 4:5).[2]

Concerning our own futures, we need not fret and worry about what may happen. Rather, let us "encourage one another day after day, as long as it is still called 'Today,' so that none of you will be hardened by the deceitfulness of sin" (Heb 3:13). As we can only be faithful to the Lord *one day at a time*, let us strive to please him *today*. "One thing I (Paul) do: forgetting what lies behind and reaching forward to what lies ahead, I press on toward the goal for the prize of the upward call of God in Christ Jesus" (Phil 3:13–14). We can imitate Brother Lawrence in saying: "Whatever becomes of me, whether I be lost or saved, I will always continue to act purely for the love of God. I shall have this good at least, that till death I shall have done all that is in me to love him."[3]

We recognize that the Lord, in his love and mercy, offers us many opportunities within his predetermined boundaries to make the right choices as mistakes are not necessarily final, and "previous successes do not guarantee future results." Therefore, every decision we make is crucial for our final destiny and needs to be decided according to the will of God, as too many "wrong" turns can lead us far away from the good outcomes (i.e., blessings and rewards) the Lord has in mind for his children (e.g., Samson chose poorly and strayed from God's perfect path).

---

2. John MacArthur said: "I do not believe it is the task of the evangelist to 'offer assurance.' That is the Holy Spirit's work." MacArthur, *The Gospel*, 273. John Piper wrote: "And perhaps, worst of all, they (some people) sometime give assurance to people who should not have it." Piper, *The Agonizing Problem*, lines 25–27.

3. Brother Lawrence, *The Practice of the Presence of God*, 3.

We may not know what the future will bring but we can surely obey our Lord, follow him, and persevere in the faith *today*. "I know whom I have believed, and I am convinced that he is able to guard what I have entrusted to him until that day" (2 Tim 1:12). Our eternal destinies (and rewards) are in God's hands and we can trust him with the final outcomes!

A STORY ON THE PERSEVERANCE OF THE SAINTS.

I was discipled by the Navigators[4] when I was in college. We had Bible studies, rallies, conferences, summer training programs, a cornucopia of wonderful opportunities to grow in the Lord. Teams of young, eager believers were helped by older, more mature leaders. Close relationships were forged over many years of shared struggles. My mentor was even the best man at my wedding! As far as I could tell, we were all striving "to know Christ and to make him known." Fast forward forty years. We have aged and gone our different ways. Have all of us persevered? Are we all walking with the Lord? I do not know since it is impossible to look inside human hearts and search for men's motives. Let us pray then that we may "all attain to the unity of the faith, and of the knowledge of the Son of God" (Eph 4:13). However, do our prayers have an impact on future events or is God's plan unalterable?

4. https://www.navigators.org/

Chapter 16

The problem of prayer

CAN OUR PRAYERS CHANGE the course of events already decreed by God? If they do, does that mean that God's foreknowledge/decree is not fixed and irrevocable? If they do not, why do we bother to pray?

THE QUANTUM PROPOSAL AS A SOLUTION.

In the Quantum Proposal, the sovereign God sometimes gives us free will choices within his preset boundaries. By exercising these God-given options (hopefully with God's input and recommendation), we will be able to progress toward our ultimate sanctification. "And your ears shall hear a word behind you, saying, "This is the way, walk in it," when you turn to the right or when you turn to the left" (Isa 30:21 ESV). When we are faced with alternative choices, we would do well to pray and ask for God's advice as a wrong decision may have long-lasting consequences (e.g., Adam's fall). We are not "doomed" to the one and only predetermined path of "God's decreed/foreknown plan." Prayer is therefore essential to the process of selecting God's best option.

What happens when we don't ask (i.e., pray)?

When Israel faced the decision to ratify a treaty with Gibeon, they "did not ask for the counsel of the Lord" (Josh 9:14) and took the wrong path. In his wisdom, the sovereign God chose not to interfere with their free will decision. They did what they desired and were not "doomed" by the Lord's foreknowledge/decree to make the poorer choice. They could (and should) have asked God for advice but they didn't.

In those days, the making of a covenant was a weighty and solemn endeavor. "It is the promise of unreserved fidelity, of whole-souled commitment, that appears to constitute the essence of the covenant."[1] No nation ever entered into such an agreement lightly without extensive deliberation. The Jews and the Canaanites were aware of God's command to "destroy all the inhabitants of the land" (Josh 9:24, Deut 20:17). Israel even had some suspicions that "perhaps you are living within our land; how then shall we make a covenant with you?" (Josh 9:7). Yet they foolishly proceeded with the planned treaty without bothering to consult their omniscient Lord. As they were free to make their decision, they had to bear full responsibility for their action and live with the long-lasting consequences.

First, they could not punish the Gibeonites "lest wrath be upon us for the oath which we swore to them" (Josh 9:20). Then, they had to defend Gibeon against its enemies because of their irrevocable covenant (Josh 10:5–7). Later, King Saul "sought to kill them (the Gibeonites) in his zeal for the sons of Israel and Judah" (2 Sam 21:2). Although God did not approve of Israel's decision to make a treaty with the Canaanites, he insisted that Israel kept its oath. "Now there was a famine in the days of David for three years, year after year; and David sought the presence of the Lord. And the Lord said, 'It is for Saul and his bloody house, because he put the Gibeonites to death'" (2 Sam 21:1). The penalty for breaking the Gibeonite covenant was the hanging deaths of seven of Saul's male descendants (2 Sam 21:6). Saul's grandson Mephibosheth (Jonathan's son) was spared "because of the oath of the Lord (the covenant) . . . between David and Saul's son Jonathan" (2 Sam 21:7). Thus were the long-term consequences of a poor free will decision made without seeking God's advice!

What happens when we do ask (i.e., pray)?

Many great books have been written about prayer.[2] The classic response to the question, "What kinds of answers can we expect from a prayer request?" is usually "yes, no, and wait."[3] Since "wait" is not really an answer

1. www.biblegateway.com/resources/encyclopedia-of-the-bible/Covenant-Old-Testament

2. Yancey, *Prayer*. Keller, *Prayer*. Hallesby, *Prayer*.

3. www.bibleinoneyear.org/bioy/commentary/1147

(i.e., no answer from God yet), let us consider the two remaining alternatives "yes and no."

Are there conditions for "yes" answers to prayer? The list of prerequisites is long. "If I regard wickedness in my heart, the Lord will not hear" (Ps 66:18). "All things for which you pray and ask, believe that you have received them, and they will be granted you" (Mark 11:24). "At all times they ought to pray and not to lose heart" (Luke 18:1). "If we ask anything according to his will, he hears us. And if we know that he hears us in whatever we ask, we know that we have the requests which we have asked from him" (1 John 5:14–15). "If you abide in me, and my words abide in you, ask whatever you wish, and it will be done for you" (John 15:7). "And without faith it is impossible to please him, for he who comes to God must believe that he is and that he is a rewarder of those who seek him" (Heb 11:6). "If you ask the Father for anything in my name, he will give it to you" (John 16:23). "But he must ask in faith without any doubting, for the one who doubts is like the surf of the sea, driven and tossed by the wind" (Jas 1:6). The word "doubts" is the Greek "diakrino (from 1223 /dia, 'thoroughly back-and-forth,' which intensifies 2919 /krino, 'to judge')—properly, investigate (judge) thoroughly—literally, judging 'back-and-forth' which can either (positively) refer to close-reasoning (discrimination) or negatively 'over-judging' (going too far, vacillating). Only the context indicates which sense is meant."[4] In the negative context of James 1:6, the meaning would be judging "back-and-forth," vacillating (between two opinions or choices).

From these verses, we gather that a "yes" answer may require "no wickedness in heart" (e.g., unconfessed sin), faith (to move mountains, Matt 17:20), belief (that the "yes" answer was already granted), persistence, a steadfast abiding in God, prayer according to God's will, prayer in Jesus' name, no doubt/vacillation between belief and unbelief . . . For many of us, these conditions are unclear and difficult to meet (e.g., how much faith is "enough" faith? How much "vacillation/doubt" is too much? How much abiding is "enough" abiding? How much "heart wickedness" is too much? What exactly is "God's will" in the matter?). If we do not meet these lofty conditions, will the answer be "no"? If so, what are the chances of getting a "yes" answer since most of us do not meet the prerequisites?

Yet, does the Lord not encourage us to pray (with the promise of "yes" answers)? "Ask, and it will be given to you; seek, and you will find;

4. http://biblehub.com/greek/1252.htm

knock, and it will be opened to you" (Matt 7:7). "For as many as are the promises of God, in him they are yes; therefore, also through him is our amen to the glory of God through us" (2 Cor 1:20).

In truth, when we pray and ask, the answer is always "yes" or "yes plus" ("yes plus" interpreted by us as "no" since it is not *what we want*).[5] Nevertheless, it is "yes plus" ("more than all we ask" Eph 3:20 NIV) for the Lord knows what is best for us and will never give us what is harmful. We need not worry about conditions to get "yes" answers *if we do not insist on getting our way.* To ask that God's will be done in our lives, as in the Lord's Prayer, will always be rewarded with the best possible choice within God's predetermined boundaries. "If you then, being evil, know how to give good gifts to your children, how much more will your Father who is in heaven give what is good to those who ask him" (Matt 7:11).

Therefore, as exhorted by our Lord, we need to "pray without ceasing," we need to "ask, seek, knock" for our Father is generous and eager to give to his children. The minimum we will receive is a "yes" (just what we ask), but even better, when we pray, we may get a "yes plus" from the one "who is able to do far more abundantly beyond all that we ask or think, according to the power that works within us, to him be the glory in the church and in Christ Jesus to all generations forever and ever. Amen" (Eph 3:20–21).

In his exile from Canaan, Jacob had asked God for safety, "food to eat and garments to wear" (Gen 28:20–21). On his safe return, he acknowledged, "for with my staff only I crossed this Jordan, and now I have become two companies" (Gen 32:10). Wasn't that much more than what he had asked? Hannah had begged the Lord for a son. God gave her a special son, the prophet Samuel! Was that not a "yes plus" answer? Solomon had petitioned the Lord for wisdom. "I will do what you have asked. I will give you a wise and discerning heart, so that there will never have been anyone like you, nor will there ever be. Moreover, I will give you what you have not asked for—both wealth and honor—so that in your lifetime you will have no equal among kings" (1 Kgs 3:12–13 NIV). Was that not "far more abundantly beyond all that" he had asked?

5. Joni Eareckson Tada said: "I used to imaging [sic] myself asking God to heal me and he never did. But you know what? I'm so glad God didn't because the 'no' answer to a prayer for healing has meant a more urgent leaning upon him every day, a more vibrant hope of heaven, a deeper sense of prayer, a more energetic love for his Word." https://billygraham.org/story/joni-eareckson-tada-on-prayer/ Not all "yes plus" are our "no" answers. For example, we may receive a five thousand dollars pay raise rather than the prayed-for two thousand dollars.

In summary, prayer occupies a prominent place in the Quantum Proposal. We are not "doomed" to the one and only path that was decreed/foreknown in eternity past, thus rendering our prayers and petitions meaningless. Since the sovereign Lord in his mercy gives us some free will choices within his preset boundaries, it is crucial that we seek the correct (and best, "yes plus") option. Prayers to determine God's will and a determination to follow God's advice, regardless of our feelings or perceived interests, will help us progress toward "the sanctification without which no one will see the Lord" (Heb 12:14).

A STORY ON PRAYER.

When I was a medical student in Houston, I was given an old bike of the "fairer sex" variety due to my "vertically challenged" stature. That was my only means of transportation to my moonlighting job at a local hospital. One evening, I sadly discovered that some miscreant stole my front wheel. Why steal such a small thing? How much could one get for that? However, to replace it would cost money, money that I could not spare. I prayed that God would somehow help me in my difficult situation for I was reluctant to ask for a handout from my friends. Soon afterward, as I was walking home late at night, I saw something lying in the gutter of the deserted street. A bicycle front wheel! Was it the right size? I took it home and sure enough, it worked just fine. The Lord also made sure that the "miracle wheel" came with the butterfly nuts fastened to its sides!

Does God bless his children in response to their prayers? Does the Lord ever need to "change his mind" and come up with a "new" plan in response to their requests? Or are all the possible scenarios created and foreknown by the omniscient God even before there is a word on their tongues (Ps 139:4)?

Chapter 17

The problem of God's immutability

"ALSO, THE GLORY OF Israel will not lie or change his mind (nacham); for he is not a man that he should change his mind" (1 Sam 15:29). "God is not Man, that he should lie, or a son of Man, that he should change his mind" (Num 23:19 ESV). It appears that the Lord never changes his mind. So, when Exodus 32:14 stated that God "changed his mind," was that just a figure of speech? Was Israel's declared punishment for worshiping the golden calf only an empty threat?

THE QUANTUM PROPOSAL AS A SOLUTION.

The Quantum Proposal suggests that the Lord in his sovereignty gave Moses two options in the episode of the golden calf: God could punish Israel and make of Moses "a great nation," or he could refrain from doing so. Moses chose to intercede for Israel and the Lord "nacham" "about the harm which he said he would do to his people" (Exod 32:14).

Just a short time before,[1] in Exodus 24:7–8, Israel solemnly agreed not to worship other gods. However, the nation promptly abandoned its covenant and followed an idol. Thus, the Lord "nacham," "suffered grief," was "sorry," but "consoled himself"[2] "about the harm which he said he

---

1. The time frame appeared to be about "forty days," Exodus 24:18.

2. "Nacham" can mean "to suffer grief, to be sorry, to console oneself, to repent of." "Nacham" in Numbers 23:19 carries the meaning of "repent." "God is not a man, that he should lie, nor a son of man, that he should repent." Thus, the omniscient and sovereign Lord *never* repents of what he has done. "Nacham" in Exodus 32 has the meaning "to be sorry, to console oneself." Brown-Driver-Briggs. http://biblehub.com/hebrew/5162.htm

would do to his people," *since he did give them fair warnings* ("He who sacrifices to any god, other than the Lord alone, shall be utterly destroyed," Exod 22:20). Was the Lord "sorry and consoled himself" by canceling the punishment? Not really! After Moses' intercession, God only delayed his judgment,[3] allowing Moses to take the alternative (not recommended) path, the option of keeping Israel alive a little longer.

Later, after the report of the twelve spies and Israel's rebellion, the Lord again said to Moses: "I will smite them with pestilence and dispossess them, and I will make you into a nation greater and mightier than they" (Num 14:12). Moses was given the same two choices. He could let God destroy Israel and make of him "a greater nation" or he could refuse God's generously renewed offer.[4] Moses again interceded for Israel and turned down God's proposal. In response, what was God's verdict for Israel? Males twenty years old or older (military service age, Num 1:3) would die in the wilderness, except for Caleb and Joshua. Moses and Aaron (both Levites) were not named in the exception. There was no need to mention them since the punishment did not include the Levites as they were exempted from the census and from serving in the army.[5] In Genesis 49, Jacob prophesied that God would "disperse them (Simeon and Levi) in Jacob and scatter them in Israel." However, "in Levi's case the curse was changed into a blessing by the faithfulness of the tribe upon a very trying occasion (Exod 32:26–28)."[6] In his omniscience, the Lord allowed some flexibility in his decree/prophecy to account for future repentance. Nevertheless, the previous declaration had to stand, and the Levites, serving as Israel's religious leaders, were "scattered up and down Palestine without territorial possession."[7]

Was God's declaration to create a "Mosite" nation a genuine offer? The Quantum Proposal suggests that the pronouncement was legitimate and not just a "test." Moses was given two alternatives and could have

---

3. Barrick, "The Openness of God," 164.

4. "When God wills to grant us a favor, it is mere pride to reject it, that God's gifts must needs be accepted, and that true humility lies in obedience and the most literal compliance with his will!" De Sales, *Introduction to the Devout Life*, 118–19.

5. Gill's Exposition of the Entire Bible. http://biblehub.com/commentaries/Num/14-29.htm

6. Ellicott's Commentary for English Readers. http://biblehub.com/commentaries/Gen/49-7.htm

7. Cambridge Bible for Schools and Colleges. http://biblehub.com/commentaries/Gen/49-7.htm

chosen either path. Was God's offer to Moses consistent with his previous promises to Israel? Could the twelve tribes be destroyed and replaced by the "Mosites"? This could not happen due to the previous pronouncements given in Genesis 49, prophesying the futures of the twelve tribes. Therefore, in Numbers 14:29, Israel's punishment for rebellion did *not* include males under the age of twenty, the Levites, Joshua, Caleb and the females of any age. God's offer to Moses, while expanding the position of the "Mosites," would still fulfill God's previous promises to Israel as young males were not included in the death sentence and could continue the tradition of the twelve tribes of Israel. However, the older men would perish, "all that had been enrolled as the soldiers of the Lord, to fight his battles and their own, but had refused, and had incurred the guilt of mutiny."[8] They would slowly die in the desert over forty years (one year for every day spent spying the land).

Was Moses wiser than God when he raised the issue of the possible loss of reputation with the Egyptians if the Lord destroyed the Israelites in the desert? Did that reason prevent God from exercising his judgment and punish Israel for its rebellion and idolatry? Obviously not! The omniscient Lord did not need Moses to point out his "deficiencies." Thus, God did not "change his mind" about punishing Israel for worshiping the golden calf. The sentence, although delayed by Moses' intercession, was inevitable once it had been pronounced!

The scenarios allowed by the Lord within his predetermined boundaries appeared to be the following. Scenario 1 (the best option): Moses accepted God's genuine offer to become "a great nation." The Israelite soldiers were destroyed. Scenario 2: Moses refused the offer and interceded for Israel. The punishment was delayed temporarily (possibly to give Moses a second chance to take God's offer?). Moses was offered the same choices later with the return of the twelve spies. Scenario 2a (the better option): Moses accepted the second offer to become "a great nation." The Israelite soldiers were destroyed. Scenario 2b: Moses refused the second offer and prayed for Israel. The Jews were forgiven (i.e., not

---

8. Pulpit Commentary. http://biblehub.com/commentaries/Num/14-29.htm

destroyed immediately?).[9] They slowly perished in the desert over forty years. Sins, though forgiven, may still have consequences in this world.

Later, the Lord told Moses to "speak to the rock" (instead of striking it like he did previously, "the rock was Christ" 1 Cor 10:4) to get water for the thirsty people. Moses was free to obey or disobey (Num 20:11). Scenario 2b alpha (the good option): Moses spoke to the rock. Water came out. Moses led the remaining Israelites into the Promised Land. Scenario 2b beta: Moses struck the rock. Water came out. Moses was disqualified and could not go into the Promised Land with the remaining Israelites.

Of the scenarios above, which one was the best for Moses? Scenario 1 (God's original recommendation) or scenario 2b beta (the one Moses ended up with by exercising his free will)? When he heard his decreed sentence, Moses desperately begged the Lord to reconsider and let him go into the Promised Land (Deut 3:23). What was God's response? Did God change his mind? "Enough! Speak to me no more of this matter" (Deut 3:26). Had Moses taken God's offer to create the "Mosites," his descendants would have prospered. They could have been "a nation greater and mightier than they (Israel)" for the Lord would always keep his word. After all, God fulfilled his promises to Abraham, Isaac, and Jacob to multiply them like "sand on the seashore" (Gen 22:17). Due to Moses' refusal of the Lord's generous offers, the "Mosites" never came into existence and the descendants of Moses faded into history.

In summary, it appears that the pronouncements of the Lord, once given, are final and irrevocable. The Lord does not change his mind and alter his promises/prophecies/decrees. "For I, the Lord, do not change" (Mal 3:6). "Every good and perfect gift is from above, coming down from the Father of the heavenly lights, who does not change like shifting shadows" (Jas 1:17 NIV). In his wisdom, God may reserve a certain amount of flexibility in his pronouncements to allow for some options within his predetermined boundaries. However, all the (future) alternative scenarios must adhere to God's previously declared decrees. Repentance (or intercession, e.g., Moses' prayer for Israel) may earn a reprieve from a previously announced punishment. Nevertheless, a sanction, once

9. While the Lord did say, "I have pardoned them according to your word" (Num 14:20), the pronouncement he previously made ("I will smite them with pestilence and dispossess them, Num 14:12) was not countermanded. The ten unfaithful spies died of the plague (Num 14:37). Pestilence struck the Israelites in the wilderness, causing many deaths (Num 16:49 and Num 25:9). The rebellious generation was dispossessed and could not enter the Promised Land.

declared, is irreversible. Therefore, it is imperative not to abuse God's patience and long-suffering.

A STORY ON GOD'S IMMUTABILITY.

As a self-employed anesthesiologist, I received most of my income from insurance companies. Occasionally, some patients without insurance would negotiate with the surgical facility for a comprehensive fee to be divided among the providers (e.g., surgeon, anesthesiologist). One day, instead of receiving a check, I was handed some cash, half of my usual pay, with the suggestion that "money under the table" was worth double its amount. However, "render to all what is due them: tax to whom tax is due" (Rom 13:7). Would the Lord change his mind and give me an exception considering my difficult circumstances (i.e., 50 percent of my fee would be only 25 percent after the tax man's cut)? Or was his command final and irrevocable? Well, 25 percent was not too bad, it could be a lot worse! "For what will it profit a man if he gains the whole world and forfeits his soul? Or what will a man give in exchange for his soul?" (Matt 16:26). In these troublesome situations, do we have the choice to freely obey and serve the Lord or not?

Chapter 18

The problem of free will choice
in serving God

DO HUMANS HAVE THE free will to serve God or not? Are we obligated to follow him if we have been "chosen" and "elected" by him? Can we choose a path different from the one that he had foreknown/decreed?

THE QUANTUM PROPOSAL AS A SOLUTION.

The Quantum Proposal advocates that, in God's sovereignty, unconditional election and irresistible grace are applied to some (e.g., John the Baptist in Luke 1, Paul in Acts 9). We can surmise that, as Paul and John the Baptist were not given a free will choice in the matter, they would not be held responsible for God's predetermined decisions. Nevertheless, they would have no cause to complain since the Lord was sovereign over his creatures. Furthermore, they reaped great benefits (forerunner of Christ, apostle, eternal life) from God's election.

Free will choices to serve God or not are given to others (e.g., Israel in Joshua 24:15, the rich young ruler in Matthew 19:21–22, the disciples in John 6). However, this God-given freedom comes with full responsibility. Men are held accountable for their decision to accept or reject the Lord.

A STORY ON THE FREE WILL CHOICE TO SERVE GOD.

When I was in medical school, I joined a Bible study group on campus. A few months later, one of the members invited everyone to stay at his family's beach house in Galveston, Texas, for the weekend. So, on a happy Friday afternoon, an excited caravan headed out to the "magic island." During the sumptuous dinner in the spacious front room overlooking the boisterous ocean, I suddenly noticed the "odd man out" among the paired visitors. Although I felt sorry for the poor devil, it was much too late to remedy his problem. After all, it was his fault for not asking about the guest list before committing himself to the junket. Probably, the appeal of "free room and board" was too much for a starving fellow to resist. After the opulent feast, everyone took off in pairs, leaving the "odd man out" to contemplate the dusky and mournful waves in the setting sun.

Being a poor foreigner and not well-developed in the physical department, I never had a date. That night, I cried out to God in my loneliness. I wondered if I was ever going to have some happiness like my Christian friends. Was God fair in blessing some of his children but not others? Submit or rebel, the choice was mine! After much struggle, I realized that Christ owed me nothing. He had already died on the cross for my sins. He had given me a good career and generous friends. Furthermore, I could come to him whenever I desired his help or needed a shoulder to cry on. O Lord, I will do what you want me to do, no matter the cost. I will be what you want me to be. I will go where you want me to go. I choose to serve you until the end!

Fast forward some years. I was an intern at a hospital in Chicago. As part of my duties, I was assigned to mentor some (female) medical students in the "fine art of medicine." I soon noticed that one of them stayed long after normal hours to "help me" care for the patients. She then intimated that she was "free on weekends" and that we "could go out to grab a bite to eat" after work. There was no restriction on interns dating medical students. In fact, it was tacitly encouraged. However, there was one problem! She was not a believer as far as I could tell. Since all my friends were blessed with wives or girlfriends, why not me? Was I doomed to stay single the rest of my life? With her phone number in hand, I had some decisions to make. Suddenly, a voice came into my head: "Son, whom do you love more, me or her?" The Galveston beach promise made long ago flooded into my mind. Would I do what my Father wanted me to do? Would I serve him or not? "Lord, you are killing me, but how can I face you in eternity if I disobey you now?" The torn phone number fluttered into the waste basket along with my only hope of escape from my drudgery.

We know that our "toil is not in vain in the Lord" (1 Cor 15:58) and that soon, we will hear, "Good and faithful servant . . . enter into the joy of your master" (Matt 25:21). Nevertheless, even "if we are faithless, he remains faithful, for he cannot deny himself" (2 Tim 2:13). If that is so, was Christ faithful to Israel in the matter of the kingdom offer? Did God really foreordain that the prize would be given to the Gentiles at Israel's expense?

Chapter 19

The problem of Jesus' offer
of the kingdom to Israel

"Jesus was going through all the cities and villages, teaching in their synagogues and proclaiming the gospel of the kingdom" (Matt 9:35). It appears that Jesus came to genuinely offer the kingdom to Israel.

However, we also read: "This man, delivered over by the predetermined plan and foreknowledge of God, you (men of Israel) nailed to a cross by the hands of godless men and put him to death" (Acts 2:23). If the Lord had foreordained that the Jews would reject the kingdom offer, was Christ's invitation genuine?

THE QUANTUM PROPOSAL AS A SOLUTION.

The Quantum Proposal affirms that Christ's offer of the kingdom to Israel was genuine. In his sovereignty, God gave two choices to the Jews within his predetermined boundaries. They could accept the Messiah who would usher in the kingdom or they could reject him, and the offer would be withdrawn.

When did the Lord take the prize away from his chosen people? Dr. Dwight Pentecost observed: "The pivotal point in the Lord's ministry to Israel was reached in the twelfth chapter (of Matthew), where the rejection of Israel by Christ, because of their announced rejection of him, and the withdrawal of the offer of the kingdom is [sic] recorded."[1] Arno Gaebelein concurred: "They rejected him, and he leaves them . . . At the end of the twelfth chapter he denies his relations and refuses to see

1. Pentecost, *Things to Come*, 463.

his own."[2] Dr. Arnold Fruchtenbaum stated: "In Matthew 12–13, Israel officially rejects the messiahship of Jesus, accusing him of demon possession and at that point, the messianic kingdom offer is withdrawn . . . The unpardonable sin, or the blasphemy of the Holy Spirit is defined, therefore, as the national rejection by Israel of the messiahship of Jesus."[3]

The novel concept of the church subsequently appeared in Matthew 16. "I also say to you that you are Peter, and upon this rock I will build my church" (Matt 16:18). In Matthew 18, Christ expounded further on church relationships and procedures. At the Last Supper, he made a new covenant with his disciples and gave them a directive for the church: "A new commandment I give to you, that you love one another" (John 13:34).

If Israel was not "doomed" to forfeit the kingdom offer, what could be the alternative? Was there more than one option within the Lord's predetermined boundaries? For example, in scenario one (a possible scenario), the Messiah came to offer the kingdom to Israel. The nation accepted Christ's offer and welcomed him to Jerusalem for the Passover. Pontius Pilate heard about "the King of the Jews," and worried about an insurrection among the crowds of pilgrims. Judas the traitor proposed to deliver Jesus to the Romans. Christ was captured, tried, and condemned to crucifixion. However, he rose after three days in the tomb. Israel received the kingdom of God.

In scenario two (the actual scenario), Jesus offered the kingdom to the Jewish nation. Sadly, the invitation was rejected. After Peter's confession of faith, Christ established the church. However, the kingdom of God would not appear immediately (Matt 24, Mark 13, Luke 21).

Are both scenarios viable considering the many messianic passages in the Old Testament and their fulfillment in the New Testament? A declaration in the Old Testament prophesying Messiah's rejection by Israel would nullify scenario one. The same pronouncement appearing early in Jesus' ministry, prior to the withdrawal of the kingdom offer (e.g., at

2. Gaebelein, "The Gospel of Matthew," IV.4.

3. Fruchtenbaum, "Doctrine of Israelology," 198. The blasphemy against the Holy Spirit is discussed in further detail in Cole, *Engaging with the Holy Spirit*, 19–34. Jesus' withdrawal of the kingdom offer is advocated by dispensationalists. See Kraus, *Jesus Christ Our Lord*, 139. "Dispensationalism is a theological system that teaches biblical history is best understood in light of a number of successive administrations of God's dealings with mankind, which it calls 'dispensations.' It maintains fundamental distinctions between God's plans for national Israel and for the New Testament Church." https://www.theopedia.com/dispensationalism

his baptism), would also make scenario one untenable. If we find these prophecies, we would have to say that scenario two was predetermined and that Messiah's offer was not genuine.

We now proceed with a *chronological* search of the Scriptures concerning Christ and his offer of the kingdom to Israel. Pronouncements from the Old Testament (especially those quoted in the New Testament) would be crucial, particularly so if they came from messianic passages. Declarations made early in the New Testament (thus qualifying them as prophecies for later events) would also be important to determine whether Christ intended to give the kingdom to Israel.

According to Daniel 9, Messiah was to come sixty-nine weeks (of years) after the decree to rebuild Jerusalem. After the sixty-nine weeks, Messiah "will be cut off and have nothing" (Dan 9:26). Since that event had been prophesied in the Old Testament, it was unchangeable by the time of Christ. Therefore, whether Israel accepted the offer of the kingdom or not, Messiah's death was inevitable and had to appear in both scenarios.

"Jesus answered them, 'Destroy this temple, and in three days I will raise it up . . . he was speaking of the temple of his body" (John 2:19, 21). This prophecy was given early in Jesus' ministry and *expanded* on the pronouncement in Daniel 9. The Messiah would be "cut off" but he would be raised up *in three days*. Messiah's rejection by Israel was not discussed.

"The spirit of the Lord is upon me, because he anointed me to preach the gospel to the poor. He has sent me to proclaim release to the captives, and recovery of sight to the blind, to set free those who are oppressed, to proclaim the favorable year of the Lord" (Luke 4:18–19 quoting Isa 61:1–2). The Old Testament passage referred to Isaiah or the anointed one.[4] Jesus applied it to himself. This event could appear in both scenarios. Isaiah 61 did not mention the Messiah being dismissed by Israel.

"This was to fulfill what was spoken through Isaiah the prophet: 'He himself took our infirmities and carried away our diseases'" (Matt 8:17 quoting Isa 53:4). The Old Testament citation spoke of the Suffering

4. http://biblehub.com/commentaries/isaiah/61–1.htm

Servant.[5] Matthew applied it to Jesus. Nothing was said in Isaiah 53:4 about the Messiah being rejected by Israel.[6]

"Behold, my servant whom I have chosen; my beloved in whom my soul is well-pleased; I will put my spirit upon him, and he shall proclaim justice to the Gentiles. He will not quarrel, nor cry out; nor will anyone hear his voice in the streets. A battered reed he will not break off, and a smoldering wick he will not put out, until he leads justice to victory. And in his name the Gentiles will hope." (Matt 12:18-21 citing Isa 42:1-4). Isaiah 42 referred to God's servant. Matthew used the quote for Jesus. Messiah's repudiation was not discussed.

"This was to fulfill what was spoken through the prophet: 'I will open my mouth in parables; I will utter things hidden since the foundation of the world'" (Matt 13:35 quoting Ps 78:2). The context of the Old Testament passage was God's dealings with Israel. Matthew applied it to Jesus. This "fulfillment" of Old Testament prophecy was "analogical or typological" rather than literal. Two possible scenarios could appear at this juncture. One path would lead to Christ's acceptance by Israel. The other would result in his rejection by the nation and the withdrawal of the kingdom offer.

"This people honors me with their lips, but their heart is far away from me. But in vain do they worship me, teaching as doctrines the precepts of men" (Matt 15:8-9 quoting Isa 29:13). According to Pentecost,[7] Gaebelein,[8] and Fruchtenbaum,[9] this declaration was given *after* the kingdom offer had already been withdrawn in Matthew 12-13. The reference from Isaiah dealt with God's repudiation by Israel. Jesus applied the quote to himself. However, nothing was said in Isaiah 29 about the

---

5. The Christian theologian Origen (184–253 AD) acknowledged that his "Jewish opponent replied, that these predictions (in Isaiah 53), bore reference to the whole people (Israel), regarded as *one individual,* and as being in a state of dispersion and suffering." Origen, *The Writings,* 458. "There has been anything but consensus on the identity of the Servant in Isa 52:13–53:12." Litwak, "The Use of Quotations," 385. Thus, the claim that Isaiah 53 is a prophecy about the Messiah is not universally accepted.

6. "He was despised and rejected by mankind" (Isaiah 53:3 NIV). "Rejected of men—This phrase is full of meaning, and in three words states the whole history of man in regard to his treatment of the Redeemer." Barnes' Notes on the Bible. http://biblehub.com/isaiah/53-3.htm. The context of Isaiah 53 is mankind's rejection of the Suffering Servant, not Israel's rejection of their Messiah.

7. Pentecost, *Things to Come,* 463.

8. Gaebelein, "The Gospel of Matthew," IV.4.

9. Fruchtenbaum, "Doctrine of Israelology," 198.

Messiah being rejected by the nation. Thus, this "fulfillment" of Old Testament prophecy was "analogical or typological" rather than literal. This event could only appear in scenario two (the actual scenario) as Christ seemingly acknowledged his dismissal by the people ("their heart is far away from me").

"From that time Jesus began to show his disciples that he must go to Jerusalem and suffer many things from the elders and chief priests and scribes, and be killed, and be raised up on the third day" (Matt 16:21, also Mark 8:31, and Luke 9:22). This pronouncement was given *after* the kingdom offer had already been withdrawn.[10] Jesus only began to speak this way "from that time." Had this pronouncement been given early in Jesus' ministry (e.g., at his baptism), scenario one would have been untenable as Jesus declared that he would "suffer many things from the elders and chief priests and scribes." This event only appeared in scenario two.

"But first he must suffer many things and be rejected by this generation" (Luke 17:25). This was declared *after* the kingdom offer had already been given to the church. Had this announcement been given at the beginning of Jesus' ministry, scenario one would not have been possible as Jesus affirmed that he would "be rejected by this generation."

"While they were listening to this, he went on to tell them a parable, because he was near Jerusalem and the people thought that the kingdom of God was going to appear at once. He said: 'A man of noble birth went to a distant country to have himself appointed king and then to return. So he called ten of his servants and gave them ten minas. 'Put this money to work,' he said, 'until I come back.' But his subjects hated him and sent a delegation after him to say, 'We don't want this man to be our king'" (Luke 19:11–14 NIV). This parable was given *after* the withdrawal of the offer. Jesus revealed that he would be rejected by his people ("We don't want this man to be our king"). The purpose of the story was to declare that the kingdom of God was *not* "going to appear at once." Events later prophesied in Matthew 24, Mark 13, and Luke 21 would have to happen *before* the Lord's return. In this scenario (scenario two) there was a

---

10. The order of the events was: Israel's rejection of the Messiah in Matthew 12–13, Peter's confession of faith in Matthew 16, Christ's creation of the church, Jesus' warning not to reveal that he was the Messiah, the announcement of his upcoming sufferings at the hands of Israel, the proclamation of his death, and his rebuke of Peter.

gap[11] between the sixty-ninth and the seventieth week of Daniel 9 since God postponed the kingdom "until the fullness of the Gentiles has come in" (Rom 11:25). Scenario one would have no gap as the kingdom was offered and accepted by Israel. Although the scenarios diverged at the point of Israel's free will choice to accept or reject the Messiah, the events *previously decreed* in the Old Testament (e.g., the Messiah will be "cut off") were unchangeable. However, the Lord allowed some flexibility in the boundaries of his prophecy in Daniel 9 (e.g., a gap in the timeline versus no gap) to cover the possibility of Messiah's rejection by Israel.[12]

"Behold your king is coming to you, gentle, and mounted on a donkey, even on a colt, the foal of a beast of burden" (Matt 21:5 quoting Zech 9:9). Zechariah prophesied the coming of Israel's king. Matthew assigned the event to Jesus. Zechariah 9 did not predict that the Messiah would be rejected. In scenario one, the king would be accepted by Israel. In scenario two, Messiah only appeared to be welcomed by Israel but was ultimately dismissed by the nation.

"The crowds going ahead of him, and those who followed, were shouting, 'Hosanna to the Son of David. Blessed is he who comes in the name of the Lord'" (Matt 21:9 quoting Ps 118:26). Psalm 118 referred to God and Israel.[13] Matthew applied it to Jesus. "According to Rabbinical writings, pilgrim caravans were thus welcomed on their arrival at Jerusalem."[14] "The Old Testament abounds in language which may thus be employed to express ideas under the Christian dispensation; but this does not prove that all such language was originally designed to refer

---

11. "The Gap Theory. The concept of the stopped prophetic clock has led to the gap theory as the explanation for Daniel 9. This theory places fulfillment of the first sixty-nine weeks of the prophecy before the death of Jesus. Then, after an approximately 2,000-year gap, comes the fulfillment of the final week (7 years) of the prophecy." Standish and Standish, *The Evangelical Dilemma*, 215–16. Also see Tanner, "Is Daniel's Seventy-Weeks," 189. The "gap theory" is not universally accepted. See Stefanovic, *Daniel: Wisdom to the Wise*, 371.

12. It is interesting to note that only sixty-nine weeks were discussed in the timeline of Daniel 9:24–27. The last week (of the seventy weeks) was not addressed in the timeline, thus allowing some flexibility for future events.

13. Psalm 118 could also refer to the post-exilic "religious community, the circle of believers," or an individual (e.g., the Davidic king). See Prinsloo, "A Contextual and Intertextual," 405.

14. Ellicott's Commentary for English Readers. http://biblehub.com/commentaries/psalms/118–26.htm

to that dispensation."[15] The passage did not state that Messiah would be rejected.

"It is written, 'My house shall be called a house of prayer'; but you are making it a robbers' den'" (Matt 21:13 quoting Isa 56:7 and Jer 7:11). This pronouncement was given during Jesus' final days in Jerusalem just before the Last Passover. The quotes in Isaiah and Jeremiah addressed God's house. Jesus ascribed them to his circumstance. Nothing was said in Isaiah 56 and Jeremiah 7 about the Messiah being dismissed by the Jews.

"And Jesus said to them, 'Yes; have you never read, 'Out of the mouth of infants and nursing babies you have prepared praise for yourself?'" (Matt 21:16, quoting Ps 8:2). The context in Psalm 8 was the Lord's glory. Jesus applied the passage to his situation. The Messiah's rejection by Israel was not discussed in Psalm 8.

"Did you never read in the Scriptures, 'The stone which the builders rejected, this became the chief corner stone; this came about from the Lord, and it is marvelous in our eyes?' Therefore, I say to you, the kingdom of God will be taken away from you and given to a people, producing the fruit of it" (Matt 21:42–43 quoting Ps 118:22–23).[16] This pronouncement was given during Jesus' final days in Jerusalem just before the Last Passover. The Messiah's rejection by Israel was inevitable at this point (i.e., "This is the heir; come, let us kill him," Matt 21:38). Psalm 118:22 referred to Israel being the "chief corner stone" of all the nations.[17] Jesus claimed the title for himself. Due to the different context in Psalm 118, this "fulfillment" of Old Testament prophecy was "analogical or typological" rather than literal.

"And he who falls on this stone will be broken to pieces; but on whomever it falls, it will scatter him like dust" (Matt 21:44 quoting Isa 8:14). In Isaiah 8:14, God was "a stone to strike and a rock to stumble over" for both Israel and Judah.[18] Jesus applied the reference to his circumstance. Nothing was said in Isaiah 8 about the Messiah being rejected by Israel.

15. Barnes' Notes on the Bible. http://biblehub.com/commentaries/psalms/118-26.htm

16. Also see Luke 20:17 and Mark 12:10.

17. Pulpit Commentary. http://biblehub.com/commentaries/psalms/118-22.htm. "We are not to suppose that this had original reference to the Messiah." Barnes' Notes on the Bible. http://biblehub.com/commentaries/psalms/118-22.htm

18. http://biblehub.com/isaiah/8-14.htm

"Then how does David in the Spirit call him 'Lord,' saying, 'The Lord said to my Lord, 'Sit at my right hand, until I put your enemies beneath your feet?'" (Matt 22:43–44 quoting Ps 110:1). Psalm 110 referred to David's Lord. Jesus claimed that designation. The passage did not mention Messiah's rejection.

"This was to fulfill the word of Isaiah the prophet which he spoke: 'Lord, who has believed our report? And to whom has the arm of the Lord been revealed?'" (John 12:38 quoting Isa 53:1). Isaiah was the subject in the original context.[19] John applied the quote to Jesus' situation. This "fulfillment" of Old Testament prophecy was "analogical or typological" rather than literal. There was no mention of Messiah's rejection by Israel in Isaiah 53:1.

"He has blinded their eyes and he hardened their heart, so that they would not see with their eyes and perceive with their heart and be converted and I heal them" (John 12:40 quoting Isa 6:9–10). The Old Testament passage addressed God's message to Israel. John used the reference for Jesus. The Messiah's repudiation was not discussed in Isaiah 6.

"It is that the Scripture may be fulfilled, 'He who eats my bread has lifted up his heel against me'" (John 13:18 quoting Ps 41:9). This happened during the Last Supper. Ps 41:9 referred to David and his false friend. Jesus applied the event to his situation. Nothing was said in Psalm 41 about the Messiah being rejected by the Jews.

"But they have done this to fulfill the word that is written in their Law, 'They hated me without a cause'" (John 15:25 quoting Ps 69:4). This pronouncement was given during the Last Supper. Psalm 69:4 addressed David and his enemies. Jesus claimed the quote for his circumstance. This "fulfillment" of Old Testament prophecy was "analogical or typological" rather than literal. The Messiah's repudiation was not mentioned in the original context.

"For I tell you that this which is written must be fulfilled in me, 'and he was numbered with transgressors'" (Luke 22:37 quoting Isa 53:12). Isaiah spoke about the Suffering Servant. Luke applied it to Jesus. Christ had been prophesied to be "cut off and have nothing" whether he would be accepted by Israel or not. This event could be in both scenarios.

"You will all fall away because of me this night, for it is written, 'I will strike down the shepherd, and the sheep of the flock shall be scattered'" (Matt 26:31 quoting Zech 13:7). The Old Testament passage referred to

19. Ellicott's Commentary for English Readers. http://biblehub.com/commentaries/isaiah/53-1.htm

a "shepherd" (any Jewish king or ruler)[20] who was struck down. *After Israel's rejection*, Jesus applied the reference to himself. Nothing was said in Zechariah 13 about the Messiah being rejected by the Jews. Meyers and Meyers commented: "This image of the slain shepherd and the consequent scattering of the flock is best understood as . . . language used to anticipate the future age when the suffering and hardships undergone by the scattered flock will at last prove to have been efficacious in . . . a renewed covenant with Yahweh."[21] They "see the reference to the shepherd in historical and eschatological, not messianic, terms. In this sense . . . this shepherd is not a positive figure."[22] In other words, the "struck down shepherd" could be a king or ruler punished by the Lord. Thus, this "fulfillment" of Old Testament prophecy was "analogical or typological" rather than literal.

"Then that which was spoken through Jeremiah the prophet was fulfilled: 'And they took the thirty pieces of silver, the price of the one whose price had been set by the sons of Israel; and they gave them for the potter's field, as the Lord directed me'" (Matt 27:9–10 quoting Zech 11:12–13 and Jer 32:6–11). This pronouncement was given *after* Jesus' trial and conviction by the Jews. As said before in the discussion about Judas, there were significant differences between the Old Testament contexts and the New Testament situation. Thus, this "fulfillment" of prophecy was "analogical or typological" rather than literal. This declaration did not appear early in Jesus' ministry. If it did, it would have pointed to a foreordained rejection of the Messiah by Israel (i.e., price "set by the sons of Israel"). The "thirty pieces of silver" could appear in both scenarios. In scenario one, the money could come from the Romans since the Jews would accept Messiah's offer of the kingdom. In scenario two, the money came from the Jews.

"They gave him wine to drink mixed with gall; and after tasting it, he was unwilling to drink" (Matt 27:34 quoting Ps 69:21). Psalm 69 referred to David. Matthew applied the quote to Jesus. Christ's crucifixion appeared in both scenarios.

"And when they had crucified him, they divided up his garments among themselves by casting lots" (Matt 27:35 quoting Ps 22:18). Psalm 22 addressed David's trials. Matthew equated them with Jesus' sufferings.

20. Cambridge Bible for Schools and Colleges. http://biblehub.com/commentaries/zechariah/13–7.htm

21. Meyers and Meyers, *Zechariah 9–14*, 388.

22. Nogalski, *The Book of the Twelve*, 57.

"And those passing by were hurling abuse at him, wagging their heads" (Matt 27:39 quoting Ps 22:7). David was the subject in the original context. Matthew used the passage to describe Jesus' crucifixion.

"He trusts in God, let God rescue him now, if he delights in him; for he said, 'I am the Son of God'" (Matt 27:43 quoting Ps 22:8). Matthew applied David's plight to Jesus.

"About the ninth hour Jesus cried out with a loud voice, saying, 'Eli, Eli, lama sabachthani?' that is, 'My God, my God, why have you forsaken me?'" (Matt 27:46 quoting Ps 22:1). Jesus used David's words when he was about to die.

"For these things came to pass to fulfill the Scripture, 'Not a bone of him shall be broken'" (John 19:36 quoting Ps 34:20). Psalm 34:20 spoke about the righteous person. John used the quote to describe Jesus' situation. "The language is of a general character, such as often occurs in the Scriptures, and it should, in all fairness, be so construed. It cannot mean that the bones of a righteous man are never broken, or that the fact that a man has a broken bone proves that he is not righteous; but it means that, as a general principle, religion conduces to safety, or that the righteous are under the protection of God."[23] Nothing was said in Psalm 34 about Messiah's rejection by Israel. This "fulfillment" was "analogical or typological" rather than literal.

"And again, another Scripture says, 'They shall look on him whom they pierced'" (John 19:37 quoting Zech 12:10). Zechariah 12 referred to God and Judah. John applied it to Jesus' situation. Did Zechariah 12:10 support the notion that Israel was predestined/foreordained to reject the Messiah by "piercing" him? Zechariah 12:9–11 stated: "And in that day I will set about to destroy all the nations that come against Jerusalem. I will pour out on the house of David and on the inhabitants of Jerusalem, the Spirit of grace and of supplication, so that they will look on me whom they have pierced; and they will mourn for him, as one mourns for an only son, and they will weep bitterly over him like the bitter weeping over a firstborn. In that day there will be great mourning in Jerusalem." The words "I" and "me" referred to God. "They" stood for "the house of David and the inhabitants of Jerusalem." "Him" was unspecified. For the sake of discussion, let us assume that "him" referred to Christ. If so, Zechariah 12:9–11 did *not* prophesy that Christ would be "pierced" (i.e., rejected) by Israel. The text clearly stated that God was pierced, and that

---

23. Barnes' Notes on the Bible. http://biblehub.com/commentaries/Pss/34-20.htm

Israel would mourn for "him." Dr. Stanley Toussaint stated: "The mourning in Zechariah 12:10 is . . . a repentant lamentation by Israel that will result in the purification of the nation."[24] However, Israel, as a nation, neither mourned for Jesus nor repented. Thus, Zechariah 12:10 cannot be construed as a prophesy of the Messiah's rejection by Israel. In my opinion, John applied Zechariah 12:10 to Jesus only in the aspect that Christ was "pierced." John did not claim that Jesus was pierced by "the house of David and the inhabitants of Jerusalem" since John already stated that "one of the (Roman) soldiers pierced his side with a spear" (John 19:34). In Daniel 9, Christ had been prophesied to be "cut off and have nothing," whether he would be accepted by Israel or not. So, the simple fact of Christ being "pierced" could appear in both scenarios.

"And Jesus, crying out with a loud voice, said, 'Father, into your hands I commit my spirit.' Having said this, he breathed his last" (Luke 23:46 quoting Ps 31:5). Psalm 31 referred to David. Jesus applied it to himself.

"And Joseph took the body and wrapped it in a clean linen cloth, and laid it in his own new tomb, which he had hewn out in the rock" (Matt 27:59–60 referring to Isa 53:9). Matthew applied the concept of the Suffering Servant to Jesus.

"This man, delivered over by the predetermined plan and foreknowledge of God, you (the Israelites) nailed to a cross by the hands of godless men and put him to death" (Acts 2:23). This pronouncement was given *after* Christ's rejection by the Jews and execution by the Romans. Israel's involvement in the crucifixion was not required by any Old Testament prophecy.[25] The verse could easily have been: "This man, delivered over by the predetermined plan and foreknowledge of God, was nailed to a cross by the hands of godless men (the Romans) who put him to death."

"For truly in this city there were gathered together against your holy servant Jesus, whom you anointed, both Herod and Pontius Pilate, along with the Gentiles and the peoples of Israel, to do whatever your hand and your purpose predestined to occur" (Acts 4:27–28). This event only appeared in scenario two. In scenario one, the verse could have been: "For truly in this city there were gathered together against your holy servant

---

24. Toussaint, "A Critique," 477.

25. Note that no Old Testament quote was given in either Acts 2:23 or Acts 4:27–28 to support the concept that Messiah's rejection by Israel was preordained.

Jesus, whom you anointed, both Herod[26] and Pontius Pilate, along with the Gentiles, to do whatever your hand and your purpose predestined to occur."

"He was led as a sheep to slaughter; and as a lamb before its shearer is silent, so he does not open his mouth. In humiliation his judgment was taken away; who will relate his generation? For his life is removed from the earth" (Acts 8:32–33 quoting Isa 53:7–8). Isaiah 53 referred to the Suffering Servant. Luke applied it to Jesus. Christ's sufferings can appear in both scenarios.

"Therefore, he also says in another Psalm, 'You will not allow your holy one to undergo decay'" (Acts 13:35 quoting Ps 16:10). David was the subject in Psalm 16. Luke applied it to Jesus. Christ prophesied early in his ministry that he would rise from the tomb after three days (John 2:19–21). Christ's resurrection was a literal fulfillment of the prophecy in John 2.[27]

In summary, there are no Old Testament prophecies or early New Testament declarations that would prevent the Lord from giving Israel a genuine offer. In his sovereignty, God gave Israel two choices within his predetermined boundaries. They could accept the Messiah who would usher in the kingdom or they could reject him, and the invitation would be withdrawn and given to the Gentiles. Christ's death on the cross was prominent in both scenarios as decreed by the prophecy in Daniel 9.

In the next sections, we will take a closer look at the scriptural evidence from the Old and New Testaments showing that the thesis of the Quantum Proposal (Man has some free will choices within the Lord's boundaries) has always been in effect in God's economy.

---

26. Herod Antipas was an Idumean (Edomite), not an Israelite, and therefore would not represent the nation.

27. The "fulfillment" of Psalm 16:10 is only "analogical or typological."

PART THREE

Scriptural Evidence from
the Old Testament

Chapter 20

The case of Adam, Eve, and the serpent.

THE SERPENT

ADAM WAS MADE IN the image of God and "became a living being" with God's "breath of life" (Gen 2:7). This "breath of life" was not unique to the human race ("Every creature that has the breath of life in it," Gen 6:17 NIV). One of the creatures, the snake ("the serpent of old, who is the devil and Satan" Rev 20:2), craftily decided to tempt Eve. Why Eve and not Adam? Possibly because she did not actually receive God's command not to eat from the tree. Probably, she only heard about the prohibition from her husband. Furthermore, the wily serpent chose to tempt Eve in Adam's absence[1] ("Two are better than one because they have a good return for their labor" Eccl 4:9).

Cunningly, Satan insinuated that the Lord was a tyrant. "Indeed, has God said, 'you shall not eat from *any* tree in the garden?'" (Gen 3:1). Then he claimed that the Lord was jealous and unwilling to share. "God knows that in the day you eat from it your eyes will be opened, and you will be like God knowing good and evil" (Gen 3:5). Finally, on his own authority, he asserted the direct negative of God's declaration. The Lord pronounced in Genesis 2:17 "mowt tamut," that is "die, you will die." The serpent proclaimed in Genesis 3:4 "lo mowt temutun," that is "*not,* die, you will die." Satan had free will to lie or not to lie within the Lord's

---

1. John Calvin said: "Some conjecture that Adam was present when his wife was tempted and persuaded by the serpent, which is by no means credible." Calvin, *Commentary on Genesis,* Genesis 3:6.

sovereign boundaries.[2] He made unwise choices and rightfully reaped the consequences. "Because you have done this, cursed are you more than all cattle" (Gen 3:14). What could be an alternative scenario? The snake could have chosen not to get involved in Man's affairs. He could have encouraged Adam and Eve to obey God. Sadly, he chose the poorer option and paid the price.

EVE.

Eve willingly conversed with the talking serpent. In response to the snake's innuendo about God's supposed "tyranny," she "inflated" God's command. "You shall not eat from it *or touch it*, lest you die" (Gen 3:3). Swayed by Satan's "ironclad" guarantee that "You surely shall not die!" and his confident assertion that she could be "like God, knowing good and evil," she mulled the option of disobeying the Lord. The snake did not force Eve to undertake any action, nor did he suggest that she should eat from the tree. He completely disappeared from the scene after his short, but eminently powerful, conversation with Eve. She was totally free to do whatever she wanted without the serpent's or God's interference.

Instead of investigating Satan's truthfulness, Eve chose to believe him and did not inquire about how he came to his lofty knowledge. Did he eat from the tree before? Was he "like God, knowing good and evil"? To her detriment, she focused on the forbidden fruit. She "saw that the tree was good for food" (Gen 3:6). Obviously, this process was only in her mind as she had never eaten the fruit before. Somehow, she reasoned that it was not poisonous, that it would be good tasting (the lust of the flesh) and that her body could handle it (even though God said it would cause death). Next, she saw "that it was a delight to the eyes" (lust of the eyes) "and that the tree was desirable to make one wise" (the boastful pride of life). Did she want to be "like God"? "For all that is in the world, the lust of the flesh and the lust of the eyes and the boastful pride of life, is not from the Father, but is from the world" (1 John 2:16).

In her desire for the fruit, she discarded the option of consulting with her husband. Even though Eve and Adam were supposed to be "one flesh" (Gen 2:24) and that "they are no longer two, but one" (Mark 10:8), she chose to make this momentous decision without her partner's input.

---

2. There is no evidence in the Scriptures that God was involved in Satan's temptation of Eve. Satan and Eve were both free to choose the path they desired.

One could see Eve weighing the advantages (good for food, delight to the eyes, becoming like God) and disadvantages (death as proclaimed by the Lord but contradicted by Satan). If she believed the serpent, she would end up with three positives and no negative. "The woman being deceived, fell into transgression" (1 Tim 2:14). "She took from its fruit and ate" (Gen 3:6). Eve had a decision to make and she chose the disobedient option.

What should she do with Adam? She could say nothing. She could tell him what she did and see what he would decide. She could confess and ask him to intercede for her. She could explain her decision and convince him to follow her example. She could also actively give him the fruit. She foolishly chose the worst option (misery loves company?). Therefore, she was held accountable and rightfully punished by God.

ADAM.

God allowed Adam and Eve to exercise their free will. Adam "listened to the voice of" his wife, and when given the fruit, he consciously chose to eat and was therefore fully responsible for his disobedience.[3] What could have been some alternative scenarios? Adam could have refused Eve's offer. He could have asked the Lord what he should do. He could have begged God to forgive his wife.

We read in Genesis 3:21, "The Lord God made garments of skin for Adam and his wife." If the "garments of skin" came from some animals, sin had repercussions on all the garden's inhabitants. "Therefore, just as through one man sin entered into the world, and death through sin, and so death spread to all men, because all sinned" (Rom 5:12). By his disobedience, Adam unleashed evil into the world and would have to live with the disastrous consequences!

The serpent, Eve, and Adam exercised their free will to choose their own paths within the omniscient Lord's predetermined boundaries. They all decided to go against God's declared will/command. Thus, the Lord rightfully held all three responsible for their respective actions.

---

3. Adam was never "deceived at all; neither by the serpent, with whom he never conversed; nor by his wife, he knew what he did, when he took the fruit of her, and ate." Gill's Exposition of the Entire Bible. https://biblehub.com/commentaries/1_timothy/2-14.htm

Chapter 21

The case of Abraham, Pharaoh, and Abimelech

ABRAHAM.

IN GENESIS 12, WE read about Abraham going to Egypt due to a famine in Canaan. Afraid of being killed by the Egyptians because of Sarah, Abraham claimed the half-truth (whole lie) that she was his sister (half-sister in Gen 20:12 or possibly his niece).[1] When Pharaoh heard about the beautiful Sarah, he wanted her for himself. Abraham had the choice to "come clean" and defend Sarah at the risk of his own life or let her go in exchange for "sheep and oxen and donkeys and male and female servants and female donkeys and camels" (Gen 12:16). Abraham chose the second option (the safer and more profitable path for him).

Though God could have intervened earlier, he allowed the patriarch to make his own decision. Afterwards, "the Lord struck Pharaoh and his house with great plagues" to rescue Sarah (Gen 12:17). God's delay in action revealed Abraham's character flaw to himself, to Sarah, to Pharaoh, and to us who could learn from other people's bad examples.

PHARAOH.

Abraham's poor decision impacted those around him. Sarah had to join a harem. Pharaoh and his people suffered "great plagues." Somehow, the

---

1. "Sarah was the grand-daughter of Terah, i.e., the daughter of Haran, and sister of Lot." Pulpit Commentary. http://biblehub.com/commentaries/Gen/20-12.htm

king found out that Sarah was Abraham's wife and not his sister. As the supreme ruler of Egypt, Pharaoh had many available options to deal with this unpleasant problem. He could pray to his gods for help. He could ask his physicians to give him remedies for the diseases. He could demand that Abraham divorce Sarah. He could "harden his heart" and stubbornly refuse to let Sarah go. He could also kill Abraham for causing him trouble. However, instead of retaliating, Pharaoh chose to let Abraham go "with his wife and all that belonged to him" (Gen 12:20).

ABIMELECH.

Later, Abraham settled in the land of Gerar. Given a second chance by God to make the right decision, he again chose to say that his wife was his "sister." When Abimelech heard about Sarah, he "sent and took her" (Gen 20:2). The Lord again had to intervene and "closed fast all the wombs of the household of Abimelech." Since God knew that Abimelech was not at fault ("in the integrity of my heart and the innocence of my hands, I have done this"), he shielded him from sin. "I also kept you from sinning against me; therefore, I did not let you touch her" (Gen 20:5–6). According to his sovereign will, the Lord could (and sometimes did) intervene to prevent evil. Even though he might allow some people to make their foolish decisions (e.g., Abraham), he was not responsible for their choices, as they acted against their creator's explicit commands (e.g., lying).

Following his predetermined boundaries (Abraham must live, and Sarah must remain pure to bear the promised son Isaac), God appeared to Abimelech in a dream to give him two choices: restore the man's wife and live or keep the man's wife and die, "you and all who are yours" (Gen 20:7). The Lord did not give Abimelech some other options: keep the man's wife and live; ask Abraham to divorce Sarah; give Abraham money to "buy" Sarah. To his credit, Abimelech made the right choice and let Sarah go free. Furthermore, he gave Abraham "sheep and oxen and male and female servants" and "a thousand pieces of silver." In return, Abraham prayed for him and God "healed Abimelech and his wife and his maids, so that they bore children" (Gen 20:17).

The sovereign Lord gave Abraham, Pharaoh, and Abimelech some alternatives within his prescribed boundaries. Abraham insisted on making the same poor choices and had to be continually rescued by the long-suffering Lord who was bound by his previous promises to the patriarch.

On the other hand, Pharaoh and Abimelech chose the correct options and were spared further sufferings. All three made their decisions freely and were therefore responsible for their actions, whether good or evil.

Chapter 22

The case of Moses and Aaron

MOSES.

IN THE ACCOUNT OF the "burning bush," God ordered Moses to go to Egypt and deliver Israel. Moses came up with five different excuses to avoid the task. First, who am I to go? (Exod 3:11). Second, what is your name? (Exod 3:13). Third, what if they will not believe me? (Exod 4:1). Fourth, I am slow of speech (Exod 4:10). Finally, please use someone else (Exod 4:13). After much patient listening and mercifully providing solemn assurances, the Lord eventually gave Moses an alternative. Aaron could be Moses' helper.[1]

This option was not a plan that God devised at the last minute. The Lord was not caught off guard by Moses' stubborn refusal. As a logical requirement for Moses to have free will, disobedience was a possibility. Therefore, a viable alternative would be required and had to be put into motion by God ahead of time. It was not pure coincidence that at the needed moment, "behold, he is coming out to meet you" (Exod 4:14). Aaron came at the right time because some days before,[2] the Lord had commanded him, "Go to meet Moses in the wilderness" (Exod 4:27).

God's instructions had to be very precise for Aaron went directly to Mount Horeb rather than to Moses' home in Midian (Exod 2:15). Had

---

1. This was done reluctantly as the Lord was not pleased by Moses' staunch resistance. "The anger of the Lord burned against Moses" (Exod 4:14).

2. "A common traveler cannot conveniently make the journey from Ramesses, or Grand Cairo (from whence it may be supposed Aaron set out), to Mount Horeb, in less than a fortnight, though he be carried on the back of a camel, and yet Aaron reached this place by the time that Moses did." Gill's Exposition of the Entire Bible. http://biblehub.com/commentaries/Exod/4-27.htm

Moses agreed to God's recommended option, Aaron would have been Moses' brother without any official position of leadership. However, since Moses refused to obey, Aaron became Moses' co-leader. Both scenarios had been created beforehand by the sovereign Lord. We could also speculate that had Moses flatly refused to go, Aaron could have been sent alone to do the task. The omnipotent Lord does *not* need any particular individual to do his work. No one, no matter how talented, is indispensable in God's economy.

The interpretation that the Lord had foreordained Moses' refusal[3] has many difficulties. First, if he had predetermined that Moses would *not* be his sole envoy, why would God offer him the position? Would that not be "disingenuous"? Would it not be simpler and more forthright to just declare, "you and your brother Aaron will be co-leaders"? Second, why would the Lord endeavor to *persistently* persuade Moses to be the sole emissary when he had already decreed otherwise? Third, why would the Lord be angry with Moses if he had predestined that outcome? Was God just "pretending" to be upset to cover up his foreordained decision? Fourth, did the Lord "entice" Moses to refuse the offer since he had no intention of giving it? Finally, why would the omniscient God choose Aaron as co-leader knowing his fickle heart? Was that the Lord's preferred option or was it the only way to convince stubborn Moses to go to Egypt?

Was Moses' choice better than the Lord's original recommendation? Aaron (and not Moses) was given the high priesthood of Israel.[4] Instead of putting down Israel's rebellion in Moses' absence, Aaron went along with the crowd and made an idol. Later, in Numbers 12, Aaron (as the older brother, Exod 7:7) challenged Moses' position of leadership, requiring a direct intervention from the Lord. Considering this outcome, would Moses have been better off to submit to God? Whose will was better? The Lord's or Man's? To his detriment, when offered a free will choice to obey or disobey, Moses chose to follow his own desires (or fears?) and was thus totally responsible for his decision.

---

3. "God knew from the beginning what Moses would do, but he reserves this motive (Aaron's arrival) to the last as the strongest to rouse his languid heart, and Moses now fully and cordially complied with the call." Jamieson-Faussett-Brown Bible Commentary. http://biblehub.com/commentaries/Exod/4-14.htm

4. In fairness to both men, God made Moses a prophet (Deut 34:10), and appointed Aaron to the high priesthood of Israel (Exod 28:1).

AARON.

Aaron became Moses' spokesman as a concession from the Lord. When Moses went up the mountain to receive God's commandments, Aaron was left in charge (together with Hur, Exod 24:14). In Moses' absence, the people asked Aaron to make an idol. Supposedly, a god that they could not see, that they could not carry around at their convenience, was no god at all. In their minds, the pillar of fire and the pillar of cloud (Exod 13:21–22) did not qualify as a "physical" god! Could this be because they were unable to *exert their will* on the cloud and the fire?

Aaron had several options to deal with Israel's request. The best approach would be to follow God's command in Exodus 20:4 ("You shall not make for yourself an idol"). As the (future) high priest, he could remind the people of their covenant and the penalty for worshiping other gods. Or he could imitate his co-leader Hur and stay out of the fray. He could also agree to the rebellious people's demand. Aaron unwisely selected the worst option. He asked the people for "the gold rings which are in the ears of your wives, your sons, and your daughters" (Exod 32:2). Was he hoping that they would put up a big fuss and refuse to part with their beloved possessions? Unfortunately, once a foothold had been given to evil, there was a good chance that it would soon grow into a flood of iniquity. The people willingly gave the gold and Aaron made the golden calf!

When the Israelites said, "This is your god, O Israel, who brought you up from the land of Egypt" (Exod 32:4), Aaron decided to build an altar for the idol. To provide some cover, Aaron declared the event, "a feast to the Lord," using God's name "Yahweh." Was the Lord fooled by the announcement that this was a celebration in his honor, even though the pagan symbol was on the altar? Hardly! "They have quickly turned aside from the way which I commanded them. They have made for themselves a molten calf and have worshiped it" (Exod 32:8). As forced love was no love at all, God allowed Israel to reject him and worship the golden image. However, the boundaries he previously established with the nation were clear: obedience brings blessings, disobedience brings curses (Deut 28). Thus, the Israelites would be judged severely for breaking their covenant.

Faced with Moses' stubborn resistance, the sovereign Lord reluctantly allowed him to select his path. The outcome of that ill-fated choice was heart-wrenching as Aaron supported Israel in its rebellion, challenged Moses' leadership, and went along with Moses' disobedience at the waters of Meribah (Num 20:2–13). Aaron and Moses were fully responsible for their poor decisions and were not allowed to enter the Promised Land with the children of Israel!

Chapter 23

The case of Israel and the twelve spies

ISRAEL AND THE MAJORITY REPORT.

AFTER A LONG TRIP from Egypt, Israel finally arrived at the border of the Promised Land. Moses then exhorted the people to move ahead with their conquest, "See, I have placed the land before you; go in and possess the land" (Deut 1:8). Israel had some choices to make. They could obey God and start the campaign; they could delay the decision until later; they could also refuse to go in. Rather than obeying immediately, they chose the second option. "Then all of you approached me (Moses) and said, 'Let us send men before us, that they may search out the land for us, and bring back to us word of the way by which we should go up, and the cities which we shall enter'" (Deut 1:22).

While this plan appeared reasonable, it was pure disobedience and unbelief. Why delay? Why bother to send men to spy out the land, risking the men's lives, when they could ask the omniscient Lord immediately about the best "way by which we should go up"? Did the decision not to proceed immediately reflect the possibility that Israel might choose not to go in after all, in case things did *not* check out to their satisfaction? Israel's crafty proposal even "hoodwinked" Moses for he said, "and the thing pleased me" (Deut 1:23). Obviously, he did not realize that Israel was going to put God's command to a popular vote! He probably assumed that Israel just wanted to find the best strategy to conquer the land.

However, God was not so easily fooled. Rather than vetoing the whole process, the sovereign Lord allowed Israel to choose its path within his prescribed boundaries. The Jews could send men to scout out the land, but each spy *had to be a leader* of his tribe. A reason for this stipulation could be to ensure that Israel would be fully represented and that their future decision (a vote of the 12 tribes)[1] would be totally democratic. Israel *as a people* would be fully responsible for its action. This was in direct contrast with the episode of the two spies sent later by Joshua to Jericho. The men were unnamed, were sent secretly, and only reported to Joshua on their return (Josh 2).

So, after forty days, the twelve spies returned and reported to Moses, Aaron, and the assembled congregation. First, they confirmed that God was correct. "It certainly does flow with milk and honey" (Num 13:27). However, it "is a land that devours its inhabitants; and all the people whom we saw in it are men of great size" (Num 13:32). What happened to the original mission to "bring back to us word of the way by which we should go up"? Instead of adhering to the initial proposal, Moses told the spies to check the accuracy of the Lord's promise of a land flowing "with milk and honey." "And how is the land, is it good or bad? Is it fat or lean?" Furthermore, Moses asked the scouts to assess the strength of their adversaries. "Are they strong or weak, few or many?" Unfortunately, there was only a short step between an appraisal of the enemy's capability and a determination not to proceed with the conquest. Israel's poor choice compounded by Moses' unfortunate decisions led to a disaster.

On their return, the ten high-profile emissaries felt entitled to give their recommendation. "We are not able to go up against the people, for they are too strong for us" (Num 13:31). On hearing the majority report, Israel trusted their tribal leaders and refused to conquer the Promised Land. Nevertheless, the ten spies were not technically wrong! They only forgot to factor in a crucial element in their appraisal. "Hear, O Israel! You are crossing over the Jordan today to go in to dispossess nations greater and mightier than you, great cities fortified to heaven, a people great and tall" (Deut 9:1–2). Yes, the Canaanites were *too strong* for them and that was exactly why they would need the Lord their God! Faithless Israel chose to forsake God's command. The people opted to rely on human leaders rather than the omnipotent Lord. Decisions were made only on the level of human strength. God allowed the Israelites to make these free will choices and rightfully held them responsible for their actions.

---

1. The tribe of Levi did not send a spy as the Levites were set aside by God to serve him and were therefore exempt from the army census (Num 1:49, Num 3:12). There were still twelve spies as the tribe of Joseph was split in two, Ephraim and Manasseh. Jacob adopted Joseph's two sons, allowing them to share equally in the inheritance with Jacob's own sons (Gen 48:5).

ISRAEL AND THE MINORITY REPORT.

After hearing the majority opinion, Israel decided: "Let us appoint a leader and return to Egypt." Supposedly, neither Moses nor Aaron would qualify for that exalted position! In an effort to dissuade the Jews from going back to Egypt, Joshua and Caleb gave their minority report: "Do not fear the people of the land, for they shall be our prey" (Num 14:9). The two men's courageous example condemned the rebels for they were sentenced to die in the wilderness (Num 14:29).[2]

The Lord gave Israel many opportunities to obey him. He used Moses, Aaron, Caleb, and Joshua to point the people toward the right path. Yet the Israelites decided to listen to their appointed leaders rather than to God's shepherds. Once the decision to go back to Egypt had been made, punishment irrevocably came as no further free will choices were given on the matter!

---

2. The decree in Exodus 32:10 (i.e., "destroy them"), while delayed (Israel was given a reprieve following Moses' intercession), was fulfilled in Numbers 14. The sentence could also be carried out with Israel's rebellions in Numbers 16, Numbers 20, Numbers 21:5, or Numbers 25.

Chapter 24

The case of Balaam and Balak

BALAAM.

WHEN BALAK, THE KING of Moab, asked Balaam to come and curse Israel, God told Balaam: "Do not go with them; you shall not curse the people; for they are blessed" (Num 22:12). Thus, Balaam declined the offer. So far so good! However, when Balak insisted and dangled the promise, "I will indeed honor you richly," Balaam had a choice to make. He could again refuse to go; he could inquire and see if the Lord had changed his mind; or he could agree to Balak's request. Balaam unwisely chose the second option. When he insisted on asking God again, the Lord "was angry because he was going" (Num 22:22). Thus God's "permission" for Balaam to go had to be understood in the context of Psalm 81:11–12. "Israel did not obey me. So, I gave them over to the stubbornness of their heart, to walk in their own devices." However, the Lord put boundaries on Balaam's options. If Balaam insisted on going, he was reluctantly allowed to go but "only the word which I speak to you shall you do" (Num 22:20). He was not to curse Israel under any condition.

Later, the angel of the Lord barred the way of Balaam's donkey. He allowed the beast to talk, a miracle that should get Balaam's attention! Subsequently, he revealed his presence, holding the "drawn sword in his hand." Furthermore, he warned: "Behold, I have come out as an adversary, because your way was contrary to me" (Num 22:32). The appearance of God's messenger, his characterization as an "adversary," and his pronouncement that "your way was contrary to me" somehow did not convince the stubborn diviner to go home. In his mercy, God gave

Balaam a "way of escape," a last warning to turn around. However, the mulish seer on a donkey persisted in his disobedience.

By pronouncing many blessings on Israel, Balaam made Balak so angry that he refused to pay. "I said I would honor you greatly, but behold, the Lord has held you back from honor" (Num 24:11). Balaam could go home empty-handed or he could try to salvage the trip somehow. Since he was prevented from cursing the Israelites, he decided, for some "wages of unrighteousness," to counsel Balak to entice Israel to sin by having "the daughters of Moab" invite the Jews to their pagan sacrifices. Israel would thus be cursed by God and not by Balaam! God's judgment was fierce on both Balak and Balaam. "Take full vengeance for the sons of Israel on the Midianites" (Num 31:2). So, Israel annihilated the kings of Midian[1] and "they also killed Balaam the son of Beor with the sword" (Num 31:8). Did Balaam exercise his God-given free will wisely? Did he profit from his "wages of unrighteousness"? "For what will it profit a man if he gains the whole world and forfeits his soul?" (Matt 16:26). Was it worthwhile for Balaam to forfeit his life in exchange for money?

BALAK.

When Israel came out of Egypt, Balak was greatly concerned that "this horde will lick up all that is around us, as the ox licks up the grass of the field" (Num 22:4). God had already warned Moses to leave Moab alone. "Do not harass Moab, nor provoke them to war, for I will not give you any of their land as a possession" (Deut 2:9). Balak "did not fear that Israel would take over Moab itself, rather he feared that they would take over the surrounding area—the grazing lands east and south of the agricultural highlands of Moab; therefore, the imagery is taken from shepherding motifs: 'as an ox licks up the grass of the field.'"[2] With the Israelites and their livestock camping near his lands (and using up the available resources), Balak had to make some decisions. He could welcome his relatives (Moabites were descendants of Lot, Abraham's nephew); he could ignore them; he could wage spiritual warfare; or he could fight them. He foolishly chose the third option.

---

1. The Moabites and the Midianites were close allies (Num 22:4) and women of both groups were enticing Israelites to sin (Num 25).

2. Ben-Yashar, "Balak, Balaam," lines 12–16.

At least, Balak did not go to war, for that would have been Moab's demise. "He (Israel) shall devour the nations who are his adversaries" (Num 24:8). Nevertheless, Balak persisted on the spiritual warfare path by enticing the Israelites to sin with Moabite and Midianite women.

God, in his mercy, gave Balaam and Balak many opportunities to repent. The Lord used a speaking donkey and an angel to get Balaam to turn from his wicked ways, to no avail. God used a disobedient prophet to warn Balak in four different prophecies, again without success. Balaam and Balak made their free will choices against the Lord's advice and were therefore totally responsible for their disastrous outcomes!

Chapter 25

The case of Barak and Jael

BARAK.

Deborah, Israel's second prophetess (the first one being Miriam, Moses' sister, Exod 15:20),[1] was the nation's only mentioned female judge. She summoned Barak, from the tribe of Naphtali, to deliver Israel from the Canaanites. "Go and march to Mount Tabor . . . I will draw out to you Sisera, the commander of Jabin's army . . . and I will give him into your hand" (Judg 4:6–7). Barak could obey and do as ordered. He could flatly refuse to go. Or he could set some conditions prior to agreeing to God's command.

Unwisely, Barak decided to bargain for his obedience. "If you (Deborah) will go with me, then I will go; but if you will not go with me, I will not go" (Judg 4:8). Would he have disobeyed the Lord had Deborah refused to go with him? Barak should have known that complete obedience would always be the best choice. Instead of submitting to God's plan, Barak insisted on choosing his own path. However, in this option, the credit of capturing Sisera would belong to someone else. "As he would not go without a woman, so a woman should take away his honor from him."[2] "It could hardly fail to be a humiliation to a great warrior to be told that the chief glory would fall to a woman."[3] Barak might have thought that the honor would fall to Deborah the prophetess. That would not have

1. https://claudemariottini.com/2013/12/16/the-seven-prophetesses-of-the-old-testament/ line 21.

2. Benson Commentary. http://biblehub.com/commentaries/Judg/4–9.htm

3. Ellicott's Commentary for English Readers. http://biblehub.com/commentaries/Judg/4–9.htm

been too embarrassing since losing the award to God's judge would have been understandable to the people of Israel. However, to further his humiliation, the prize went to a foreign woman, Jael of the Kenites.

The sovereign Lord allowed Barak to make some free will choices within his predetermined boundaries. The option that Barak selected fell far short of the Lord's best plan for him and for that, Barak had only himself to blame!

JAEL.

Jael was the wife of Heber and "there was peace between Jabin the king of Hazor and the house of Heber" (Judg 4:17). In the decisive battle, "all the army of Sisera fell by the edge of the sword" (Judg 4:16). Sisera escaped without his bodyguards. This obviously was arranged by the sovereign Lord to facilitate Jael's task. When Sisera came to ask for shelter and protection, Jael had to decide on how to proceed. She could ask him to wait until her husband's return. After all, it would be immodest and dangerous to welcome a fierce warrior in her spouse's absence. She could refuse his request, since she knew that Barak was on his trail. She could give him some provisions and ask him to leave before his pursuers arrived and caused trouble for her family.

Instead of these reasonable options, Jael chose a very strange approach. Without her husband's consent, she "went out to meet Sisera" and encouraged him to come into *her* tent. "Sisera went, not to Heber's tent, but to Jael's, as more secure from pursuit. Women occupied a separate tent. Gen 18:6, Gen 18:10; Gen 24:67."[4] While it would be safer for him to hide in her quarters, since men might be reluctant to search there for cultural reasons, how would she explain that to her husband? Even if given hospitality, male guests were not allowed to stay in the women's dwellings or even converse with the women directly. For example, the Lord only talked obliquely to Sarah while she was hiding inside the tent, eavesdropping on the conversation between God and Abraham about the prophesied birth of a son (Gen 18).

Jael "covered him (Sisera) with a blanket," and gave him milk to drink. He admonished her to lie to protect him. "It shall be if anyone comes and inquires of you and says, 'Is there anyone here?' that you shall say, 'No'" (Judg 4:20). Then, while he was sleeping, "she struck Sisera, she

4. Barnes' Notes on the Bible. http://biblehub.com/commentaries/Judg/4-19.htm

smashed his head" (Judg 5:26). The laws of hospitality required the hosts to protect their guests, even to their own detriment. For example, Lot tried to protect his guests by offering his two daughters to the Sodomites (Gen 19:8). Was there a breach of hospitality, a most severe transgression of cultural norms, in this case? Most likely not, for only the male head of the household could extend hospitality and protection to strangers (Abraham rather than Sarah in Gen 18; Laban rather Rebekah in Gen 24; Jethro rather than his daughters in Exod 2).

Jael was blessed by God for her courageous, unorthodox, and clever actions. Sisera died and, by a fate worse than death, was humiliated for he was killed by a woman with a tent peg. "A certain woman threw an upper millstone on Abimelech's head . . . 'Draw your sword and kill me, so that it will not be said of me, 'A woman slew him'" (Judg 9:53–54). Sisera died "between her feet he bowed, he fell, he lay," a humiliating posture in death for a great warrior. "Thus, the glory, such as it was, of having slain the general of the enemy passed to a woman."[5]

The Lord called Barak to a great endeavor, a victory over the Canaanites and the honor of capturing their commander Sisera. Regrettably, Barak chose a lesser path within the Lord's boundaries and, as a result, only attained part of what God had in store for him. Jael chose wisely, was blessed for her courage, and her exploit was forever immortalized in the prophetess Deborah's song.

---

5. Ellicott's Commentary for English Readers. http://biblehub.com/commentaries/Judg/4-22.htm

Chapter 26

The case of Israel and Saul

ISRAEL.

GOD WAS ISRAEL'S KING. Nevertheless, the Israelites demanded a human ruler. "Give us a king to judge us" (1 Sam 8:6). Obviously, this did not take the omniscient Lord by surprise for he had long before decreed requirements for a king (i.e., a monarch must be chosen by God, must be an Israelite, and must not accumulate horses, wives, silver and gold for himself. He must write a copy of the Law and read it all the days of his life, Deut 17:14–20).

During the days of the Judges, Israel wanted to make Gideon its ruler after the victory over Midian. Wisely, Gideon refused, knowing that the Lord was their sovereign. "I will not rule over you, nor shall my son rule over you; the Lord shall rule over you" (Judg 8:23). Soon afterward, the people of Shechem made Abimelech king and "Abimelech ruled over Israel three years" (Judg 9:22). The Shechemites chose to ignore the command that a monarch must be appointed by God.

Israel gave Samuel, the Lord's prophet, several reasons why they wanted to have a human ruler. Samuel was getting old and his sons were not following in his ways. Israel desired to "be like all the nations" around them. They wanted a king who would judge them and fight for them. Obviously, they did not think that God had done an adequate job! The Lord clearly understood the slight. "They have rejected me from being king over them" (1 Sam 8:7). In his mercy, God endeavored to explain the disadvantages of having a human ruler and the serious consequences of their foolish desires. The monarch would take their sons, their daughters, their servants, the best of their fields, a tenth of their seed, and a tenth of their flocks. Furthermore, the Lord warned them that their decision would be irrevocable. There would be no return to a theocracy. "Then you will cry out in that day because of your king whom you have chosen for yourselves, but the Lord will not answer you in that day" (1 Sam 8:18). The "no return policy" was necessary since God would have to promise the new king a *guaranteed succession* of his heirs to the throne in return for loyalty and obedience (a standard suzerain-vassal covenant prevalent in those days).[1]

The Lord then allowed Israel to freely choose between the two paths: retain God as their sovereign or have a human king. The Lord set some boundaries and did not offer the following options: let Israel choose its own ruler; forbid the human monarch from taking Israel's sons, daughters, fields, servants and flocks; have God keep a "veto" power over the king's decisions. After listening to God's dire warnings, Israel made its stubborn choice and went down the irrevocable kingship path, relying on fallible humans rather than the infallible God. "No, but there shall be a king over us" (1 Sam 8:19). For that disastrous decision, they only had themselves to blame!

SAUL.

God chose Saul of the tribe of Benjamin to be the first monarch of Israel. However, did Jacob not prophesy in Genesis 49:10 that the kingship belonged to Judah? "The scepter shall not depart from Judah." The scepter or the ruler's staff "probably indicates here tribal rather than royal rank, and means that Judah would continue, until the time indicated, to be a self-governed and legally-constituted tribe."[2] Thus, the Lord was free to appoint a ruler from the tribe of Benjamin. Saul's kingdom would be "forever" on the condition of obedience. The word "forever" is the Hebrew "olam" meaning long duration, antiquity, and futurity. In 1 Sam 13:13, the meaning is "continuous existence (of) . . . the dynasty of Saul."[3] God gave Saul a magnificent promise that his kingdom would endure if he obeyed the Lord his God.

---

1. "The Hittite suzerainty treaty/covenant form consisted of six sections . . . These are the stipulations of the covenant consisting of obligations, such as tribute . . . (and) guarantees of succession." Harless, *How Firm a Foundation*, 13.

2. Ellicott's Commentary for English Readers. http://biblehub.com/commentaries/Gen/49–10.htm

3. Brown-Driver-Briggs. http://biblehub.com/hebrew/5769.htm

Saul's faithfulness was quickly tested. At his anointment, he was instructed by Samuel: "You shall wait seven days until I come to you and show you what you should do" (1 Sam 10:8). Soon after, Saul was at war with the Philistines and anxiously awaited the prophet's arrival. "Now he waited seven days, according to the appointed time set by Samuel, but Samuel did not come to Gilgal" (1 Sam 13:8). Saul could be patient and wait a little longer, or he could do whatever he thought was best. He chose to disobey the Lord's command and "offered the burnt offering" (1 Sam 13:9). Samuel was not late in coming but Saul was too afraid to delay.[4] Thus, Saul forfeited the bountiful promise God had given him. "Now your kingdom shall not endure" (1 Sam 13:14).

The Israelites were given the choice to keep the Lord as their sovereign or to have a human king with all its problems. They foolishly decided to imitate the nations around them and demanded a human ruler against God's advice. Their appointed monarch, Saul, although promised a kingdom for himself and his descendants forever, disobeyed God and forfeited his prize. The sovereign Lord gave Israel and Saul freedom to choose their own paths within God's predetermined boundaries. They exercised their free will unwisely and suffered the dreadful consequences of their ill-conceived actions!

4. Gill's Exposition of the Entire Bible. http://biblehub.com/commentaries/1_samuel/13-11.htm

Chapter 27

The case of David and Keilah

DAVID.

DAVID WAS HIDING IN the forest of Hereth when he heard that the Philistines were attacking Keilah. He could choose to ignore the problem. He could go fight the Philistines. Or he could tell the people to notify Saul and have him come to Keilah's rescue. By putting the burden on Saul, David would be able to protect his men. If Saul refused to do his duty, his kingship would suffer irreparable harm. If Saul decided to fight the Philistines and was defeated, his kingdom would be destroyed. However, if Saul won the battle, the honor of rescuing the city would go to him.

By taking his small band against the Philistines, David would be able to show his concern for Israel and further his claim to the throne. A victory over the Canaanites would cement his reputation as a mighty warrior and contrast his skills with Saul's. "Saul has slain his thousands and David his ten thousands" (1 Sam 18:7). However, his six hundred men might not be enough to vanquish the enemies and a defeat would be disastrous for his people's morale.

After considering his options, David leaned toward rescuing Keilah. However, before deciding, he wisely inquired of the omniscient Lord. "Your ears will hear a word behind you, 'This is the way, walk in it,' whenever you turn to the right or to the left" (Isa 30:21). God's answer was clear: "Go and attack the Philistines and deliver Keilah" (1 Sam 23:2). Nevertheless, the Lord did not force David to take his advice. David was free to listen to his men, consider his overall situation, and then make up his mind. "Behold, we are afraid here in Judah. How much more then if we go to Keilah against the ranks of the Philistines?'" (1 Sam 23:3).

David's soldiers believed that they would be defeated in the unequal fight, no matter what God said. Obviously, this reasoning struck a chord with David who was aware of his men's skills (or lack thereof) in a formal battle (rather than just a run-and-hide tactic against Saul).

Swayed by the people and unsure of God's counsel, "David inquired of the Lord once more" (1 Sam 23:4). Fortunately, God "knows our frame; he is mindful that we are but dust" (Ps 103:14). The Lord graciously answered David and reiterated his previous promise: "Arise, go down to Keilah, for I will give the Philistines into your hand" (1 Sam 23:4). Upon being asked, God narrowed his boundaries and removed two of David's options: do nothing or tell Saul to go rescue the city. The choice became to obey or disobey. Once we seek God's advice and "best plan," the other options will automatically be labeled as "subpar."

At this juncture, David had to decide. He could trust God and proceed, or he could listen to the people and refuse to go. David chose to obey and was blessed with a great victory. He delivered Keilah and resided in the town rather than in the forest of Hereth. One could hardly blame him since the amenities would be much more pleasant in a walled city than in the middle of the woods. However, the wily Saul saw a golden opportunity to seize David who had eluded capture by moving from place to place (Gath, the cave of Adullam, Mizpah, "the stronghold," and the forest of Hereth). "Saul said, 'God has delivered him into my hand, for he shut himself in by entering a city with double gates and bars'" (1 Sam 23:7). Both Saul and David believed that God was on their side. Of course, one was right and the other wrong!

When David heard that Saul was coming "for certain," he had to make some decisions. He could remain and fight or he could depart quickly. Obviously, David's spies had warned him about Saul's plans. However, how reliable was that information? David also had some doubts about Keilah's loyalty in the event of a battle. He had reasons to believe that the people might make a deal and deliver him to Saul.

Instead of relying on men's information and guesswork, David decided as before to seek advice from the omniscient Lord. "He (Saul) will come down . . . They (Keilah's people) will surrender you" (1 Sam 23:11, 12). God did not (explicitly) recommend any course of action. He left it up to David to decide what he thought would be best for him. David could elect to get rid of the potential traitors in the city, firm up his control, and prepare for battle. After all, had he not defeated the mighty Philistines? Had the Lord not promised him the kingdom and therefore ultimate victory? Instead, David decided to leave and "go wherever they could go" (1 Sam 23:13). A possible reason for this behavior was stated later. "May the Lord judge between you and me, and may the Lord avenge me on you; but my hand shall not be against you" (1 Sam 24:12). David, out of respect for Saul, the Lord's anointed, refused to fight his lawful king.

David was given many free will choices within the Lord's boundaries. He wisely asked for God's advice to choose the best available option. David's obedience was greatly blessed by the Lord who, in due time, fulfilled the promise to make him king over Israel and Judah.

KEILAH.

Keilah was raided by the Philistines during the harvest, when the mature crops were left unprotected outside the city walls. David learned about the incursion and took great risks to come to the rescue while King Saul remained strangely uninvolved. However, when Saul heard that David was staying in the town, he decided to attack his own city to capture his son-in-law. Thus, Keilah had a choice to make. It could show its gratitude by defending its guest or it could choose to betray its benefactor. To its shame, Keilah opted to surrender David to Saul. Although the decision was secret, yet it was known by God for "I am he who searches the minds and hearts" (Rev 2:23).

Keilah's treacherous plan failed for David wisely inquired of the omniscient Lord and departed before it could be put into action. Obviously, no matter what Keilah or Saul decided, God's promises to his future king would still stand. The boundaries previously set by the Lord (David must live, and David must become king) would prevent any harmful actions against God's anointed.

David and Keilah were given many options. David chose wisely by following the Lord's counsel. Keilah chose poorly by going against God's desire for his people to show gratitude and hospitality. David was blessed and Keilah would have to face the Lord's judgment. "Vengeance is mine, I will repay" (Heb 10:30).

Chapter 28

The case of Nabal, David, and Abigail

NABAL.

NABAL (MEANING FOOL, "PROBABLY a nickname given him on account of his well-known stubborn folly")[1] was a very rich man. During sheep shearing time, "usually a time of lavish hospitality,"[2] Nabal received envoys from David who requested a gift, not "anything extraordinary of him, or to put him to any expense, but what was at hand, and he could spare."[3] The justification for the request was that David and his men protected Nabal's shepherds and their flocks from harm. "We hurt them not . . . This, considering the licentiousness of soldiers, and the necessities David and his men were exposed to, was no small favor, which Nabal was bound both in justice and gratitude, and prudence, to requite."[4] Furthermore, David humbled himself before his kinsman (since they were both from the tribe of Judah, Nabal being a descendant of Caleb), calling his men and himself, "your servants" and "your son David."

Nabal could choose to personally deliver a generous gift and earn some good will from the future king. He could offer an acceptable donation. He could hand out a token amount since the request was left open-ended. He could give nothing with some excuses to let both parties save

---

1. Ellicott's Commentary for English Readers. http://biblehub.com/commentaries/1_samuel/25-3.htm

2. Pulpit Commentary. http://biblehub.com/commentaries/1_samuel/25-2.htm

3. Gill's Exposition of the Entire Bible. http://biblehub.com/commentaries/1_samuel/25-8.htm

4. Benson Commentary. http://biblehub.com/commentaries/1_samuel/25-7.htm

face, a crucial Middle Eastern consideration. Or he could rudely spurn the request.

Unwisely, Nabal chose to rebuff David's petition with gratuitous comments about him ("Who is David?") and his father ("And who is the son of Jesse?"). Furthermore, he accused David and his men of being runaway servants and renegades, "men whose origin I do not know" (1 Sam 25:11). While that might be true of some of David's men, that surely did not apply to all his followers and especially not to David (the king's son-in-law). By committing these outrageous deeds, Nabal joined himself with Saul against the Lord and his future king.

While Nabal was not killed by David in revenge for the slight, he did not escape God's swift judgment. "And about ten days later, it happened that the Lord struck Nabal, and he died" (1 Sam 25:38). Nabal was graciously given an opportunity to be an early follower of the future king (a great privilege accorded to few), yet unwisely rejected it and went to his death. He chose poorly and thus, only had himself to blame for his folly!

DAVID.

When David heard about Nabal's taunts, he gathered his men to exact swift revenge. "May God do so to the enemies of David, and more also, if by morning I leave as much as one male of any who belong to him" (1 Sam 25:21). In anger, David took an oath to destroy Nabal's household, with a curse on the "enemies of David" if the vow was not fulfilled. "Unto the enemies of David, i.e., unto David himself. But because it might seem ominous and unnatural to curse himself, therefore by a figure called euphemismus, instead of David, he mentions David's enemies."[5] Obviously, that was a rash vow, since the murder of innocent people was forbidden. Such an atrocity could disqualify David from future acceptance by the people. Thus, while God gave the future king the freedom to vow revenge on Nabal or to humbly swallow the insults, the two options led to different scenarios within the Lord's predetermined boundaries. If David had chosen to keep the peace, God would not have needed to intervene. In the actual scenario, the Lord had to step in to prevent the wholesale slaughter.

---

5. Matthew Poole's commentary. http://biblehub.com/commentaries/1_samuel/25–22.htm

Upon receiving Abigail's gifts and entreaty, David faced a difficult choice. He could swallow his hurt pride and go home. Or he could avenge himself and destroy Nabal's household despite the appeals for mercy. Wisely, he selected the first option. "Blessed be the Lord God of Israel, who sent you this day to meet me . . . Unless you had come quickly to meet me, surely there would not have been left to Nabal until the morning light as much as one male" (1 Sam 25:32, 34). God mercifully restrained David from committing bloodshed. The Lord provided his anointed with a way of escape and spared him much future heartache and grief.

ABIGAIL.

Abigail could have ignored David's spurned request and her husband's rude answers as these issues were men's problems. She could have tried to convince Nabal to relent "for evil is plotted against our master" (1 Sam 25:17). Or she could have hastened to do what needed to be done. Knowing the imminent dangers and realizing that Nabal could not be persuaded, Abigail hurriedly gave David a generous gift. The presents were sent ahead to mollify him (as did Jacob with Esau), and prepare the way for her appeal to spare the household. She begged him to forgive and reminded the future king of the consequences of such a murderous course of action. Unlike Nabal, Abigail sided with the Lord and asked for David's favor: "When the Lord shall deal well with my lord, then remember your maidservant" (1 Sam 25:31). David granted her request and more, for after Nabal's death, David married Abigail, Nabal's "intelligent and beautiful" widow.

Nabal, David, and Abigail were given many choices within God's predetermined boundaries. Some selected wise options, others acted foolishly. All were held accountable for their actions. The sovereign Lord, in his mercy, offered everyone a way of escape but left it up to the individual to freely decide his/her path and live with the consequences, whether good or evil!

Chapter 29

The case of David, God, and the census

DAVID.

"THEN SATAN STOOD UP against Israel and moved David to number Israel" (1 Chr 21:1). God permitted the enticement as a form of discipline. "Now again the anger of the Lord burned against Israel" (2 Sam 24:1). "No doubt there was cause for it (God's anger), though it is not expressed."[1] Thus, when the Lord allowed Satan to tempt his people, he did not act without good reasons.[2]

David chose to be "carried away and enticed by his own lust," in this case, by his pride over his military power. God mercifully provided David with a way of escape through Joab, the army's commander. "Now may the Lord your God add to the people a hundred times as many as they are . . . but why does my lord the king delight in this thing?" (2 Sam 24:3). Thus, David had a face-saving way to revoke his order. After all, what was the need to know the number of soldiers in the army since God could increase it a hundred times if necessary?

After providing the way of escape, the Lord allowed David to make up his own mind. Unwisely, David "doubled down" on his decision. "Nevertheless, the king's word prevailed against Joab" (2 Sam 24:4). "God was displeased with this thing, so he struck Israel" (1 Chr 21:7). Since the Lord was "displeased" with David's decision, it was obvious that he did not "approve" or "decree" this course of event. God's preferred option was

---

1. Gill's Exposition of the Entire Bible. http://biblehub.com/commentaries/2_samuel/24-1.htm

2. God also allowed Satan to tempt Job. Nevertheless, God always wanted his people to resist the temptations and remain faithful.

for David to realize his boastful pride, repent, and cancel the order for a census. Regrettably, David ignored God's way of escape and was thus totally responsible for his actions.

If the census was David's fault, why was Israel struck? "When the head suffers, all the members suffer along with it."[3] After their demand to be like the nations around them, the Israelites were no longer in a theocracy but in a monarchy where they would have to suffer for their king's poor decisions. To his credit, David acknowledged full responsibility for the action and repented when he saw God's displeasure. "I have sinned greatly" (1 Chr 21:8). However, sin, even after repentance, still brought consequences.

The sovereign Lord graciously gave David a choice of punishment: three years of famine (seven years listed in 2 Sam 24:13 was probably due to a scribal error),[4] three months of being pursued by his foes, or three days of pestilence (i.e., three *different* paths with three different outcomes, although all three were created and known by God). David chose the third option for "let us now fall into the hand of the Lord for his mercies are great" (2 Sam 24:14). "War would place the nation at the mercy of its enemies; famine would make it dependent on corn-merchants, who might greatly aggravate the miseries of scarcity; only in the pestilence— some form of plague sudden and mysterious in its attack, and baffling the medical knowledge of the time—would the punishment come directly from God, and depend immediately upon his will."[5] "And it may be noted also that he chooses that form of punishment from which his own royal position would afford him no immunity."[6]

"So the Lord sent a pestilence upon Israel from the morning until the *appointed* time; and seventy thousand men of the people from Dan to Beersheba died. When the angel stretched out his hand toward Jerusalem to destroy it, the Lord relented from the calamity and said to the angel who destroyed the people, 'It is enough! Now relax your hand!'" (2 Sam 24:15–16). The word "appointed" is the Hebrew "moed" meaning

3. Jamieson-Fausset-Brown Bible Commentary. http://biblehub.com/commentaries/2_samuel/24-17.htm

4. http://www.kjv-only.com/2sam24_13.html

5. Cambridge Bible for Schools and Colleges. http://biblehub.com/commentaries/2_samuel/24-14.htm

6. Ellicott's Commentary for English Readers. http://biblehub.com/commentaries/2_samuel/24-14.htm

"appointed time, place or meeting."[7] The same word "moed" was used in Samuel's command for Saul to wait seven days. If the pestilence lasted until the appointed time (i.e., three days), in what way did the Lord "relent" (nacham) and say, "It is enough"? Did the Lord change his mind and shorten the duration to less than three days as suggested by several commentators?[8] The plain reading of the text suggested that the duration was not changed as it lasted "until the appointed time" as already decreed and therefore unchangeable. What was not decreed was the *place* where the destroying angel held sway.

"And the angel of the Lord was standing by the threshing floor of Ornan" (1 Chr 21:15). The compassionate God saw Jerusalem's impending doom, was sorry (nacham) for their plight and restrained the angel, thus justifying David's trust that "his mercies are great." Nevertheless, although Jerusalem and David's house were spared, seventy thousand men from the rest of the country died in the pestilence. So much for knowing the exact strength of the army!

That same day, David was commanded to build an altar on the threshing floor of Ornan. Even though Ornan (Araunah in 2 Sam 24) offered to give the land free of charge, David insisted on paying for it "for I will not offer burnt offerings to the Lord my God which cost me nothing" (2 Sam 24:24). David paid fifty shekels of silver for the threshing floor and the oxen and probably[9] six hundred shekels of gold by weight for the whole site. "David built there an altar to the Lord and offered burnt offerings and peace offerings" (2 Sam 24:25). As a result, the plague ended with no further loss of life as "the Lord commanded the angel, and he put his sword back in its sheath" (1 Chr 21:27). While told to "relax your hand," the angel still had his sword out. He would have unleashed further punishment had David refused to obey the order to offer sacrifices. God's command to the angel appeared to be only a temporary stay, contingent on David's decision. The injunction only became permanent (put the sword back in its sheath) *after* David's compliance. "And he (David) called to the Lord and he answered him with fire from heaven on the altar of burnt offering" (1 Chr 21:26). "Thus, the Lord was moved by prayer for the land, and the plague was held back from Israel" (2 Sam 24:25). Also,

7. http://biblehub.com/hebrew/4150.htm

8. http://biblehub.com/commentaries/2_samuel/24-15.htm

9. Jamieson-Fausset-Brown Bible Commentary. http://biblehub.com/commentaries/1_chronicles/21-25.htm

God did not give David any other alternative to end the plague but by the offering of sacrifices.

The choices given to Man are always within God's strict confines. Man is not free to make any decision he pleases. Bad decisions made against the Lord's advice reap disastrous consequences. Good choices made in obedience garner great rewards and mercies. Both paths are possible in God's omniscience and sovereignty.

GOD.

The Lord allowed Satan to entice David to number the people. In his mercy, God provided David with a way of escape through the respectful appeal of Joab. However, David indulged his pride, overruled his general, and ignored God's command that a king should not trust in his power. Disobedience had to bring about discipline. Yet, the merciful Lord graciously allowed David to choose his own punishment. Once David had selected the option, it was carried out as decreed.

Nevertheless, within the Lord's boundaries (i.e., three days of deadly pestilence), there could be a variety of possible scenarios (two full days and one hour, two full days and twenty hours, one thousand dead, ten thousand dead, pestilence all over Israel from Dan to Beersheba, or pestilence in only parts of Israel with Jerusalem being spared, plague killing people from every family as in Egypt, or plague sparing some families like David's family). In his mercy, the Lord felt sorry for Jerusalem, temporarily stayed the punishment, and gave David the option to atone for his sin by offering sacrifices, thus ending the plague early in the appointed three days (e.g., two days and a few hours).[10] The prophet Gad was sent to David "that day" and David obeyed promptly so "that the plague may be restrained from the people" (1 Chr 21:22).

Satan's enticement to carry out a census was allowed by God to discipline disobedient Israel. Nevertheless, the Lord wanted David to overcome the temptation and provided him with a way of escape. Sadly, David ignored Joab's advice and had to live with the dire consequences! Even then, the compassionate Lord was willing to lighten the punishment

---

10. It could not have been a full three days (seventy-two hours) when David was given a temporary stay since the angel stood ready to *resume* the plague (sword still out of its sheath) if necessary.

in response to David's heartfelt repentance. What more could one ask of God?

Chapter 30

The case of Solomon and David

SOLOMON.

IT IS NOT OFTEN that God would come to a man and grant him a wish. "Ask what you wish me to give you" (1 Kgs 3:5). Solomon could ask for riches, honor, long life, life of his enemies, wisdom . . . He chose to ask for "an understanding heart to judge your people" (1 Kgs 3:9). So, the Lord unconditionally gave Solomon "a wise and discerning heart." He also gave the king what he did not ask, "riches and honor," "and if you walk in my ways . . . then I will prolong your days" (1 Kgs 3:13–14). By every standard, Solomon was given much, as the Lord appeared to him not once but twice (1 Kgs 3:5 and 1 Kgs 9:2). However, would he be a faithful steward of God's blessings? How would he respond when the Lord asked for his obedience?

The Lord commanded that a king "must not acquire great numbers of horses for himself or make the people return to Egypt to get more of them" (Deut 17:16 NIV). Yet, "Solomon had forty thousand stalls of horses for his chariots and twelve thousand horsemen" (1 Kgs 4:26). "Also, Solomon's import of horses was from Egypt and Kue" (1 Kgs 10:28).

The monarch "must not take many wives or his heart will be led astray" (Deut 17:17 NIV). Yet, Solomon married foreign women (forbidden by the Lord, Deut 7:3) and "held fast to these in love." "He had seven hundred wives, princesses, and three hundred concubines" (1 Kgs 11:3).

The sovereign "must not accumulate large amounts of silver and gold" (Deut 17:17 NIV). "All King Solomon's drinking vessels were of gold" (1 Kgs 10:21). "I amassed silver and gold for myself" (Eccl 2:8 NIV).

The ruler must "not consider himself better than his fellow Israelites" (Deut 17:20 NIV). Yet, the Jews bitterly complained about Solomon's tyrannical reign and oppression. "Your father made our yoke hard; therefore, lighten the hard service of your father" (1 Kgs 12:4).

Solomon was unconditionally given "a wise and discerning heart," riches, and honor. However, all these gifts had to be exercised within God's boundaries in the Law. Solomon chose to rebel, held fast to his foreign wives, and "went after Ashtoreth the goddess of the Sidonians and after Milcom the detestable idol of the Ammonites" (1 Kgs 11:5). The Lord's judgment was swift. "I will surely tear the kingdom from you and will give it to your servant" (1 Kgs 11:11). The Lord raised up adversaries for Solomon, Hadad the Edomite of the royal line of Edom, Rezon the son of Eliada, and Jeroboam the future king of the northern kingdom of Israel. Thus, Solomon reigned for forty years and died. He forfeited a longer life due to his disobedience. He also relinquished God's promise given in 1 Kings 9: 4–5 (NIV). "If you walk before me faithfully . . . I will establish your royal throne over Israel forever." God, in his omniscience, did not grant Solomon "the life of your enemies" (1 Kgs 3:11). Had that been given, the scenarios of Hadad, Rezon, and Jeroboam would have been impossible as Solomon could have "wished them away."

What was the difference between Solomon and David? After all, unlike David, Solomon did not rape any woman, nor did he murder anyone's husband. Obviously, in the Lord's eyes, not all sins were equal in severity. It all amounted to a matter of the heart. "His heart was not wholly devoted to the Lord his God, as the heart of David his father had been" (1 Kgs 11:4). For all his faults, David never wavered from his loyal devotion to the Lord and never worshiped other gods.

The Lord gave Solomon a wish, (supposedly) anything he desired. He chose "an understanding heart" which the Lord granted him together with riches and honor. Although that was a good choice, as God was pleased with it, was that the best request he could have made? What did his father David ask from the Lord?

DAVID.

"*One* thing I have asked from the Lord, that I shall seek: that I may dwell in the house of the Lord all the days of my life, to behold the beauty of the Lord and to meditate in his temple" (Ps 27:4). "Only a few things are necessary, really *only one*; for Mary has chosen the good part, which shall not be taken away from her" (Luke 10:42). Although David had committed many sins (e.g., Bathsheba, the census), he had always repented and returned to the Lord his God in love and humility. On his deathbed, David reminded Solomon of the most important thing in life: "Keep the charge of the Lord your God, to walk in his ways" (1 Kgs 2:3). David learned that there would be no blessings without love and obedience. "He who has My commandments and keeps them is the one who loves Me" (John 14:21).

David asked for one thing from the Lord, an eternal love relationship with the Almighty. As he asked wisely, like Paul, he finished the course and kept the faith (2 Tim 4:7). Sadly, Solomon chose to ignore his father's admonition and suffered the disastrous consequences of his free will actions!

Chapter 31

The case of Jeroboam and God

JEROBOAM.

JEROBOAM, FROM THE TRIBE of Ephraim, was given a kingdom and a similar promise to the ones offered to Saul, David, and Solomon ("an enduring house" on the condition of obedience). Due to Solomon's unfaithfulness, "I (God) am going to tear the kingdom out of Solomon's hand and give you (Jeroboam) ten tribes. But for the sake of my servant David and the city of Jerusalem, which I have chosen out of all the tribes of Israel, he will have one tribe" (1 Kgs 11:31–32 NIV). "But ten plus one doesn't equal twelve! What happened to the last piece? The answer is simple. Rehoboam was of the tribe of Judah. He retained that tribe and was given one more, which turns out to be the tribe of Benjamin."[1] Since the Lord previously decreed, "Your (David's) house and your kingdom shall endure before me forever" (2 Sam 7:16), David's descendants could not be completely dispossessed. One had to appreciate the incomparable favor granted to David. However, the Lord's promise was broad enough to cover the possibility of a temporary hiatus, with the kingship resuming after a certain time.[2]

Jeroboam, a young man with a widowed mother, was appointed by Solomon to supervise the construction of the Millo (probably a fortification)[3] in Jerusalem. Since he was totally dependent on the king for his livelihood, one would expect complete loyalty and gratitude for the sovereign's beneficence. Therefore, even though promised a kingdom,

1. http://lavistachurchofchrist.org/LVanswers/2008/08–24a.html

2. David's kingdom will resume with the return of Christ.

3. Smith's Bible Dictionary. http://biblehub.com/topical/m/millo.htm

shouldn't he stay faithful to his monarch and wait for God's timing to assume his reign? Given free will to decide, he could choose to be patient, or he could take matters into his own hands, reject his lawful sovereign, and carve out a realm at his convenience. Unwisely, Jeroboam repaid Solomon's goodness with evil for he "rebelled against the king" (1 Kgs 11:26). Furthermore, once declared ruler over the ten northern tribes, he chose to lead the people astray by making two golden calves and proclaiming: "It is too much for you to go up to Jerusalem; behold your gods, O Israel, that brought you up from the land of Egypt" (1 Kgs 12:28).

The Lord would have been justified in swiftly punishing Jeroboam. Nevertheless, God mercifully gave him a warning and a way of escape from his disastrous course of action. A "man of God" was sent from Judah to prophesy against Jeroboam's altar: "Behold, a son shall be born to the house of David, Josiah by name; and on you he shall sacrifice the priests of the high places who burn incense on you, and human bones shall be burned on you" (1 Kgs 13:2). To underline the certainty of the oracle and its divine origin, he further declared, "Behold, the altar shall be split apart and the ashes which are on it shall be poured out" (1 Kgs 13:3), pronouncements that were immediately fulfilled. When Jeroboam ordered the arrest of the prophet, the king's hand "dried up" and was only restored after the seer's entreaty to God.

In the Lord's mercy, Jeroboam was afforded an opportunity to repent. Would he confess his sins, turn back, and salvage what he could of the situation? Or would he ignore the Lord's admonition and persist in disobedience? "After this event Jeroboam did not return from his evil way, but again he made priests of the high places from among all the people; any who would, he ordained, to be priests of the high places" (1 Kgs 13:33). Jeroboam was given many free will choices within God's boundaries. He unwisely decided not to listen to the Lord's warnings and was therefore totally responsible for his evil actions.

GOD.

God fully intended to keep his promises to David and Solomon. However, while the pledge of an eternal royal line for David was unconditional, the pronouncement of "a royal throne over Israel forever" for Solomon was conditioned on his obedience. Solomon, in rebellion, forfeited the Lord's generous offer.[4] The unalterable grant to David, though narrowing God's boundaries and limiting what he could bestow to later kings,[5] still allowed room for many possible scenarios. For example, God could have chosen to chastise Solomon alone and not his descendants. The Lord could have used other forms of punishments for Solomon's misdeeds (e.g., famine, war, plague, leprosy).

While God could have divided the nation immediately under Solomon, he gave a reason why he chose not to do so. "Nevertheless I will not do it in your days for the sake of your father David, but I will tear it out of the hand of your son (ben)" 1 Kgs 11:12. Thus, the Lord decided to take some of the realm away from Solomon's descendants (not necessarily his son since "ben" in Hebrew can mean descendant).[6] God could choose any kind of apportionment he desired as long as the House of David still had a kingdom (a one to eleven split, an even split, or an eleven to one split). In his wisdom, the Lord decreed a ten to two split, giving Jeroboam ten tribes.

God promised Jeroboam that "I will be with you and build you an enduring house as I built for David" if he obeyed the Lord. Regrettably, Jeroboam chose to rebel against Solomon, established his own kingdom in northern Israel, and set up the worship of the golden calves, reasoning that "if this people go up to offer sacrifices in the house of the Lord at Jerusalem, then the heart of this people will return to their lord, even to Rehoboam king of Judah; and they will kill me and return to Rehoboam king of Judah" (1 Kgs 12:27).

God was merciful and gave Jeroboam warnings through a prophet, even healing Jeroboam's hand when he was beseeched by the king. However, Jeroboam stubbornly persisted in his insubordination. "Therefore

4. The Lord Jesus, the king of Israel, was not from the line of Solomon (Luke 3:31). He was a descendant of Nathan, Solomon's older brother (1 Chr 3:5). Thus, God's promise to David was fulfilled but the promise to Solomon was forfeited! Had Solomon been faithful, his descendants would have been *guaranteed* a "royal throne over Israel forever" (1 Kgs 9:5 NIV). Had he obeyed God, Jesus the King would have been his direct descendant. Instead, Solomon's rebellion allowed the ending of his royal line with Zedekiah. Although each one of us is responsible for his own sins (Deut 24:16), there are nevertheless long-term consequences of disobedience and rebellion in a family! "I, the Lord your God, am a jealous God, visiting the iniquity of the fathers on the children, on the third and the fourth generations of those who hate me" (Exod 20:5).

5. Since David's descendants could not be *totally* dispossessed, other kings could not be given the whole kingdom.

6. Brown-Driver-Briggs. http://biblehub.com/hebrew/1121.htm

behold, I am bringing calamity on the house of Jeroboam, and will cut off from Jeroboam every male person" (1 Kgs 14:10). Jeroboam was given many unearned privileges, favors not accorded to many. However, instead of loving God and obeying him out of gratitude, Jeroboam chose to rebel and refused to change his evil ways. Therefore, the sovereign Lord gave him the full wages of his defiance!

Chapter 32

The case of Rehoboam and God

REHOBOAM.

BY THE TIME OF Solomon's death and Rehoboam's ascension to the throne, events had already been set in motion to fulfill the Lord's decree to sever the kingdom in two. Ahijah the prophet had been sent to Jeroboam to give him ten tribes, confirming his God-given right to the kingdom of Israel. Solomon subsequently sought to put Jeroboam to death, causing him to flee to Egypt. While the Lord had determined by his decree the boundaries for Israel's future (i.e., two kingdoms), he nevertheless gave Rehoboam and Jeroboam much freedom to decide their free will actions within these confines.

After Solomon's death, Jeroboam could have decided not to defy Rehoboam and start a civil war. He could have stayed in Egypt until the Lord's call to return (like Joseph in Matt 2:19). Instead he chose to go home and lead the northern tribes. "We see another suspicious sign in the recall of Jeroboam, and his selection as spokesman; for he had been in rebellion against Solomon (1 Kgs 11:26), and therefore an exile. Probably he had now been the instigator of the discontent of which he became the mouthpiece; and, in any case, his appearance as the leader was all but a declaration of war."[1]

The succession of kings in the line of David had never been subjected to a popular vote (e.g., Solomon's ascension to power was decided

---

1. McLaren's Expositions. http://biblehub.com/commentaries/1_kings/12-1.htm

by David). The Davidic kings had always been enthroned in Jerusalem,[2] the capital of the nation and the place chosen by God for his temple. However, with Rehoboam, "all Israel had come to Shechem to make him king" (1 Kgs 12:1). The demand for him to go to Shechem (a major city in Ephraim territory, the tribe of Jeroboam) to meet with the northern tribes was ominous. Jeroboam the rebel would be safe among his kinsmen while Rehoboam would be vulnerable as he was far away from his Judean base of support. Nevertheless, it appeared that he had no choice but to agree to the ultimatum. "Rehoboam was obliged to go there, if he would not at once provoke a civil war."[3]

At the meeting, some demands were made (i.e., lighten the hard service) with the implied threat of rebellion if the northern tribes were not satisfied ("do this and we will serve you"). Rehoboam could agree to the people's requests. He could reject them out of hand. Or he could delay his decision. He chose the third option and asked for three days to consider the issue.

God mercifully gave the king a way of escape from the imminent disaster of a civil war by providing him with wise counsel from the elders who had served under his father Solomon. "If you will be *a servant* to this people today, and will serve them and grant them their petition, and speak good words to them, then they will be your servants forever" (1 Kgs 12:7). Apparently not pleased with that advice, he sought a second opinion from his young peers who counseled him to declare: "My father disciplined you with whips, but I will discipline you with scorpions'" (2 Chr 10:11). Rather than taking the way of escape, Rehoboam foolishly challenged the northern tribes. Had he not done so, they would have been responsible for rebelling without a cause. He unwisely chose to provoke them with his threats and therefore shared the blame for the ensuing debacle.

Had he agreed to the people's request, perhaps the kingdom would not have been divided during his reign[4] as the Lord's decree concerning

2. "In *Jerusalem*, he (David) reigned thirty-three years over all Israel and Judah," 2 Sam 5:5. "Then Absalom and all the people, the men of Israel, entered *Jerusalem*. . . Hushai said to Absalom, "Long live the king!" 2 Sam 16:15–16. "And Zadok the priest and Nathan the prophet have anointed him (Solomon) king in Gihon (a spring in *Jerusalem*)," 1 Kgs 1:45.

3. Cambridge Bible for Schools and Colleges. http://biblehub.com/commentaries/1_kings/12-1.htm

4. "It is very doubtful if concession would have conciliated them." McLaren's Expositions. http://biblehub.com/commentaries/1_kings/12-1.htm

the partition could have referred to any descendant of Solomon, not necessarily Rehoboam. Had he been a good and obedient king, the Lord could have delayed the dissolution of the realm until later[5] without contradicting his promise to Jeroboam. However, Rehoboam acted foolishly and brought God's declared prophecy on his reign. "So the king did not listen to the people; for it was a turn of events from the Lord" (1 Kgs 12:15). The words "turn of events" is the Hebrew "sibbah" meaning "a turn,"[6] appearing only here in the Old Testament. "Sibbah" does not necessarily indicate that this was the one and only possible scenario, and that Jeroboam's rebellion and Rehoboam's harsh insults were decreed by the Lord. "God did not inspire Rehoboam's proud and despotic reply."[7] Thus, Jeroboam would have been better served by imitating David's restraint and Rehoboam would have been wiser to humble himself before his countrymen. God's will (i.e., two kingdoms) had to be done God's way (without rebellion and brotherly strife).

Rehoboam's harsh answer incited Israel into open rebellion. This eerily resembled the insurrection led by Sheba against David. "We have no portion in David, nor do we have inheritance in the son of Jesse" (2 Sam 20:1). In anger, the northern tribes rejected not just Rehoboam but the whole Davidic dynasty as legitimate kings of Israel.

Rehoboam rashly sent Adoram (who supervised the forced labor, a point of great contention with the northern tribes) to manage the conflict. Murder ensued as Israel stoned the envoy to death. The king himself felt so threatened that he "made haste to mount his chariot to flee to Jerusalem" (1 Kgs 12:18). So much for the king's empty threats to discipline Israel with scorpions! God allowed Rehoboam to consider his few remaining options. He could bow to the inevitable and acquiesce to a formal division of the kingdom. He could refuse to recognize the legitimacy of the partition, keeping the status quo without resorting to violence. Or he could gather his army and start a war. Rehoboam unwisely chose the third option.

In his mercy, the Lord gave Rehoboam another way of escape. He sent the prophet Shemaiah to dissuade Judah and Benjamin from going to war against their brothers. Rehoboam could listen to God and disband his army, or he could persist in his plan to regain the kingdom, a task

---

5. For example, the partition could happen at the end of Rehoboam's reign, yet within Jeroboam's lifetime.

6. http://biblehub.com/hebrew/5438.htm

7. Pulpit Commentary. http://biblehub.com/commentaries/1_kings/12–15.htm

against God's will and thus doomed to failure. The prophesied partition had been carried out during his reign and was therefore irreversible. This time, to his credit, Rehoboam chose to obey the Lord, thus avoiding (temporarily) a destructive civil conflict. However, the truce did not last long for "there was war between Rehoboam and Jeroboam continually" (1 Kgs 14:30).

GOD.

As the result of Solomon's unfaithfulness, God decreed that the kingdom would be divided, and ten tribes given to Jeroboam. However, the partition had to be done God's way, without violence and bloodshed. In a possible scenario that would have been more consistent with God's Law, Rehoboam could have inquired of the Lord about the best course of action when challenged by the northern tribes. If not previously aware of God's decree to divide the kingdom, he would have learned that resistance was futile and that the best option would have to be an amicable parting of ways between relatives (like Abraham and Lot in Gen 13:11), either during his or his heir's reign, as Jeroboam had already been promised a kingdom. An alliance treaty against outside foes could have been forged between the two realms. The unrestricted travel of pilgrims to Jerusalem for the required Passover feasts could have been guaranteed, thus negating the need for the golden calves in Israel's territory. Obviously, the actual scenario (war between brothers) was never God's choice.

The Lord allowed Jeroboam and Rehoboam to make their decisions within his predetermined boundaries. He mercifully provided them with wise counsel and ways of escape, but ultimately, he let them choose their paths without interference. Therefore, the Lord rightfully held them responsible for their actions and gave them both their deserved punishments!

Chapter 33

The case of the disobedient prophet, the lying prophet, and God

THE DISOBEDIENT PROPHET.

AN UNNAMED PROPHET FROM Judah was sent by the Lord to pronounce judgment on Jeroboam and his altar at Bethel, ten miles north of Jerusalem. The seer was clearly commanded by God, "You shall eat no bread, nor drink water, nor return by the way which you came" (1 Kgs 13:9). These solemn instructions could be explained by the fact that the Lord abhorred the worship of the golden calf in Bethel and disallowed any fellowship (e.g., a meal) between his prophet and the Bethelites. The seer was also told to take a different way to return to Judah, probably as a precaution against being detained by Jeroboam (likewise, the magi were warned and went home "by another way," Matt 2:12). Since Bethel was near the border between the kingdoms of Israel and Judah, the task could be done quickly.

The prophet pronounced judgement against the altar. In retaliation, Jeroboam ordered his arrest, prompting God to wither the king's hand. Jeroboam entreated the seer for mercy and was healed. When the monarch wanted to reward him for the miraculous cure by offering him refreshment and hospitality, he rightfully declined, citing God's commands. He then "went another way and did not return by the way which he came to Bethel" (1 Kgs 13:10). So far, so good! The Lord's command not to take food and water was not unreasonable since this should be a very short trip. The directive would have been much more difficult to follow had God decided to act against the other golden calf altar in far north Israel.

The prophet knew that Jeroboam wanted to arrest him for daring to challenge the king in public. Furthermore, the seer realized that he embarrassed the monarch by refusing his offer of hospitality. Thus, Jeroboam had many reasons to have him jailed and punished for the affront to the king's dignity and honor. Knowing all these dangers, the prophet had some decisions to make. He could hurry back to Judah (the safest approach and the earliest opportunity to get some food and water). He could walk home at a reasonable pace and get some refreshment when he arrived (not as tiring but not as safe for it would take longer). He could take his time and get home whenever (not ideal considering the risk of being captured). God did not specify how fast the prophet had to travel, like he did with Paul later. "Make haste, and get out of Jerusalem quickly, because they will not accept your testimony about me" (Acts 22:18).

The seer unwisely chose to take his time on his return trip to Judah. He was found "sitting under an oak" (1 Kgs 13:14) by an old prophet on a donkey. If so, how much faster would he have been found and captured by Jeroboam's soldiers on horses had they gone after him? When told a lie (i.e., "an angel spoke to me by the word of the Lord, saying, 'Bring him back with you to your house, that he may eat bread and drink water,'" 1 Kgs 13:18), he could abide by the terms of the original instructions. He could also ask the Lord whether the new guidance was correct. Or he could believe the lying prophet. God did not intervene at this juncture. The Lord allowed the seer to freely choose his path of obedience or disobedience.

Like Jesus who later quoted the Lord's words to counter the devil's lies, the seer recited God's commands to answer the lying prophet's offer. However, besides repeating the Lord's instructions, would he actually obey them? The seer chose to disregard God's directions and went back to Bethel to eat and drink. The Lord's judgment was swift, "your body shall not come to the grave of your fathers" (1 Kgs 13:22). "To the ancient Hebrew, to die was 'to be gathered unto his people' and to lie with his fathers . . . to be buried in the grave of his father and mother was his fondest wish."[1] This severe punishment was only meted out as a result of shameful acts that would bring dishonor to the whole clan, requiring a

---

1. http://www.jewishencyclopedia.com/articles/3842-burial

sanction equivalent to the erasure of one's name from the family register.[2] The disobedient prophet made his foolish free will choice and suffered the dire consequences!

THE LYING PROPHET.

When Solomon's kingdom was divided into Israel and Judah, "the priests and the Levites who were in all Israel stood with him (Rehoboam) . . . and came to Judah and Jerusalem" (2 Chr 11:13–14). However, the old prophet chose to remain at Bethel in the northern kingdom. Furthermore, his sons appeared to be present[3] during the worship at the altar of the golden calf as they "came and told him all the deeds which the man of God had done that day in Bethel" (1 Kgs 13:11). "Like Balaam, he (the lying prophet) united true prophetic gifts with a low worldliness of temper, capable on occasion of base subterfuge and deceit."[4]

The old seer chose to lie to get the prophet from Judah to return to Bethel. He did so out of his own free will as he received no instructions from the Lord. God did not interfere and let both prophets make their own decisions. However, once the choices had been made, the Lord decreed the death of the disobedient seer. "It must be acknowledged, however, to be strange, that the lying prophet should escape, while he, who, notwithstanding this error, was truly a man of God, is so severely punished."[5] Nonetheless, "from everyone who has been given much, much will be required" (Luke 12:48). The prophet from Judah was given much (the honor of being God's ambassador to a king), therefore the Lord expected much from him (a complete obedience to the commands).

After leaving the lying prophet's house, the seer from Judah was killed by a lion. When he heard about the misfortune, the old prophet

2. This harsh sentence was pronounced on seven kings of Judah for their utterly dishonorable reigns: Jehoram (2 Chr 21:20), Joash (2 Chr 24:25), Uzziah (2 Chr 26:23), Ahaz (2 Chr 28:27), Manasseh (2 Kgs 21:18), Amon (2 Kgs 21:26) and Jehoiakim (Jer 22:18–19). Three Judean kings died in exile and were not even buried in the Promised Land: Jehoahaz, Jehoiachin, and Zedekiah.

3. "Though not present himself at the sacrifice, he permitted his sons to be there, is a sufficient index to his character." Pulpit Commentary. https://biblehub.com/commentaries/1_kings/13–11.htm

4. Ellicott's Commentary for English Readers. http://biblehub.com/commentaries/1_kings/13–11.htm

5. Benson Commentary. http://biblehub.com/commentaries/1_kings/13–23.htm

could wash his hands of the whole matter. He could bury him where he died. He could take the body to Judah and give it to the man's relatives. He could inter the remains somewhere on his land. Or he could lay the man in his own prepared grave. In recognition that "the thing shall surely come to pass" (i.e., the bones of idolatrous priests would be burned by Josiah on the altar), he wisely ordered his sons: "When I die, bury me in the grave in which the man of God is buried" (1 Kgs 13:31). Three hundred years later, "when Josiah came to burn the bones of the priests, he would spare the bones of this man of God (the disobedient prophet's); and so, his (the old prophet's bones), lying by them, and mingled with them, would be spared also."[6] No one, not even an old, idolatrous priest, would want his grave disturbed and his bones desecrated!

GOD.

God gave the prophet from Judah clear instructions for his mission to pronounce judgment on Jeroboam. In his mercy, he also provided the envoy with safeguards (i.e., short distance, different return path) from the dangers of traveling in a hostile country. Then he allowed the seer to use his judgment to handle the events of his journey. Sadly, the prophet chose to disobey the Lord's commands and suffered a gruesome death in a foreign land. The old seer elected to lie and deceive. Yet, in the end, he wisely chose to believe God's prophecy and therefore avoided the desecration of his tomb. The Lord allowed each person to make his free will decisions and live with the consequences, whether good or evil!

6. Gill's Exposition of the Entire Bible. http://biblehub.com/commentaries/1_kings/13-31.htm

Chapter 34

The case of Ahab, Jezebel, and God

AHAB AND JEZEBEL.

AHAB EARNED THE INFAMOUS reputation of being "evil in the sight of the Lord more than all who were before him." Furthermore, "he married Jezebel . . . and went to serve Baal and worshiped him" (1 Kgs 16:31). Although repeatedly rebuked by God, he stubbornly persisted in his ways. Driven by covetousness, he desired Naboth's vineyard for a vegetable garden and obtained it through murder (Jezebel had Naboth stoned to death outside the city of Jezreel). The Lord finally pronounced Ahab's punishment in three parts. First, "in the place where the dogs licked up the blood of Naboth the dogs will lick up your blood." Second, "I will bring evil upon you, and will utterly sweep you away, and will cut off from Ahab every male, both bond and free in Israel." Finally, "the dogs will eat Jezebel in the district of Jezreel" (1 Kgs 21:19–23).

These were dire pronouncements. Once decreed, were they irreversible? Was there any hope that the Lord would "change his mind" and revoke the edicts? Surprisingly, "it came about when Ahab heard these words, that he tore his clothes and put on sackcloth and fasted" (1 Kgs 21:27). What could the Lord do at this juncture? "Because he has humbled himself before me, I will not bring the evil in his days, but I will bring the evil upon his house in his son's days" (1 Kgs 21:29). God's prophecy of the annihilation of the house of Ahab had some built-in flexibility to account for future repentance (e.g., an immediate or a delayed fulfillment). Likewise, the declaration of "dogs licking Ahab's blood" could include various alternatives. The possible scenarios could be dogs eating the corpse *and* licking the blood or just doing the latter. Because of his contrition, Ahab was spared the indignity of having his body unburied and eaten by scavengers.[1] In the Lord's mercy, Ahab's corpse was interred in Samaria (1 Kgs 22:37).

The first prophecy was fulfilled when "they washed the chariot by the pool of Samaria, and the dogs licked up his (Ahab's) blood," though not in Jezreel, "in the place where the dogs licked up the blood of Naboth." However, Jehu later killed Ahab's son, Jehoram, and threw his body "into the property of the field of Naboth the Jezreelite"[2] (2 Kgs 9:25). "Here (in Jezreel) did dogs lick Ahab's blood, that is, his son's blood, the execution of the full retaliatory sentence having been deferred to the days of his son."[3] Did God change his mind and revoke his decree after Ahab's penitence? "This was not a pardon, only a reprieve; the sentence pronounced on him and his family was not taken off, nor countermanded, only the execution of it prolonged."[4] Since Ahab repented, the merciful Lord allowed a slightly less onerous alternative.[5]

The fulfillment of the second prophecy was deferred until the time of Ahab's son Jehoram. In his omniscience, the Lord created some slightly different scenarios within his predetermined boundaries. However, all the possible paths had to include the annihilation of Ahab's descendants as decreed by the Lord.[6] "So Jehu killed all who remained of the house of Ahab . . . until he left him without a survivor" (2 Kgs 10:11).

Concerning the third decree, as Jezebel did not repent, the punishment was carried out as pronounced. "They went to bury her, but they found nothing more of her than the skull and the feet and the palms of her hands" (2 Kgs 9:35). She was eaten by stray dogs in the district of Jezreel.

---

1. "Naboth's body was left for the dogs to eat." Barnes' Notes on the Bible. http://biblehub.com/commentaries/1_kings/21–19.htm

2. Naboth was stoned outside the city of Jezreel (1 Kgs 21:13), probably somewhere near his vineyard since Jehoram's body was thrown in Naboth's field.

3. Barnes' Notes on the Bible. http://biblehub.com/commentaries/1_kings/21–19.htm

4. Gill's Exposition of the Entire Bible. http://biblehub.com/commentaries/1_kings/21–29.htm

5. Interpretations of Elijah's prophecy in 1 Kgs 21:19 are detailed in Foreman, "The Blood of Ahab," 249–64.

6. A scenario *without* Ahab's repentance would have been the destruction of his entire family *during his lifetime*. Both paths had the same ending as required by the Lord's previous prophesy/decree.

Ahab was given many opportunities to change his mind through the ministry of Elijah (1 Kgs 17:1, 1 Kgs 18, 1 Kgs 21:17). Sadly, he persisted in his stubborn rebellion until the day the Lord pronounced judgment on his house. Nevertheless, even then, in the Lord's mercy, he was able to salvage something by repenting of his misdeeds.

GOD.

God was patient with Ahab and Jezebel, "not wishing for any to perish but for all to come to repentance" (2 Pet 3:9). However, at long last, the Lord had to judge their sins. Yet, the merciful Lord was still willing to lessen the dire consequences when Ahab finally chose to show contrition. In his wisdom, the Lord allowed some flexibility within the boundaries of his decrees as God's pronouncement also served as a final call to penance. For her part, Jezebel stubbornly refused to repent and therefore went to her predicted doom. The sovereign Lord allowed his creatures to make some free will decisions. Some made the right choices and lived; others persisted in disobedience and suffered their full deserved penalties.

Chapter 35

The case of Jehoshaphat, Ahab, the evil spirit, and God

JEHOSHAPHAT.

JEHOSHAPHAT "ALLIED HIMSELF BY marriage with Ahab" (2 Chr 18:1). Jehoshaphat's son Jehoram married Ahab and Jezebel's daughter Athaliah. During a lavish state visit in Samaria, Ahab "induced" Jehoshaphat to help him retake Ramoth-gilead from the Syrians. The word "induce" is the Hebrew "suth" meaning "to incite, to allure, to instigate." In 2 Chronicles 18:2, "suth" means "instigate, in bad sense."[1] As the honored guest at a state banquet, Jehoshaphat was under pressure to agree to the request of his host and in-law. "This royal hospitality is here represented as part of a deliberate plan for obtaining the cooperation of Jehoshaphat in the projected campaign."[2] Nevertheless, Jehoshaphat had many viable alternatives. He could gently decline the offer. He could come up with some face-saving excuses to delay the decision (e.g., he needed to consult with his generals). Or he could consent to go with Ahab.

Jehoshaphat unwisely chose the last option. "I am as you are, my people as your people, my horses as your horses" (1 Kgs 22:4). Jehoshaphat knew that Ahab and Jezebel were worshipers of Baal and that they were persecuting the prophets of God. Why would he ally himself with them? "Do not be bound together with unbelievers; for what partnership have righteousness and lawlessness, or what fellowship has light

---

1. http://biblehub.com/hebrew/5496.htm

2. Ellicott's Commentary for English Readers. http://biblehub.com/commentaries/2_chronicles/18-2.htm

with darkness?" (2 Cor 6:14). While it was true that Ahab had repented, events soon showed that it was only temporary.

After agreeing to go with Ahab, Jehoshaphat asked for a prophet to inquire "for the word of the Lord." Since he had already committed himself, what was he hoping to hear from God? Or was it a case of "buyer's remorse" for "jumping the gun" and acting rashly without thinking? Ahab was happy to oblige Jehoshaphat's request. After all, he had already obtained what he wanted. Four hundred "prophets of the Lord" were quickly rounded up. "Shall we go against Ramoth-gilead to battle, or shall I refrain?" (2 Chr 18:5a). Unsurprisingly, the opinion of the "prophets" was unanimous: "Go up, for God will give it into the hand of the king" (2 Chr 18:5b). Note that "king" was singular, indicating that Jehoshaphat was now a subordinate ally of Ahab and would have to do whatever Ahab decided.

Belatedly, Jehoshaphat recognized that something was amiss and that the men might not be true prophets of the Lord. He could beg leave of Ahab and go seek God's advice through the High Priest in Jerusalem or he could ask: "Is there not yet a prophet of the Lord *here*, that we may inquire of him?" (1 Kgs 22:7). God, in his mercy, provided the prophet Micaiah and a way of escape for Jehoshaphat. Contrary to the previous oracle, Micaiah prophesied utter defeat for Israel and Judah. He also revealed that the Lord had allowed a spirit to entice Ahab to go to battle. Furthermore, Micaiah asserted his status as a true prophet of God by declaring in the presence of all that "if you (Ahab) indeed return safely the Lord has not spoken by me" (1 Kgs 22:28).

Given all these facts, Jehoshaphat could swallow his pride and take back his previous commitment to join Ahab. He could come up with some face-saving excuses to delay the venture until later (e.g., due to the conflicting "words from the Lord," we will need to seek a third opinion in Jerusalem). Or he could just ignore God's prophecy and go to war. Unwisely, Jehoshaphat chose the third option. Furthermore, he agreed to wear his royal robes (to act as a target?) while Ahab disguised himself. Sure enough, the Syrian king "commanded the captains of his chariots, saying, 'Do not fight with small or great, but with the king of Israel alone'" (2 Chr 18:30). Seeing Jehoshaphat in regal attire, they mistook him for Ahab and tried to kill him. However, the merciful Lord intervened and "diverted them" (2 Chr 18:31).

As declared by Micaiah, Israel and Judah were utterly defeated. Jehoshaphat barely escaped to Jerusalem. Once there, he was rebuked for his poor choices. "Should you help the wicked and love those who hate the Lord and so bring wrath on yourself from the Lord?" (2 Chr 19:2). God called Ahab "the wicked" and "those who hate the Lord" despite the previous (and probably brief) repentance. The Lord further revealed the reason why he chose to protect Jehoshaphat. "But there is some good in you, for you have removed the Asheroth from the land and you have set your heart to seek God" (2 Chr 19:3). Obedience brought blessings, disobedience brought curses.

The sovereign Lord gave Jehoshaphat many options/ways of escape within his predetermined boundaries. For some reason, Jehoshaphat continually made unwise decisions. Would he eventually learn his bitter lesson?

AHAB.

In a previous battle, Ahab was able to defeat Syria with the Lord's help (1 Kgs 20). Three years later, Ahab wanted to retake Ramoth-gilead. God, through Micaiah, declared that Israel would be defeated, Ahab would be killed in battle, and a spirit[3] had been allowed by the Lord to entice Ahab into this disastrous course of action. Contrary to what he did before when he gave Ahab an opportunity to repent, this time, the sovereign Lord pronounced final judgment on Ahab with no chance of reprieve. He said to the spirit: "You are to entice him and *also prevail*" (1 Kgs 22:22).

Undaunted, Ahab prepared for battle and ordered Micaiah sent to prison. "Feed him sparingly with bread and water until I return safely" (1 Kgs 22:27). Nevertheless, the Lord's words did not totally fall on deaf ears since Ahab took some measures to protect his life. He disguised himself and wore body armor. Despite these precautions, the prophecy of the Lord was fulfilled as "a certain man drew his bow at random and struck the king of Israel in a joint of the armor" (1 Kgs 22:34). Ahab died of his injuries and the dogs licked his blood.

God does use "evil" as a tool to punish disobedience. Although the Lord is long-suffering, the time may come when his patience is exhausted,

---

3. "On the one hand, it is hard to suppose one of the holy angels a 'lying spirit;' on the other, hard to find Satan, or an evil spirit, included among 'the host of heaven' 1 Kings 22:19 and acting as the minister of God. Still, Job 1:6; Job 2:1, lend countenance to the latter point, and 2 Thessalonians 2:11 to the former." Barnes' Notes on the Bible. http://biblehub.com/commentaries/1_kings/22-22.htm

and final judgment is pronounced on the guilty parties. Therefore, we need to listen closely to his rebuke and quickly change our ways!

THE EVIL SPIRIT.

In a scene reminiscent of Job 1, Micaiah described an event taking place in heaven. "I saw the Lord sitting on his throne, and all the host of heaven standing by him on his right and on his left. And the Lord said, 'Who will entice Ahab to go up and fall in Ramoth-gilead?'" (1 Kgs 22:19–20). God was asking for a volunteer to bring about Ahab's downfall. In Isaiah 6:8, the Lord also asked: "'Whom shall I send, and who will go for us?' Then I said, 'Here am I. Send me!'"

There was some discussion among the spirits as "one said this while another said that" (1 Kgs 22:20). "Then a spirit came forward" and volunteered to do the job. He proposed to be a deceiving spirit in the mouth of Ahab's prophets. The Lord accepted the plan and declared that it would "prevail." Spirits were sometimes given free will choices. However, their actions had to be preapproved by the Lord.

GOD.

The sovereign Lord granted mercy and protection to some (e.g., Jehoshaphat) and withheld the same favors from others (e.g., Ahab). Nevertheless, he acted righteously as Ahab had been given many opportunities to repent. Ahab's death was a consequence of his continued disobedience and he had no one to blame but himself.

God is in full control of the spirits as they must live and act within God's strict boundaries. Satan and his demons must ask God's permission before they can tempt humans. Children of God should not fear these powers for "greater is he who is in you than he who is in the world" (1 John 4:4).

Chapter 36

The case of Jehoshaphat and God

JEHOSHAPHAT.

JEHOSHAPHAT MADE A POOR decision in joining Ahab, was defeated at Ramoth-gilead, and barely escaped. He was soon given a second chance to show that he had learned his lesson. After Ahab's death, Ahaziah became king. "And he did evil in the sight of the Lord" (1 Kgs 22:52). Like his father, Ahaziah sought an alliance with Judah. Jehoshaphat could decline the offer with some face-saving statements. He could propose a friendly relationship between the two kingdoms without having a formal collaboration. He could delay the decision until later. Or he could agree to the partnership. Disregarding God's previous rebuke, he joined forces with Ahaziah to build ships for the gold trade of Ophir. The Lord's discipline came quickly. "'Because you have allied yourself with Ahaziah, the Lord has destroyed your works.' So the ships were broken and could not go to Tarshish" (2 Chr 20:37).

Jehoshaphat was soon given a third opportunity to do the right thing. When Ahaziah died for inquiring of Baal-zebub, his brother Jehoram became king since Ahaziah had no son. "And he (Jehoram) did evil in the sight of the Lord" (2 Kgs 3:2). Jehoshaphat was asked to go with Jehoram against Moab. As before, he had many options. He could flatly decline the offer as alliances with Israel had been disastrous for his kingdom. He could delay the decision until later. Or he could agree to the partnership. Incredibly, Jehoshaphat again chose the last option. Using the identical speech in his alliance with Ahab, he agreed to join Jehoram ("I will go up; I am as you are, my people as your people, my horses as your horses" 2 Kgs 3:7).

Jehoshaphat did not ask the Lord's advice and decided to take the allied armies (Judah, Israel, and Edom) through the wilderness. Unfortunately, the water they needed was not available. In desperation, the three kings called on Elisha for help. In God's mercy, water was provided miraculously. Furthermore, the Lord promised that "he shall also give the Moabites into your hand" (2 Kgs 3:18). "Then you shall strike every fortified city and every choice city and fell every good tree and stop all springs of water and mar every good piece of land with stones" (2 Kgs 3:19). As prophesied, the allied armies had a great victory. Then, they did what was commanded by cutting down the trees, stopping the springs of water, and marring the land with stones. The Moabites retreated to their stronghold of Kir-hareseth where they were besieged. In desperation, their king offered his eldest son to Chemosh as a burnt offering. "And there came great wrath against Israel, and they departed from him (Moab) and returned to their own land" (2 Kgs 3:27). The word "wrath" is the Hebrew "qetseph" meaning wrath (of God or of man).[1]

The commentators are divided on the meaning of the verse. Some believe that the Lord was angry with Israel for causing Moab to offer a human sacrifice.[2] This is not likely as God had commanded the allied armies to strike every fortified city including Kir-hasereth. Furthermore, it was Moab's idea to offer a human sacrifice. Others opine that it was the wrath of Chemosh against Israel.[3] Since there was no other god but the God of Abraham, the wrath of the non-existent Chemosh was not real and could not have forced Israel to lift the siege. Others think that it was the wrath of Moab against Israel.[4] Although the loss of their crown prince would cause great anger among the Moabites, that would not have driven the allied armies to depart. Others conclude that it was the wrath of Edom and Judah against Israel for involving them in this barbaric incident.[5] This was not likely for all three armies went home, not just Edom and Judah. A decision to leave had to be made unanimously by all three kings. "The most likely reason seems to be that Israel feared the retribution of

1. http://biblehub.com/hebrew/7110.htm

2. Jamieson-Fausset-Brown Bible Commentary. http://biblehub.com/commentaries/2_kings/3-27.htm

3. Ellicott's Commentary for English Readers. http://biblehub.com/commentaries/2_kings/3-27.htm

4. Pulpit Commentary. http://biblehub.com/commentaries/2_kings/3-27.htm

5. Barnes' Notes on the Bible. http://biblehub.com/commentaries/2_kings/3-27.htm

Chemosh, and so they fled!"[6] Even though Chemosh did not exist, he still had great powers *in people's minds*, especially in the imaginations of Jehoram and the Edomite king, neither of whom served the Lord. The siege was lifted in disobedience of God's command to "strike every fortified city," due to a *greater* fear of Chemosh, and for that action, God's "great wrath against Israel" was well-deserved!

Jehoshaphat was given many opportunities to learn not to ally himself with wicked kings. Sadly, he kept repeating the same mistake with disastrous results. He was almost killed in Ramoth-gilead. He lost all his ships at Ezion-geber. He failed in his conquest of Moab. Since he made all these decisions against the Lord's counsel, he only had himself to blame for the dire consequences!

GOD.

Since Jehoshaphat was a good ruler and "sought the God of his father" (2 Chr 17:4), the Lord was gentle and patient with him. In his mercy, God sent Micaiah to dissuade the king from allying himself with the wicked Ahab. On his safe return from the disaster at Ramoth-gilead, the prophet Jehu admonished him about the danger of loving "those who hate the Lord." After the loss of his ships at Ezion-geber, the prophet Eliezer proclaimed: "Because you have allied yourself with Ahaziah, the Lord has destroyed your works" (2 Chr 20:37).

Nonetheless, when his army was caught without water in the wilderness, God mercifully rescued him through the prophet Elisha and granted him victory over the Moabites. However, he did not fulfill the task to "strike every fortified city" in Moab and, like the Israelites in the conquest of Canaan, came far short of what the Lord had offered, allowing Moab to survive until the time of the Babylonians.[7]

The sovereign Lord gave Jehoshaphat many opportunities to do the right thing. Furthermore, he sent prophet after prophet to counsel, warn, and rescue the wayward monarch. God was gracious, merciful, patient, and long-suffering with the slow-to-learn king. What more could one ask of a Father?

---

6. Harton, "The Meaning of 2 Kings 3:27," 39.

7. Moab "was conquered by the Babylonians in 582 BC, upon which the Moabites disappeared from history." https://www.britannica.com/topic/Moabite

Chapter 37

The case of Jehoiada, Joash, and God

JEHOIADA.

WHEN KING AHAZIAH, ATHALIAH's son, died, Athaliah "rose and destroyed all the royal offspring of the house of Judah" (2 Chr 22:10),[1] and took over the throne. Jehoiada the priest and his wife Jehosheba, Ahaziah's sister, could "live and let die," or they could take great personal risks and try to thwart Athaliah's plans. To their credit, they chose to rescue Joash, the only remaining son of Ahaziah, and hid him in the house of the Lord for six years. When Joash was seven years old, Jehoiada sought the support of the people, put Athaliah to death, and restored Joash to the throne. Jehoiada knew the promise God had made to David and was working in obedience to bring about God's will. "Behold, the king's son shall reign, as the Lord has spoken concerning the sons of David" (2 Chr 23:3). Had Jehoiada not risked his life to protect one of David's descendants, the Lord would have used someone else to carry out the task (e.g., Jael rather than Barak).

Jehoiada served as the king's counselor and "Joash did what was right in the sight of the Lord all the days of Jehoiada the priest" (2 Chr 24:2). "Now when Jehoiada reached a ripe old age he died; he was one hundred and thirty years old at his death. They buried him in the city of David among the kings" (2 Chr 24:15–16). Jehoiada obeyed the Lord, made the right choices, and was therefore blessed with a long life when compared to David's (seventy years), Solomon's (fifty-nine years), Rehoboam's (fifty-eight years), Jehoshaphat's (sixty years), Jehoram's (forty

---

1. Only the royal line from Solomon was destroyed by Athaliah since Nathan's line continued with Mary and Jesus.

years) and Ahaziah's (twenty-three years) lifespans.[2] Furthermore, Jehoiada was greatly honored by the people and was buried with the kings,
a privilege given to no other commoner!

JOASH.

After Jehoiada's death, the king had some decisions to make. He could
continue in the teachings of his mentor or he could do whatever he
pleased. God gave Joash free will to decide without any interference. Unwisely, Joash chose the second option. "But after the death of Jehoiada the
officials of Judah came and bowed down to the king, and the king listened
to them. They abandoned the house of the Lord, the God of their fathers,
and served the Asherim and the idols" (2 Chr 24:17–18). In his mercy,
God "sent prophets to them to bring them back to the Lord; though they
testified against them, they would not listen" (2 Chr 24:19). God was patient and did not yet pronounce judgment on Joash, a decree that would
make some events irrevocable.

The Lord sent Zechariah, Jehoiada's son, to call Joash to repentance.[3] If the king would listen to anyone, it would have been the son of
his benefactor Jehoiada and the king's own cousin. Zechariah faithfully
delivered the Lord's message: "Why do you transgress the commandments of the Lord and do not prosper? Because you have forsaken the
Lord, he has also forsaken you" (2 Chr 24:20). Joash could listen to God's
warning and repent. He could ignore God's message. Or he could kill
God's messenger and thus despise the Lord (i.e., teach the Lord not to
mess with him)! Joash foolishly commanded the people to stone Zechariah "to death in the court of the house of the Lord." "He murdered his
(Jehoiada's) son. And as he (Zechariah) died he said, "May the Lord see
and avenge!" (2 Chr 24:22). For his own reasons, God did not intervene
to prevent Zechariah's murder but allowed Joash to do what he wanted.

God's judgment came swiftly for "at the end of the year the army of
the Syrians came up against Joash. They came to Judah and Jerusalem and
destroyed all the princes of the people" (2 Chr 24:23 ESV). "His (Joash's)
own servants conspired against him because of the blood of the son of

---

2. Castellano, "Revised Chronology of the Monarchies of Israel and Judah."

3. In a parable later given by Jesus ("Last of all, he sent his son to them. 'They will
respect my son,'" Matt 21:37 NIV), the landowner (i.e., God) sent his son (i.e., Jesus) as
the last resort to call the vine-growers to repentance.

Jehoiada the priest and murdered him on his bed. So he died, and they buried him in the city of David, but they did not bury him in the tombs of the kings" (2 Chr 24:25). While Jehoiada was buried with the kings, Joash was excluded! The Lord gave Joash many opportunities to choose the right path, culminating with Zechariah's ultimate appeal. Undaunted, Joash killed the last messenger, spurned all of God's entreaties, refused to repent, and therefore suffered the due consequences of his actions!

GOD.

In his faithfulness to David, the Lord protected Joash from his murderous grandmother. Jehoiada and Jehosheba willingly chose to be God's instruments in this hazardous rescue. They hid the boy in the temple for six long years. Finally, Athaliah was killed and Joash acceded to the throne. The Lord mercifully gave the new king a counselor that served him faithfully for a long time as Jehoiada lived for one hundred and thirty years. Did the king internalize what he needed to know under this extended apprenticeship? Sadly, no! He quickly turned to other gods after Jehoiada died. The Lord sent many prophets to call Joash to repentance. At long last, God sent his cousin Zechariah to give him a final warning. Undeterred, he stubbornly refused to listen and, to add insult to injury, murdered God's messenger in God's own house. The temple was normally a place of sanctuary, immune to the shedding of human blood (1 Kgs 1:50).[4] The Lord's retribution was swift. As Joash murdered Zechariah, so he was murdered by his own servants on his bed.

In his wisdom, God allowed men and women to make choices within his narrow boundaries. No one was "doomed" to commit sin and evil! Athaliah made the decision to murder her own offspring and usurp the throne. For these depraved deeds, she was condemned to death. Jehoiada made good decisions and was blessed with a long life. Joash acted unwisely and died in dishonor. They were all held responsible for their actions, whether good or evil!

---

4. except in the case of a willful murderer (Exod 21:14, 1 Kgs 2: 29–34).

Chapter 38

The case of Jehoash and God

JEHOASH.

JEHOASH (JOASH) "BECAME KING over Israel in Samaria and reigned sixteen years. And he did evil in the sight of the Lord" (2 Kgs 13:10–11). Nevertheless, when the prophet "Elisha became sick with the illness of which he was to die," Jehoash went to see him. "The visit of a king to a prophet, in the way of sympathy and compliment, would be a very unusual occurrence at any period of the world's history."[1] Jehoash chose to humble himself and show concern for God's prophet. The king wept over the seer, using Elisha's own words at Elijah's departure, "My father, my father, the chariots of Israel and its horsemen!"[2] (2 Kgs 2:12, 2 Kgs 13:14).

The ongoing war with the Syrians had been going badly since the time of Jehoash's father, Jehoahaz, with the army so depleted that it only had "fifty horsemen, ten chariots and ten thousand footmen" (2 Kgs 13:7). Now Elisha was dying without leaving a successor. "'How will I defeat Syria with no army and Elisha dead?' is the question haunting the king. Elisha represented the only hope that Joash had left of ever utterly defeating Syria."[3]

In response to Jehoash's desperate cry about the imminent departure of Israel's power, God mercifully gave the king a parting gift. The prophet instructed Jehoash to take a bow and arrows (the weapons of

1. Pulpit Commentary. http://biblehub.com/commentaries/2_kings/13-14.htm

2. The chariots of Israel and its horsemen represented Israel's power (i.e., the Lord's power as symbolized by the presence of his prophets). Thus, Elisha's death would remove Israel's strength.

3. Bailey, "Elijah and Elisha," 21.

war of charioteers and horsemen), point toward the east (where Syria was) and shoot while he "laid his hands on the king's hands" (signifying the transfer of the prophet's power onto the king). To make the symbolism crystal clear, Elisha exclaimed: "The Lord's arrow of victory, even the arrow of victory over Syria; for you shall defeat the Syrians at Aphek" (2 Kgs 13:17). Thus, the Lord equated a shot arrow with a victory over the enemy.

To continue the symbolism, Elisha told Jehoash to take the arrows and strike the ground (by shooting with a bow or by directly striking the ground was unclear). Nevertheless, the imagery was the same. Every time an arrow struck the ground, one battle victory was granted to Jehoash. The king could ask Elisha how many projectiles he needed to use. He could strike/shoot his darts until the prophet ordered him to stop or until he ran out of shots. Or he could pick a random number and do whatever he wanted to do.

Neither God nor Elisha told Jehoash how many arrows he should use. The offer of victories was freely given by the Lord, but it was up to the king to appropriate it in full or partial measure. As a chariot was equipped with five quivers each holding thirty arrows,[4] one would expect Jehoash to shoot a multitude of darts at the Syrians to annihilate them. Unfortunately, he chose to strike the ground only three times, and for that limited action, he was granted three victories. "If he had been earnestly desirous of victory and had had faith in the symbolical action as divinely directed, he would have kept on smiting till the prophet told him it was enough."[5] "So the man of God was angry with him and said, "You should have struck five or six times, then you would have struck Aram (Syria) until you would have destroyed it. But now you shall strike Aram only three times" (2 Kgs 13:19). In God's compassion for the king's predicament, Jehoash was given the freedom to decide his own number of blessings. He chose poorly and suffered the consequences as he only defeated Syria three times.

GOD.

Even though Jehoash "did evil in the sight of the Lord," the merciful God was willing to grant the king deliverance from the Syrians in response to

---

4. Maidman, *Nuzi Texts*, 37.

5. Pulpit Commentary. http://biblehub.com/commentaries/2_kings/13-19.htm

his visit to the dying Elisha. The Lord made clear to him that the arrows represented battle successes over the enemy. God then allowed him to freely choose the number of victories he desired.

In his sovereignty, the Lord did not give Jehoash other options within his predetermined boundaries. For example, the arrow shot together by Jehoash and Elisha could have represented the complete destruction of the Syrians. The three darts used by the king could have been deemed sufficient to annihilate Syria. The king could have been allowed to launch more projectiles. Elisha could have told him the exact number of arrows he needed to use. Elisha could have ordered him to keep striking until he was told to cease. Elisha could have said, "do not strike just a few," a recommendation which Elisha gave to the widow with the oil. "Go, borrow vessels at large for yourself from all your neighbors, even empty vessels; *do not get a few*" (2 Kgs 4:3). Blessed by the merciful Lord with a generous opportunity to destroy his enemies, Jehoash made a poor decision and had to settle for much less than God's best!

Chapter 39

The case of Amaziah and God

AMAZIAH.

WHEN AMAZIAH BECAME KING of Judah, "he did right in the sight of the Lord, yet not with a whole heart" (2 Chr 25:2). In due course, he mobilized his troops to go against Edom. However, he deemed his army's strength of three hundred thousand men insufficient to assure victory. Thus, he had some difficult choices to make. He could call off the war and sue for peace. "Or what king, when he sets out to meet another king in battle, will not first sit down and consider whether he is strong enough with ten thousand men to encounter the one coming against him with twenty thousand?" (Luke 14:31). He could strengthen his forces by adding chariots and horses. He could hire mercenaries to supplement his soldiers. He could ally himself with other kings (e.g., Egypt). Or he could beseech the Lord for help.

Instead of seeking God, Amaziah chose to hire one hundred thousand mercenaries from Israel. The Lord's response was swift. "Do not let the army of Israel go with you . . . But if you do go, do it, be strong for the battle; yet God will bring you down before the enemy" (2 Chr 25:7–8). The sovereign Lord gave Amaziah two alternatives: defeat with the Israelites or victory without them. However, God's approach would create a problem. "What shall we do for the hundred talents which I have given to the troops of Israel?" (2 Chr 25:9). Hearing God's answer that "the Lord has much more to give you than this," Amaziah followed the Lord's advice and dismissed the Israelites.

As expected, this created much trouble as the mercenaries went home in fierce anger, "because they were both disgraced by this rejection, and disappointed of that spoil which they hoped to gain, whereas now they are sent away empty; for the hundred talents, probably, were given to their officers only to raise men for this service."[1] So, in revenge, they "raided the cities of Judah" and "plundered much spoil." These were the consequences of making decisions without seeking the Lord's counsel!

Nevertheless, by obeying the Lord, Amaziah gained a great victory over the Edomites. "He killed of Edom in the Valley of Salt 10,000 and took Sela by war" (2 Kgs 14:7). Surprisingly, he then decided to worship the gods of the vanquished nation. The Lord promptly sent a prophet to rebuke him. "Why have you sought the gods of the people who have not delivered their own people from your hand?" (2 Chr 25:15). Amaziah could heed the warning, repent, and put away the foreign gods. Or he could insist on his evil ways and spurn God's counsel. Unwisely, he selected the second option and threatened the prophet with bodily harm. "Have we appointed you a royal counselor? Stop! Why should you be struck down?" (2 Chr 25:16a). The parting words of the Lord's envoy sealed Amaziah's fate. "I know that God has planned to destroy you, because you have done this, and have not listened to my counsel" (2 Chr 25:16b). No further warning would be given. Disaster was inevitable!

After his victory over Edom, Amaziah, in boastful pride, wanted to start a war with King Jehoash of Israel.[2] To avert a destructive conflict, Jehoash sent a message to Amaziah. "Behold, you have defeated Edom. And your heart has become proud in boasting. Now, stay at home; for why should you provoke trouble that you, even you, should fall and Judah with you?" (2 Chr 25:19). In fulfillment of God's decree, "Amaziah would not listen, for it was from God, that he might deliver them into the hand of Joash because they had sought the gods of Edom" (2 Chr 25:20). The Lord let him be deaf and "not listen" to reason. Whether God did this actively (by hardening Amaziah's heart and preventing his ears from hearing) or passively (allowing Amaziah to harden his own heart) was not addressed. If the Lord did the hardening actively, it was only after a punishment had been decreed and had to be carried out. If God only passively allowed Amaziah to harden his own heart, Amaziah's demise was a result of his own pride and stubbornness. In either case, Amaziah did spurn God's warning about the worship of idols. He threatened God's

1. Benson Commentary. http://biblehub.com/commentaries/2_chronicles/25-1 0.htm

2. Amaziah might have thought that victory was assured since he had three hundred thousand men (2 Chr 25:5) to fight Jehoash's depleted army.

prophet with death, insisted on his evil ways, and was therefore totally responsible for his destruction. Amaziah was defeated by Jehoash and later assassinated by some of his own people "who conspired against him in Jerusalem" (2 Chr 25:27).

GOD.

The Lord is always righteous and deals fairly and patiently with his people. Obedience brings blessings and disobedience discipline. Amaziah knew that he was not to trust in his own strength and worship other gods. Yet, when warned by a prophet, he chose to ignore the Lord's counsel and persist in disobedience. God's judgment, once pronounced, becomes irrevocable. Further free will choices may not be offered. Therefore, it is imperative for God's people to respond quickly to God's rebuke, repent, and change their ways.

Chapter 40

The case of Uzziah and God

UZZIAH.

Uzziah, Amaziah's son, "did right in the sight of the Lord" and "as long as he sought the Lord, God prospered him" (2 Chr 26:4–5). However, "when he became strong, his heart was so proud that he acted corruptly . . . for he entered the temple of the Lord to burn incense on the altar of incense" (2 Chr 26:16).

Only descendants of Aaron could be priests in the temple. Twenty-four priestly divisions, each serving in a weekly rotation system, attended to the various duties. Of these thousands of priests, only one, taken by lot like Zechariah in Luke 1:9, was given the honor of burning the morning or evening daily incense. "The office of burning incense gave the priest to whom this important lot fell, the right of entering the holy place. It was the most coveted of all the priestly duties."[1] "For the first time in his life, and for the last, would this service devolve on him"[2] as the other priests would want an opportunity to enter the Holy Place once in their lifetime.

In his pride, Uzziah, wanting the privileges of a priest as well as that of a king, went into the temple to burn incense. He was opposed by Azariah the high priest. "It is not for you, Uzziah, to burn incense to the Lord, but for the priests . . . Get out of the sanctuary, for you have been unfaithful, and will have no honor from the Lord God" (2 Chr 26:18). The merciful Lord gave Uzziah a warning to spare him from the fate of Nadab and Abihu who were killed when they offered "strange fire before the Lord" (Lev 10:1).

1. Pulpit Commentary. http://biblehub.com/commentaries/luke/1–9.htm
2. Edersheim, *The Temple: Its Ministry and Services*, 129.

Thus, Uzziah could cut his losses and depart. Some judgment had already been pronounced at this stage (i.e., "unfaithful" and "will have no honor from the Lord"). Uzziah could also choose to persist in his folly. After all, wasn't he the all-powerful king of Judah? Who were those worthless priests who dared to oppose his royal will? Uzziah refused to leave and "was enraged with the priests" for opposing him. The Lord's punishment came swiftly as "leprosy broke out on his forehead" and he "hastened to get out" (2 Chr 26:19–20). He died a leper and was buried separately from the rest of the kings of Judah, lest his leprosy defiled their tombs.

GOD.

God was always faithful with his people. The Lord helped Uzziah against the Philistines, the Arabians, the Meunites, the Ammonites, "and his fame extended to the border of Egypt, for he became very strong" (2 Chr 26:8). However, his heart became proud and he willfully disobeyed God's strict commands concerning the incense offering. "Pride goes before destruction, and a haughty spirit before stumbling" (Prov 16:18). Warned by the Lord to desist, he stubbornly refused. Thus, he took the forbidden path that led to his destruction for which he only had himself to blame!

Chapter 41

The case of Hezekiah and God

HEZEKIAH.

HEZEKIAH WAS A GOOD king of Judah for "he did right in the sight of the Lord" (2 Chr 29:2). Therefore, the Lord delivered him from the Assyrians. Their besieging army was destroyed by an angel, and their king was murdered.

"In those days Hezekiah became mortally ill . . . 'Set your house in order, for you shall die and not live'" (2 Kgs 20:1). One should not take this pronouncement as God's irrevocable decree but rather as God's chosen option for Hezekiah. The alternative scenario was there *if the recommended path was rejected.* Unwisely, Hezekiah turned down God's choice for him, prayed (begged?) for a longer life, cited his past faithfulness, and "wept bitterly," preferring this fallen world to the heavenly realm.[1]

Thus, God gave him what he craved, fifteen more years of life. The sovereign Lord did not give the king other options (e.g., twenty or thirty more years). There were a *limited* number of choices within God's predetermined boundaries, in this case only two. "But Hezekiah gave no return for the benefit he received, because his heart was proud; therefore, wrath came on him and on Judah and Jerusalem" (2 Chr 32:25). After Hezekiah recovered from his illness, he received some envoys from Babylon. "The ostensible business of the embassy was to congratulate Hezekiah on his recovery . . . but the Assyrian records make it pretty clear that the real object was to ascertain the extent of Hezekiah's resources, and to secure

---

1. "If that which God himself chooses for you does not content you, from whom do you expect to obtain what you desire?" De Caussade, *Abandonment*, 11.

his alliance against the common enemy."[2] Hezekiah had a choice to make. He could trust the Lord, or he could rely on the Babylonians. "Do not trust in princes, in mortal man, in whom there is no salvation" (Ps 146:3). In his wisdom, "God left him, to try him, that he might know all that was in his heart" (2 Chr 32:31 KJV), "not that God might know, who knows all things . . . but rather that Hezekiah might know the pride lurking in his heart."[3]

Hezekiah chose to ally himself with Babylon. "There was nothing in his house nor in all his dominion that Hezekiah did not show them" (2 Kgs 20:13). The Lord's judgment was swift. "Behold, the days are coming when all that is in your house, and all that your fathers have laid up in store to this day will be carried to Babylon; nothing shall be left . . . Some of your sons who shall issue from you, whom you will beget, will be taken away; and they will become officials[4] in the palace of the king of Babylon" (2 Kgs 20:17–18). However, this decree did not prophesy that Judah would no longer exist as a nation as only *some* of the royal family would be taken captives.

Hezekiah could submit to the Lord's decision, and salvage what he could from God's dire pronouncement. Or he could strike back at God in anger and rebellion like his father Ahaz ("Now in the time of his distress this same King Ahaz became yet more unfaithful to the Lord" 2 Chr 28:22). Wisely, "Hezekiah humbled the pride of his heart, both he and the inhabitants of Jerusalem" (2 Chr 32:26a). In response to Hezekiah's repentance, the Lord granted a less onerous alternative within his preset confines. The decree that Judah would be conquered by Babylon could not be changed. However, Hezekiah obtained a reprieve, "that the wrath of the Lord did not come on them in the days of Hezekiah" (2 Chr 32:26b). Hezekiah meekly accepted his deserved punishment and was thankful (and probably relieved)[5] that the decreed disaster would not

2. Ellicott's Commentary for English Readers. http://biblehub.com/commentaries/2_kings/20–12.htm

3. Gill's Exposition of the Entire Bible. http://biblehub.com/commentaries/2_chronicles/32–31.htm

4. "Keil and Bahr translate 'sarisim' in this place by 'chamberlains' or 'footmen,' but there is no reason why the word should not have its ordinary sense of 'eunuchs.'" Pulpit Commentary. http://biblehub.com/commentaries/2_kings/20–18.htm

5. "While there is resignation, there is no doubt something also of selfishness, in Hezekiah's acceptance of the situation." Pulpit Commentary. http://biblehub.com/commentaries/Isa/39–8.htm

happen in his days.[6] Was Hezekiah's chosen scenario (i.e., live a little longer) better than God's recommended option? Is Man's demand for "free will" to make his decisions a good idea, or should he submit and pray that God's "will be done"?

GOD.

Learning of his imminent death, Hezekiah resisted the Lord and begged for a longer life. When the Israelites in the wilderness demanded meat, God "gave them their request; but sent leanness into their soul" (Ps 106:15 KJV). Likewise, at Hezekiah's insistence, the Lord reluctantly gave him what he wanted. However, the sovereign Lord's judgment for pride and unbelief came swiftly. In bitter irony, Judah was decreed to be given to the Babylonians, its supposed "friends" and allies. Everything shown to them in boastful pride would be taken away, including some of Hezekiah's descendants. What would be left there to boast about? Even repentance could not reverse God's decree. Hezekiah got a reprieve, not a cancellation of the punishment. This should serve as a warning to us not to resist God's will as declared in his Word!

---

6. "All that the passage fairly implies is, that he saw that it was right; and that it was proof of great mercy in God that the punishment was deferred." Barnes' Notes on the Bible. http://biblehub.com/commentaries/Isa/39-8.htm

Chapter 42

The case of Manasseh and God

MANASSEH.

MANASSEH SUCCEEDED HIS FATHER Hezekiah and "did evil in the sight of the Lord" (2 Chr 33:2). "He sacrificed his children in the fire in the Valley of Ben Hinnom, practiced divination and witchcraft, sought omens, and consulted mediums and spiritists" (2 Chr 33:6 NIV). "Then he set the carved image of Asherah that he had made in the house" of the Lord (2 Kgs 21:7). Furthermore, "Manasseh seduced them (Israel) to do evil more than the nations whom the Lord destroyed before the sons of Israel" (2 Kgs 21:9). In his mercy, the Lord gave Manasseh and Israel a warning. "The Lord spoke to Manasseh and his people" (2 Chr 33:10a). Manasseh could repent and turn from his wicked ways or he could ignore the Lord's rebuke and persist in his rebellion. Sadly, Manasseh and Israel "paid no attention" to the Lord's admonitions (2 Chr 33:10b).

The Lord's judgment came without further warning. "Behold, I am bringing such calamity on Jerusalem and Judah, that whoever hears of it, both his ears will tingle . . . I will wipe Jerusalem as one wipes a dish, wiping it and turning it upside down. I will abandon the remnant of my inheritance" (2 Kgs 21:12–14). This pronouncement shared a common aspect with the one previously given to Hezekiah. Judah would be plundered by the Babylonians. This edict also increased the sanctions because of the added sins of Manasseh. Judah would *cease to exist as a nation*. This calamity would be so disastrous that "ears will tingle" on hearing the dreaded account. However, the annihilation of Judah could not happen until the time of Josiah at the earliest, due to a prophecy given two hundred and fifty years before. "Behold, a son shall be born to the house of David, Josiah by name" (1 Kgs 13:2).

In his great mercy, the Lord gave Manasseh another opportunity to repent. "Therefore, the Lord brought the commanders of the army of the king of Assyria against them, and they captured Manasseh with hooks, bound him with bronze chains and took him to Babylon" (2 Chr 33:11). In hooks and chains, Manasseh could humble himself, repent, and salvage something out of this disaster, or he could "curse God and die" (Job 2:9) as a prisoner in Babylon. To his credit, Manasseh finally learned his lesson and chose the better option. In this case, the Lord's discipline fulfilled its desired purpose of rehabilitating the wayward king. "When he was in distress, he entreated the Lord his God and humbled himself greatly before the God of his fathers" (2 Chr 33:12). Like Hezekiah, Manasseh was shown mercy, had a reprieve from the decreed punishment, and was restored to the throne (2 Chr 33:13). However, the die was cast, and the nation was irrevocably doomed!

GOD.

As a righteous Lord, God took pains to give his people fair warnings to heed his counsel. When Manasseh foolishly persisted in his disobedience, the Lord was forced to decree a just punishment. Even so, the merciful God still provided "a way of escape," an opportunity for Manasseh to repent. Mistakes might not necessarily be final. Contrition, however late, was still better than continued disobedience. The Lord, in response to repentance, might "make up to you for the years that the swarming locust has eaten" (Joel 2:25). Despite his heinous sins ("more evil than the Amorites who preceded him" 2 Kgs 21:11 NIV), when Manasseh repented, God graciously restored him to the throne where he reigned for fifty-five years, the longest in the history of Judah, died in peace, and was succeeded by his son Amon.

Chapter 43

The case of Josiah and God

JOSIAH.

IN ACCORDANCE WITH THE prophecy given concerning Josiah, the decreed punishments of Hezekiah and Manasseh did not happen in the time of Amon. He "did evil in the sight of the Lord" (2 Kgs 21:20) and was murdered by his servants after only two years on the throne. His son "Josiah was eight years old when he became king" (2 Kgs 22:1).

The new king had a decision to make. Should he follow in the footsteps of his father or should he obey the Lord his God? Wisely, Josiah chose to do "right in the sight of the Lord and walked in all the way of his father David" (2 Kgs 22:2). He purged Judah of the high places, eradicated the shrines, and repaired the temple of the Lord. He then tore down "the altar that was at Bethel and the high place which Jeroboam the son of Nebat, who made Israel sin, had made" (2 Kgs 23:15). "He sent and took the bones from the graves and burned them on the altar and defiled it according to the word of the Lord" (2 Kgs 23:16). Josiah then celebrated a lavish Passover in Jerusalem. "Before him, there was no king like him who turned to the Lord with all his heart and with all his soul and with all his might, according to all the law of Moses; nor did any like him arise after him" (2 Kgs 23:25).

Considering Josiah's exemplary faithfulness, did the Lord change his mind and countermand the decreed disasters? "The Lord did not turn from the fierceness of his great wrath with which his anger burned against Judah, because of all the provocations with which Manasseh had provoked him" (2 Kgs 23:26). Thus, a decree, once pronounced, was irrevocable. However, Josiah got a reprieve from the prophesied calamities.

"Because your heart was tender, and you humbled yourself . . . you shall be gathered to your grave in peace, so your eyes will not see all the evil which I will bring on this place and on its inhabitants" (2 Chr 34:27–28).

"After all this . . . Neco king of Egypt came up to make war at Carchemish on the Euphrates, and Josiah went out to engage him" (2 Chr 35:20). Pharaoh Neco II was marching north to give aid to the Assyrian king Ashur-Uballit II against the Babylonians.[1] "Josiah went out against him; or to meet him, and stop him from going through his land, which lay between Egypt and Syria."[2] "But Neco sent messengers to him, saying, "What have we to do with each other, O King of Judah? I am not coming against you today but against the house with which I am at war, and God has ordered me to hurry. Stop for your own sake from interfering with God who is with me, so that he will not destroy you" (2 Chr 35:21). Was Neco telling the truth? Should Josiah ask the Lord about Neco's claim? Or should he go to war despite what Neco had said?

Josiah chose not to inquire of the Lord and "would not turn away from him (Neco)" (2 Chr 35:22), "being, peradventure, encouraged to go out against him by a misinterpretation of that promise made to him."[3] The Lord's prophecy that Josiah would die "in peace" only meant that he received a reprieve, not that he would be invulnerable in battle. In any case, he took precautions "and disguised himself" (2 Chr 35:22). The consequences for not asking the Lord's counsel came swiftly. At the battle of Megiddo, Pharaoh's archers shot Josiah despite his concealment, for he did not "listen to the words of Neco from the mouth of God" (2 Chr 35:22). Thus "he died and was buried in the tombs of his fathers" (2 Chr 35:24).

Josiah was warned not to go to battle. Had he doubted Pharaoh's words, he could have sought a confirmation from the Lord. He unwisely chose to ignore the warning and went to war against Egypt (and against God). Thus, he was fully responsible for his disobedience and untimely death!

1. Horn, "The Babylonian Chronicle," 12–27.

2. Gill's Exposition of the Entire Bible. http://biblehub.com/commentaries/2 _chronicles/35-20.htm

3. Benson Commentary. http://biblehub.com/commentaries/2_chronicles/ 35-22.htm

GOD.

The Lord was gracious to Josiah and gave him a reprieve. Nevertheless, God did not "change his mind" and revoke his decrees. Furthermore, past performances never guaranteed future results. When Josiah disregarded God's warning, the Lord had to discipline him. Due to his poor free will choice, Josiah died of his arrow wounds at the young age of thirty-nine. Was that punishment much too harsh for one mistake? "From everyone who has been given much, much will be required" (Luke 12:48). Was Josiah given much? Therefore, much was expected of him, as of Moses (no entrance to the Promised Land due to the one rebellious act of striking the rock), and of Hezekiah (everything in Hezekiah's house would be taken away, including some of his descendants for some boastful pride). Obedience and faithfulness are always required of the people of God!

Chapter 44

The case of Jehoiakim and God

JEHOIAKIM.

JOSIAH DIED FROM HIS arrow wounds in 609 BC[1] and was replaced by his son Jehoahaz who only reigned three months before he was deposed by Pharaoh Neco and replaced by Jehoiakim, Jehoahaz's older brother. Like his forebears before him, Jehoiakim was given a free will choice by the sovereign Lord. He could follow the good example of his father Josiah or he could forsake his God. "He (Jehoiakim) did evil in the sight of the Lord" (2 Kgs 23:37). Jehoiakim became a vassal of Egypt and "gave the silver and gold to Pharaoh, but he taxed the land in order to give the money" (2 Kgs 23:35). However, the Egyptians were soon defeated by the Babylonians at the battle of Carchemish in 605 BC,[2] clearing the way for Babylon to conquer Judah.

"In the third year of the reign of Jehoiakim king of Judah, Nebuchadnezzar king of Babylon came to Jerusalem and besieged it. The Lord gave Jehoiakim king of Judah into his hand, along with some of the vessels of the house of God . . . including some of the royal family" (Dan 1:1–3). "Now among these there were four of the family of Zedekiah, of most excellent dispositions, one of whom was called Daniel, another was called Ananias, another Misael, and the fourth Azarias."[3] Thus, the decree of the Lord given in the time of Hezekiah (about eighty years earlier) was fulfilled. Furthermore, Nebuchadnezzar "bound him (Jehoiakim) with bronze chains to take him to Babylon" (2 Chr 36:6). "But he did not

---

1. www.britannica.com/biography/Josiah

2. www.britannica.com/topic/Battle-of-Carchemish

3. Josephus, *Antiquities of the Jews,* Book 10, section 186.

carry him thither, for Nebuchadnezzar altered his mind, and permitted him to reign at Jerusalem as his tributary,"[4] a vassal king in Judah.[5]

"In the fourth year of Jehoiakim," Jeremiah was instructed by God to "take a scroll and write on it all the words which I have spoken to you concerning Israel and concerning Judah . . . Perhaps the house of Judah will hear all the calamity which I plan to bring on them, in order that every man will turn from his evil way; then I will forgive their iniquity and their sin" (Jer 36:1–3). Thus, the merciful Lord gave his people another opportunity to repent. A reprieve could be obtained with heartfelt repentance. Baruch, Jeremiah's scribe, "read from the book the words of Jeremiah . . . to all the people" (Jer 36:10). "Jehudi read it to the king as well as to all the officials who stood beside the king" (Jer 36:21). "When Jehudi had read three or four columns, the king cut it with a scribe's knife and threw it into the fire that was in the brazier, until all the scroll was consumed in the fire that was in the brazier. Yet the king and all his servants who heard all these words were not afraid, nor did they rend their garments . . . And the king commanded Jerahmeel the king's son . . . to seize Baruch the scribe and Jeremiah the prophet, but the Lord hid them" (Jer 36:23–26).

The Lord's punishment came swiftly. "He (Jehoiakim) shall have no one to sit on the throne of David, and his dead body shall be cast out to the heat of the day and the frost of the night" (Jer 36:30). Besides what had already been pronounced in the previous decrees against Hezekiah and Manasseh, the Lord added further judgments against Jehoiakim for desecrating his Word. Jehoiakim's kingly line of succession would end.[6] Jehoiakim would die and his body would be left uncollected in the open field. "The Lord sent against him bands of Chaldeans, bands of Arameans, bands of Moabites, and bands of Ammonites. So, he sent them against Judah to destroy it" (2 Kgs 24:2). "Either in an engagement with some of these forces or else by the hand of his own oppressed subjects, Jehoiakim came to a violent end . . . His body was cast out ignominiously

---

4. Benson Commentary. http://biblehub.com/commentaries/2_chronicles/36–6.htm

5. From 2 Kings 24:1, it appears that Jehoiakim rebelled three years later.

6. Since Solomon forfeited the Lord's promise of "a forever throne," Jehoiakim, Solomon's descendant, could be dispossessed by the Lord.

on the ground, and then was dragged away and buried 'with the burial of an ass,'"[7] in other words, unburied.[8]

In God's mercy, Jehoiakim was given many opportunities to repent, yet he persisted in his destructive behavior, showing contempt for the Lord by burning his Word and trying to harm his envoys. His shameful death was well deserved, and he had only himself to blame!

GOD.

Jehoiakim was free to follow his father Josiah's good example or stray away from the right path. He foolishly chose to do evil. The Lord had to discipline him by delivering him to Nebuchadnezzar. Yet, the merciful Lord still endeavored to call the nation to penance and contrition through the warnings in Jeremiah's scroll. When his Word was burned, God rightfully decreed Jehoiakim's shameful death, as no further opportunity was given for repentance!

7. Smith's Bible Dictionary. http://biblehub.com/topical/j/jehoiakim.htm

8. Pulpit Commentary. http://biblehub.com/commentaries/jeremiah/22–19.htm

Chapter 45

The case of Jehoiachin and God

JEHOIACHIN /JECONIAH.

JEHOIAKIM WAS SUCCEEDED BY his son Jehoiachin who "was eighteen years old when he became king" (2 Kgs 24:8). 2 Chronicles 36:9 stated: "Jehoiachin was eight years old when he became king." This discrepancy is most likely due to a scribal error.[1] Even though Jehoiakim had rebelled against Babylon, "Nebuchadnezzar did not promptly march against Jehoiakim to suppress his rebellion."[2] As the new king, Jehoiachin could follow his father's footsteps into disaster or he could repent and turn to the Lord for help against Babylon. He made his choice and "did evil in the sight of the Lord" (2 Kgs 24:9).

God's pronouncement against him came swiftly. "Even though Coniah the son of Jehoiakim king of Judah were a signet ring on my right hand, yet I would pull you off; and I will give you over . . . into the hand of Nebuchadnezzar . . . I will hurl you and your mother who bore you into another country where you were not born, and there you will die" (Jer 22:24–26). Not surprisingly, "the king of Egypt did not come out of his land again, for the king of Babylon had taken all that belonged to the king of Egypt" (2 Kgs 24:7). Thus, Jehoiachin was left without a key ally.

---

1. Critchlow, *Looking Back for Jehoiachin*, 12–13.

2. Pulpit Commentary. http://biblehub.com/commentaries/2_kings/24–2.htm

"And Nebuchadnezzar the king of Babylon came to the city, while his servants were besieging it. Jehoiachin the king of Judah went out to the king of Babylon, he and his mother and his servants and his captains and his officials. So, the king of Babylon took him captive in the eighth year of his reign" (2 Kgs 24:11–12). Jerusalem and the temple were not burned since Jehoiachin had surrendered peacefully.

The prophecies given to Hezekiah, Jehoiakim, and Jehoiachin were all fulfilled. "Though Jehoiachin his son succeeded him (Jehoiakim), yet because he reigned but three months, it was esteemed as no reign."[3] Since the Lord had already decreed that Jehoiakim "shall have no one to sit on the throne of David" (Jer 36:30), the reign of Jehoiachin could not be long no matter what he decided.[4] One could speculate that had Jehoiachin chosen to follow the Lord, he could have been given an early peaceful death and been buried in honor, like Jeroboam's unnamed child in 1 Kings 14:13. "All Israel shall mourn for him and bury him, for he alone of Jeroboam's family will come to the grave, because in him something good was found toward the Lord God." Instead, due to his rebellion against the Lord, Jehoiachin died as a captive in Babylon and was not buried with his ancestors.

Furthermore, as a punishment for all the perpetrated evils (and to reaffirm what he had previously decreed to Jehoiakim), the Lord declared concerning Jehoiachin, "'Write this man down childless, a man who will not prosper in his days; for no man of his descendants will prosper sitting on the throne of David or ruling again in Judah'" (Jer 22:30). Since Jehoiachin/Jeconiah was in the genealogy of Jesus (Matt 1:11–12), how could Christ inherit David's throne? As it turned out, Jesus was *not* in the *physical* lineage of Jeconiah. He was instead a descendant of Nathan, David's other son (Luke 3:31). "Matthew gives the legal pedigree through Solomon down to Joseph; Luke the real pedigree, from Mary, the real parent, through Nathan, brother of Solomon."[5] Thus, the Israelites would be satisfied that Jesus had a right to the throne of David (through Solomon down to Joseph in Matthew's genealogy) as kingship could only be transferred through the male line (by adoption as in the case of Joseph

---

3. Geneva Study Bible. http://biblehub.com/commentaries/Jer/36–30.htm

4. The Lord's punishment of a father (e.g., Jehoiakim) obviously has consequences for a son (e.g., Jehoiachin). Our actions cause repercussions on those around us.

5. Jamieson-Fausset-Brown Bible Commentary. http://biblehub.com/commentaries/Jer/22–30.htm

and Jesus).[6] The Lord's decree would also stand as Jesus was not in the blood line of Jeconiah and Jehoiakim.

In his mercy, the Lord lightened Jehoiachin's punishment in Babylon. "Now it came about . . . that Evil-merodach king of Babylon, in the year that he became king, released Jehoiachin king of Judah from prison; and he spoke kindly to him and set his throne above the throne of the kings who were with him in Babylon. Jehoiachin changed his prison clothes and had his meals in the king's presence regularly all the days of his life" (2 Kgs 25:27–29). Nevertheless, the Lord's decree was irrevocable for Jehoiachin died in exile in Babylon.[7]

GOD.

God, in his wisdom, allowed Jehoiachin to select his own path. Since reprieves were given to Hezekiah, Manasseh, and Josiah, a less onerous scenario could have been available for Jehoiachin had he decided to follow the Lord his God. Sadly, Jehoiachin chose the evil way and was therefore totally responsible for his disastrous outcome. Even so, the Lord was still gracious to him for, after thirty-seven years as a captive, he was released from prison and treated kindly by the Babylonian king. Nevertheless, as decreed by the Lord, he could not go home and be buried with his fathers in the tombs of the kings of Judah.

6. "'Is not this Jesus, the son of Joseph,' John 6:42. Jesus must have been adopted by Joseph. Such an adoption with full inheritance rights can be found in Gen 48:5. 'Ephraim and Manasseh . . . are mine; as Reuben and Simeon, they shall be mine,' which indicates that the writer was probably acquainted with adoption in the legal sense, such as would give to the chosen children the right of inheriting from the person adopting them; for the obvious intent of the passage is to account for the establishment of two tribes, Ephraim and Manasseh, with distinct territories, on an equality with the tribes claiming descent from Jacob's sons." Dembitz and Kohler, "Adoption," lines 59–63.

7. International Standard Bible Encyclopedia. http://biblehub.com/topical/j/jehoiachin.htm

Chapter 46

The case of Zedekiah and God

ZEDEKIAH.

WHEN JEHOIACHIN WAS TAKEN captive in 597 BC,[1] "the king of Babylon made his uncle Mattaniah king in his place and changed his name to Zedekiah" (2 Kgs 24:17). Nebuchadnezzar "made a covenant with him, putting him under oath" (Ezek 17:13) and "made him swear allegiance by God" (2 Chr 36:13). Thus, the prophecy of the Lord was fulfilled. No descendant of Jehoiachin and Jehoiakim ever sat on the throne of Judah again.

Zedekiah was urged to submit to Nebuchadnezzar. "It will be, that the nation or the kingdom which will not serve him, Nebuchadnezzar . . . I will punish that nation with the sword, with famine and with pestilence" (Jer 27:8). However, in 594 BC, the false prophet Hananiah declared, "Thus says the Lord of hosts, the God of Israel, 'I have broken the yoke of the king of Babylon. Within two years I am going to bring back to this place all the vessels of the Lord's house, which Nebuchadnezzar king of Babylon took away from this place and carried to Babylon. I am also going to bring back to this place Jeconiah the son of Jehoiakim, king of Judah, and all the exiles of Judah who went to Babylon'" (Jer 28:2–4). "Then Jeremiah the prophet said to Hananiah . . . 'the Lord has not sent you, and you have made this people trust in a lie.' Therefore, thus says the Lord, 'Behold, I am about to remove you from the face of the earth. This year you are going to die, because you have counseled rebellion against the Lord.' So Hananiah the prophet died in the same year in the seventh month" (Jer 28:15–17). Sadly, Zedekiah chose to listen to the dead

---

1. The dates are taken from http://nabataea.net/jeremiah.html

Hananiah rather than to the living God. "The beginning of Zedekiah's reign was memorable for the gathering at Jerusalem of ambassadors from the kings of Edom, Moab, Ammon, Tyre, and Zidon, obviously for the purpose of forming a confederacy against Nebuchadnezzar."[2]

In 594 BC, Zedekiah went to Babylon. "It is probable that Nebuchadnezzar summoned the king of Judah to Babylon to question him as to this scheme (rebellious confederacy), and to demand an act of renewed homage."[3] Jeremiah sent along a scroll prophesying the future judgment of Babylon (Jer 51:60). Later, two envoys carried a letter from Jeremiah to the captives in Babylon, encouraging them to "seek the welfare of the city where I have sent you in exile," promising them a return to the land after "seventy years," and warning them against false prophets (Jer 29:7–10).

Undeterred by the summon to appear before Nebuchadnezzar, Zedekiah proceeded with his rebellious plans, "sending his envoys to Egypt that they might give him horses and many troops" (Ezek 17:15). "He stiffened his neck and hardened his heart against turning to the Lord God of Israel. Furthermore, all the officials of the priests and the people were very unfaithful following all the abominations of the nations . . . the God of their fathers sent word to them again and again by his messengers . . . but they continually mocked the messengers of God, despised his Word and scoffed at his prophets, until the wrath of the Lord arose against his people, until there was no remedy" (2 Chr 36:13–16).

At long last, the Lord's judgment came. "As I live, surely my oath which he despised and my covenant which he broke, I will inflict on his head . . . Then I will bring him to Babylon and enter into judgment with him there . . . All the choice men in all his troops will fall by the sword, and the survivors will be scattered to every wind" (Ezek 17:19–21). God pronounced through the prophet Ezekiel in exile in Babylon that Judah's army would be destroyed, and Zedekiah would die in Babylon.

In 589 BC, "Nebuchadnezzar king of Babylon came, he and all his army, against Jerusalem, camped against it and built a siege wall all around it" (2 Kgs 25:1). In great distress, Zedekiah called on Jeremiah to intercede with God. "Please inquire of the Lord on our behalf, for Nebuchadnezzar king of Babylon is warring against us; perhaps the Lord will deal with us according to all his wonderful acts, so that the enemy will

2. Ellicott's Commentary for English Readers. http://biblehub.com/commentaries/Jer/51–59.htm

3. Ellicott's Commentary for English Readers. http://biblehub.com/commentaries/Jer/51–59.htm

withdraw from us" (Jer 21:2). However, God declared: "I will give over Zedekiah king of Judah and his servants and the people, even those who survive in this city from the pestilence, the sword and the famine, into the hand of Nebuchadnezzar king of Babylon" (Jer 21:7). Nevertheless, the merciful Lord still provided a "way of escape" for Judah. "Behold, I set before you the way of life and the way of death. He who dwells in this city will die by the sword and by famine and by pestilence; but he who goes out and falls away to the Chaldeans who are besieging you will live" (Jer 21:8–9). The way of life, for the people as well as for the royal family, would be an unconditional surrender to the Babylonians. Any resistance would lead to the way of death.

Later, Jeremiah went again to Zedekiah with further words from God. "You will see the king of Babylon eye to eye, and he will speak with you face to face, and you will go to Babylon . . . You will not die by the sword" (Jer 34:3–4). Probably to encourage Zedekiah to surrender, the Lord decreed that the king would be able to see Nebuchadnezzar face to face and that he would die in peace in Babylon. Jerusalem would fall but Zedekiah would survive. However, God did not promise that Zedekiah's eyesight would be preserved.

"And I shall bring him (Zedekiah) to Babylon in the land of the Chaldeans; yet *he will not see it*, though he will die there" (Ezek 12:13). If this prophecy was given early, then whether Zedekiah surrendered or not, the punishment for rebellion would still entail the loss of his eyesight. If this prophecy was given after he had made the decision to ignore God's advice, then the loss of his eyes could be the further result of his stubborn disobedience. Yet God's decree to spare his life would stand. No matter what he decided, he would not be killed.

Zedekiah foolishly chose to wait for rescue from Egypt. As the siege went on, he "made a covenant with all the people who were in Jerusalem to proclaim release to them: that each man should set free his male servant and each man his female servant . . . And all the officials and all the people obeyed . . . and set them free" (Jer 34:8–10). "The step was probably not without its influence in giving fresh energy to the defenders of the city"[4] as free people had much more to lose than slaves. Freed slaves would defend the city with vigor as they would not want to be re-enslaved by the victorious Babylonians.

---

4. Ellicott's Commentary for English Readers. http://biblehub.com/commentaries/Jer/34-8.htm

Meanwhile, Pharaoh's army had set out from Egypt to fight Nebu-chadnezzar. When the Babylonians heard about the attempted rescue, they lifted the blockade. Zedekiah then beseeched Jeremiah, "Please pray to the Lord our God on our behalf" (Jer 37:3). "This petition to the prophet was to pray that the king of Egypt . . . get the victory over the Chaldean army . . . Thus, wicked men will desire the prayers of good men in times of distress, when their words, their cautions, admonitions, exhortations, and prayers too, are despised by them at another time."[5] The Lord's answer was swift. "Behold, Pharaoh's army which has come out for your assistance is going to return to its own land of Egypt. The Chaldeans will also return and fight against this city, and they will capture it and burn it with fire" (Jer 37:7–8). The Lord again reiterated that resistance was futile and could only bring more death and destruction.

With the siege temporarily lifted, the slave owners "took back the male servants and the female servants whom they had set free" (Jer 34:11). God was not pleased with that decision. "You have not obeyed me in proclaiming release each man to his brother and each man to his neighbor. Behold, I am proclaiming a release to you, declares the Lord, to the sword, to the pestilence and to the famine" (Jer 34:17). "I will bring them back to this city; and they will fight against it and take it and burn it with fire" (Jer 34:22).

Aware of the impending doom, Jeremiah tried to leave the city but was thrown in jail for desertion. "Now King Zedekiah sent and took him out; and in his palace the king secretly asked him and said, 'Is there a word from the Lord?' And Jeremiah said, 'There is!' Then he said, 'You will be given into the hand of the king of Babylon!'" (Jer 37:17), meaning that the Egyptian rescue mission would surely fail. Zedekiah was given a chance to voluntarily surrender on reasonably good terms since the Babylonians were not besieging the city and might be willing to be more magnanimous with their demands. Unfortunately, hoping for an Egyptian victory, Zedekiah again refused to submit.

However, Pharaoh soon withdrew, and the Babylonians resumed the siege in 587 BC. Jeremiah declared to the people: "He who stays in this city will die by the sword and by famine and by pestilence, but he who goes out to the Chaldeans will live and have his own life as booty and stay alive'" (Jer 38:2). The same two options were offered to anyone willing to listen and obey. As a punishment for undermining Israel's war

5. Gill's Exposition of the Entire Bible. http://biblehub.com/commentaries/Jer/37-3.htm

effort by counseling an unconditional surrender, Jeremiah was thrown into a dry cistern to die.

With no hope of rescue, Zedekiah had Jeremiah brought to him in secret. "Then Jeremiah said to Zedekiah . . . 'If you will indeed go out to the officers of the king of Babylon, then you will live, this city will not be burned with fire, and you and your household will survive. But if you will not go out to the officers of the king of Babylon, then this city will be given over to the hand of the Chaldeans; and they will burn it with fire, and you yourself will not escape from their hand'" (Jer 38:17–18). Even at this very late date, in the Lord's mercy, the same two options were still offered. If the Israelites submitted to the Babylonians, they would live, and the city would not be burned. Otherwise, death and destruction would await, except for Zedekiah who had been promised life.

"Then King Zedekiah said to Jeremiah, 'I dread the Jews who have gone over to the Chaldeans, for they may give me over into their hand and they will abuse me.' But Jeremiah said, 'They will not give you over. Please obey the Lord in what I am saying to you, that it may go well with you and you may live'" (Jer 38:19–20). Since some Israelites had already capitulated, the king was worried that they might do him harm, blaming him for the disaster. Jeremiah reiterated that the king would be safe if he obeyed and surrendered.

Despite all the admonitions, Zedekiah foolishly chose to continue the fight. In 586 BC, the Babylonians captured him and killed his sons "before his eyes, then put out the eyes of Zedekiah" (2 Kgs 25:7). "Then they burned the house of God and broke down the wall of Jerusalem and burned all its fortified buildings with fire and destroyed all its valuable articles" (2 Chr 36:19). The prophecy given to Manasseh sixty years earlier was fulfilled as Judah was erased as a nation.

The better option for Zedekiah and the nation also vanished. Although Judah's fall was inevitable, the death of many Jews including Zedekiah's sons, and the destruction of the city could have been avoided. "The ark, containing the two tables of the law, disappeared at the Babylonian captivity, and was not restored to the second temple."[6] All the prophecies of the Lord were fulfilled. Zedekiah's life was spared. He did

---

6. Jamieson-Fausset-Brown Bible Commentary. http://biblehub.com/commentaries/Jer/3–16.htm. What would have happened had Zedekiah surrendered? God's "way of life" prophesied the preservation of Jerusalem, its temple, and the survival of Zedekiah's sons (Jer 38:17). Zedekiah and Judah were not "doomed" to take the "way of death."

see Nebuchadnezzar "face to face," eye to eye before they took out his eyes. The people who surrendered lived and those who did not, perished. The city and its temple were ransacked and burned. Obedience brought blessings and disobedience brought curses!

GOD.

God gave Zedekiah and Judah many opportunities to repent. Jeremiah, the Lord's prophet, remained with them through the whole siege, endeavoring to change their minds, to no avail. Ezekiel prophesied to them from Babylon, also without success. In response to his repeated warnings, the Jews threw Jeremiah in jail. When the seer faithfully persisted in proclaiming the truth, they condemned him to death by casting him into a dry cistern. Nevertheless, the long-suffering Lord still endeavored to help them by holding out the two options, the way of life and the way of death, until the final moment. Due to their stubborn disobedience, Zedekiah and Judah only had themselves to blame for the loss of their beloved Promised Land!

Chapter 47

The case of Jonah, Nineveh, and God

JONAH.

"THE WORD OF THE Lord came to Jonah the son of Amittai saying, Arise, go to Nineveh the great city and cry against it" (Jonah 1:1–2). In God's sovereignty, Jonah was given some free will choices, albeit within God's strict confines (i.e., Jonah must go to Nineveh, more or less willingly), limits much stricter than those given to others (e.g., Zedekiah). Jonah could obey and go as ordered. He could stay wherever he was and see what the Lord would do. He could bargain with God and delay his departure. He could suggest that the Lord would be better off sending someone else to Nineveh (a more willing and better qualified messenger like his contemporary prophets Hosea and Amos?). He could also run far away from God and hopefully escape.

Jonah chose the last option. "So, he went down to Joppa, found a ship which was going to Tarshish, paid the fare and went down into it to go with them to Tarshish from the presence of the Lord" (Jonah 1:3). Of course, Tarshish, a sea destination, was nowhere near Nineveh, the modern city of Mosul, Iraq. However, "the Lord hurled a great wind on the sea and there was a great storm on the sea so that the ship was about to break up. Then the sailors became afraid and every man cried to his god, and they threw the cargo which was in the ship into the sea to lighten it for them" (Jonah 1:4–5a).

According to the Jewish commentator Ibn Ezra, Jonah was not asleep before the storm. "Jonah goes to sleep in order to hide 'from the danger of the sea and his (God's) anger.'"[1] This was a more likely explanation than

---

1. Bob, *Jonah and the Meaning of Our Lives*, 38.

the scenario of Jonah blissfully sleeping in the cargo hold, completely oblivious to the thunderous storm, the howling winds, the loud cries of the terrified sailors in the foundering ship, and the tumultuous stampede of people frantically running in and out of the cargo hold to throw the merchandise overboard! If Ibn Ezra was correct, the sovereign Lord gave Jonah another free will choice with the arrival of the storm. He could repent, confess his sin of disobedience, beg the Lord to calm the seas and save the lives on the ship. He could also bury his head in the sand, persist in his rebellion, and go to sleep. "But Jonah had gone below into the hold of the ship, lain down and fallen sound asleep" (Jonah 1:5b). This unconcerned attitude would explain the captain's sharp reproof: "How is it that you are sleeping? Get up, call on your god" (Jonah 1:6). "It is an exclamation of indignant surprise at the unreasonableness of Jonah's conduct."[2]

We do not know whether Jonah prayed to God or not. In any case, the storm was not abating and the sailors perceived "something very uncommon and extraordinary in the tempest, and all means, both natural and religious, failing to help them . . . they supposed there must be some . . . notorious sinner among them, that had committed some very enormous crime, which had drawn the divine resentment upon them to such a degree."[3] Therefore, "each man said to his mate, 'Come, let us cast lots so we may learn on whose account this calamity has struck us'" (Jonah 1:7a). Jonah could confess that he was the culprit responsible for the disaster befalling his shipmates or he could stand by and wait for the verdict. In a scene reminiscent of Achan being unmasked (Josh 7:16–18), he kept silent until the "lot fell on" him (Jonah 1:7b). Being fingered as the culprit, he could admit his sins, acknowledge his responsibility, and make amends (e.g., leave the ship to save his shipmates). Or he could claim that the lot divination was faulty and blame the storm on someone else! Belatedly, Jonah owned up to his mistakes. "Pick me up and throw me into the sea. Then the sea will become calm for you, for I know that on account of me this great storm has come upon you" (Jonah 1:12). In his mercy, "the Lord appointed a great fish to swallow Jonah" (Jonah 1:17), saving him from drowning. After three days and three nights in the stomach of the fish (prefiguring the death and burial of Jesus, Matt 12:40), "it vomited Jonah up onto the dry land" (Jonah 2:10).

2. Cambridge Bible for Schools and Colleges. http://biblehub.com/commentaries/jonah/1–6.htm

3. Gill's Exposition of the Entire Bible. http://biblehub.com/commentaries/jonah/1–7.htm

"Now the word of the Lord came to Jonah the second time, saying, 'Arise, go to Nineveh the great city and proclaim to it the proclamation which I am going to tell you'" (Jonah 3:1–2). Did Jonah learn his lesson? This time, he decided to go "to Nineveh according to the word of the Lord" (Jonah 3:3). One could quibble whether Jonah made his choice "freely" considering the Lord's strong "pressure" tactics. Nevertheless, Jonah could possibly choose not to go to Nineveh, if he was willing to pay the price (e.g., another extended "cruise" in the belly of the fish)!

Jonah proclaimed God's message and Nineveh repented. He could rejoice that his ministry was successful, or he could be resentful as he really did not want Nineveh to escape God's wrath. Unwisely, Jonah chose to be angry. "Please Lord, was not this what I said while I was still in my own country? Therefore, in order to forestall this, I fled to Tarshish, for I knew that you are a gracious and compassionate God, slow to anger and abundant in lovingkindness, and one who relents concerning calamity" (Jonah 4:2).

Thus, the Lord had to teach him a lesson about compassion. God provided a shrub to shade Jonah from the sun. Then, he appointed a worm to kill the plant. This loss of cover made Jonah angry. "Then the Lord said, 'You had compassion on the plant for which you did not work and which you did not cause to grow, which came up overnight and perished overnight. Should I not have compassion on Nineveh, the great city in which there are more than one hundred twenty thousand persons who do not know the difference between their right and left hand, as well as many animals?'" (Jonah 4:10–11).

Jonah was given free will to decide among God's given options. He made some unwise decisions and had to live with the consequences. By setting strict boundaries, the Lord carried out his sovereign will to give the Ninevites a fair warning, in the hope of bringing them to repentance and avoiding the destruction of one hundred twenty thousand innocent children.[4]

---

4. "This number of infants, 120,000, according to the usual reckoning, gives a population of 600,000." Ellicott's Commentary for English Readers. http://biblehub.com/commentaries/jonah/4–11.htm

NINEVEH.

"Arise, go to Nineveh the great city and cry against it, for their wickedness has come up before me" (Jonah 1:2). The depravity of Nineveh was legendary. "The head of the Elamite king was struck off and later brought to Ashurbanipal[5] as he banqueted with his queen in the palace gardens, whereupon the head was raised on a pole in front of the guests later to be fixed over the gate of Nineveh to rot away. Dananu, the famous Elamite general, was flayed alive and then bled like a lamb; his brother, perhaps more fortunate, had his throat cut before his body was chopped into pieces for distribution as souvenirs throughout the land."[6]

"So, Jonah arose and went to Nineveh according to the word of the Lord. Now Nineveh was an exceedingly great city, a three days' walk. Then Jonah began to go through the city one day's walk; and he cried out and said, 'Yet forty days and Nineveh will be overthrown.'" (Jonah 3:3–4). If Nineveh persisted in its evil ways, the city would be destroyed in forty days. If it repented, mercy might be given. No clear promise was made, but since a warning was given, repentance might bring a reprieve. "Then the people of Nineveh believed in God; and they called a fast and put on sackcloth from the greatest to the least of them. When the word reached the king of Nineveh, he arose from his throne, laid aside his robe from him, covered himself with sackcloth and sat on the ashes." (Jonah 3:5–6).

The fact that Jonah only preached in a third of the city (one day's walk) "enhances the idea of the impressibility of the Ninevites, and their readiness to believe and repent . . . while the preacher himself was seen and heard in only a portion of the vast city, his message was taken up and repeated, and sped and bore fruit rapidly in every direction, till tidings of what was happening came to the king himself."[7] Nineveh wisely chose the better alternative. In his compassion, the Lord granted them a reprieve (Nineveh was not destroyed until 612 BC,[8] about one hundred fifty years later). God did not "change his mind" about Nineveh's destruction. The

---

5. "Ashurbanipal (Akkadian: Assur-bani-apli; 685 B.C.E. – 627 B.C.E.), was the last great king of ancient Assyria . . . Ashurbanipal created the first known systematically collected library at Nineveh." http://www.newworldencyclopedia.org/entry/Ashurbanipal

6. Simons, *Iraq from Sumer to Saddam*, 127.

7. Cambridge Bible for Schools and Colleges. http://biblehub.com/commentaries/jonah/3-4.htm

8. http://www.bible-history.com/biblestudy/nineveh.html

option of repentance was always there as shown by Jonah's proclamation and warning.

GOD.

God was gracious and merciful to both Jonah and Nineveh. Despite their sins and mistakes, the Lord patiently gave them ways of escape and opportunities to repent. Jonah and Nineveh freely chose their paths and had to live with the consequences, whether good or evil.

In summary, the evidence from the Old Testament supports the premise that the Lord, in his sovereignty, gives Man free will choices within his predetermined boundaries. Man can make his decisions and is thus fully responsible for his actions, especially if he ignores God's counsel. Obviously, once Man has selected a path, the other possible scenarios disappear. However, in God's mercy, future options may be given so that mistakes, if made, would not be final. Let us now go to the New Testament and see if Man has the same freedom to choose among various alternatives within God's sovereign confines.

PART FOUR

Scriptural Evidence from
the New Testament

Chapter 48

The choices

DOES GOD GIVE MEN free will to decide between options or are they restricted to the one and only path foreknown/decreed in eternity past? "Live as free people, but do not use your freedom as a cover-up for evil" (1 Pet 2:16 NIV). Are men free to do good or to commit evil? Is the principle that "Man has free will within God's sovereign boundaries" exemplified in the New Testament? Do we live within the "boundaries of freedom"?

ROCK OR SAND.

Christ, in the Sermon on the Mount, gave his audience the choice to build on a strong or weak foundation. "Therefore, everyone who hears these words of mine, and acts on them, may be compared to a wise man who built his house on the rock . . . And everyone who hears these words of mine, and does not act on them, will be like a foolish man who built his house on the sand" (Matt 7:24, 26). The sovereign Lord's pronouncements are not open to negotiation. The list of those who are blessed (i.e., the Beatitudes, Matt 5:3–11) is complete and not susceptible to future amendments. The commands given in the Sermon on the Mount are explicit (e.g., "love your enemies," "you cannot serve God and mammon"). The consequences of one's actions are inevitable. Obedience brings blessings and safety. "And the rain fell, and the floods came, and the winds blew and slammed against that house; and yet it did not fall, for it had been founded on the rock" (Matt 7:25). Disobedience brings disaster. "The rain fell, and the floods came, and the winds blew and slammed against that house; and it fell— and great was its fall" (Matt 7:27). Thus, the people of God have a decision to make. "Why do you call me, 'Lord,

Lord,' and do not do what I say?" (Luke 6:46). In the New Testament as in the Old, we are free to obey or disobey God's commands and live with the consequences, whether good (i.e., rock) or evil (i.e., sand). No one is forced to follow the Lord.

One of the theological questions raised in our discussion of God's sovereignty and Man's free will is whether God ever changes his mind. We read in the Sermon on the Mount, "You have heard" or "It was said" (in the Old Testament), "but I say to you" (in the New Testament).[1] Did the Lord "change his mind" when he saw that the Old Testament edicts were not adequate and therefore had to come up with a new set of rules in the New Testament? Did the Lord come up with a "better" plan since the previous scheme failed? Paul said that "we are not under law but under grace" (Rom 6:15). Are we no longer obligated to keep the commandments in the Old Testament Law? Why then did our Lord say, "Do not think that I came to abolish the Law or the Prophets; I did not come to abolish but to fulfill. For truly I say to you, until heaven and earth pass away, *not the smallest letter or stroke shall pass from the Law*" (Matt 5:17–18)?

Paul explained the problem using an analogy. The Old Testament Law acted like a tutor (Greek "paidagogos," "a *legally appointed overseer*, authorized to train (bring) up a child by administering discipline, chastisement, and instruction, i.e., doing what was necessary to promote development").[2] "But now that faith has come, we are no longer under a tutor" (Gal 3:25). For example, a tutor trains a five-year-old child by giving him a simple rule: "Do not eat cookies before dinner!" However, does a father give that same direction to his adult son? Obviously not! The father would give the guideline "Eat healthily!" for that is the actual principle underlying the more elementary "law." The precept "Eat healthily!" covers a multitude of rules such as "Do not eat unwashed vegetables," "Do not eat fatty foods," "Do not eat with dirty hands." Is the tutor right in admonishing the child, "Do not eat cookies before dinner"? Of course! "So then, the Law is holy, and the commandment is holy and righteous and good" (Rom 7:12). However, since the child is now an adult, he needs to know, from his father and not the tutor, the *underlying principle* of the rules. "When I was a child, I used to speak like a child, think like a child, reason like a child; when I became a man, I did away with childish

---

1. Matt 5:21–22, 5:27–28, 5:31–32, 5:33–34, 5:38–39, 5:43–44.

2. http://biblehub.com/greek/3807.htm

things" (1 Cor 13:11). Thus, our Lord, in the Sermon on the Mount, gave the underlying principles of the previous Old Testament rules while affirming the Law's validity.

The Old Testament requires "circumcision of the flesh" to separate/ differentiate God's people from the other nations around them. This is something easy to understand and not too difficult to follow, especially if the "procedure" is done on the eighth day after birth (thus, no memory of the "traumatic" experience). Is "circumcision of the flesh" a good thing? Of course! The American Academy of Pediatrics[3] in 2012 and the Centers for Disease Control (CDC) in 2014 affirmed its health benefits.[4] However, the underlying principle is the "circumcision of the heart." "But he is a Jew who is one inwardly; and circumcision is that which is of the heart, by the Spirit, not by the letter" (Rom 2:29). This principle of "circumcision of the heart" is much higher and much more difficult to follow than the rule/law of "circumcision of the flesh" which can be done to any baby boy. Thus, the New Testament principle encompasses the Old Testament law, broadens, fulfills but does not abolish it. The differentiation and separation of God's people from the rest of the world are still necessary. "Therefore, come out from their midst and be separate" (2 Cor 6:17).

The Old Testament orders the consumption of only "clean" foods (e.g., no pig, hare, or camel). The reasons for this diet are variously thought to be health related,[5] culture related,[6] or possibly other issues.[7] Eating "clean" food is good and holy. However, the underlying principle is not just "no unclean food in," but it is also "no unclean speech out." "Do you not understand that everything that goes into the mouth passes into the stomach, and is eliminated? But the things that proceed out of the mouth come from the heart, and those defile the man. For out of the heart come evil thoughts, murders, adulteries, fornications, thefts, false

3. Blank et al., "Circumcision Policy Statement," 585.

4. CDC, Department of Health and Human Services. "Recommendation for Providers Counseling Male Patients and Parents Regarding Male Circumcision and the Prevention of HIV Infection, STIs, and Other Health Outcomes." www.scribd.com/document/248978688/CDC-proposal-on-male-circumcision-December-2-2014#scribd

5. Winnail, "Bible Health Laws," March-April 2004.

6. Biblical Archaeology Society, "Making Sense of Kosher Laws," 2017. www.biblicalarchaeology.org/daily/ancient-cultures/daily-life-and-practice/ making-sense-of-kosher-laws/

7. Key and Allen, "The Levitical Dietary Laws," 61–64.

witness, slanders" (Matt 15:17–19). This principle of "no unclean speech out" is much more advanced than the law of "no unclean food in" as anyone can eat Kosher foods (and can still choose to do so for religious or other reasons).

The Old Testament commands, "You shall not murder" (Exod 20:13). The New Testament proclaims, "But I say to you that everyone who is angry with his brother shall be guilty before the court" (Matt 5:22). This underlying precept of "no anger" is much deeper than the rule of "no murder."

The Old Testament mandates, "You shall not commit adultery" (Exod 20:14). The New Testament declares, "But I say to you that everyone who looks at a woman with lust for her has already committed adultery with her in his heart" (Matt 5:28). This instruction of "no thought adultery" is much broader than the law of "no physical adultery."

The Old Testament prescribes animal sacrifices for the forgiveness of sins. This is not to say that offerings take away sins "for it is impossible for the blood of bulls and goats to take away sins" (Heb 10:4). "We know that sin offerings were shadows of the real sacrifice for sin, Jesus Christ (Heb 10:1–3). Now that the real sacrifice for sin has been made, the physical symbolism does not need to be reenacted."[8]

What then is the New Testament underlying principle corresponding to the Old Testament's sacrifice requirements? "One died for all, therefore all died; and he died for all, so that they who live might no longer live for themselves, but for him who died and rose again on their behalf" (2 Cor 5:14–15). "The Christian's life of sacrifice is the logical consequence of Christ's sacrificial death. The Christ who sacrificed himself for the believer is now continuing the sacrifice in the believer's life."[9] The Apostle Paul declared, "I have been crucified with Christ; and it is no longer I who live, but Christ lives in me; and the life which I now live in the flesh I live by faith in the Son of God, who loved me and gave himself up for me" (Gal 2:20). "Therefore, I urge you, brethren, by the mercies of God, to present your bodies a living and holy sacrifice, acceptable to God, which is your spiritual service of worship" (Rom 12:1). This injunction of "a personal living sacrifice/personal crucifixion" in the New Testament is much more profound than the law of "animal sacrifices" in the Old Testament. "If anyone wishes to come after me, he must deny himself, and take

8. Joseph Tkach, "Are Old Testament Laws," lines 29–31.

9. http://www.biblestudytools.com/encyclopedias/isbe/sacrifice-in-the-new-testament-2.html

up his cross daily and follow me" (Luke 9:23). This is a voluntary act as no one is forced to follow Jesus! However, if we choose to be a Christ's follower, we *must* deny ourselves and take up our cross daily. God's sovereign boundaries and requirements are firm and non-negotiable.[10] As it was for ancient Israel, the free will decision to obey or disobey is ours to make!

Thus, the Lord did not "change his mind" in the New Testament. He did not try to improve on his Law by canceling the old, "non-workable" rules and initiate some "new" requirements. The underlying principles have always been there, just not communicated due to the maturity level of the listeners and the lack of the Helper, the Holy Spirit, in the lives of the believers. In the New Testament period, with the power of the Holy Spirit, the believer is able to keep Christ's commandments as expressed in the New Testament teachings. "You will receive power when the Holy Spirit has come upon you" (Acts 1:8). Since the people of God are now considered to be "mature," and no longer under a tutor, much more is expected of them (i.e., obey the underlying principles). Thus, the elementary rules of the Old Testament have been raised to the lofty requirements of the New Testament Law, the "Law of Liberty." Nevertheless, the Lord's expectation is the same, as obedience to the commandments is the desired goal. "But one who looks intently at the perfect law, the law of liberty, and abides by it, not having become a forgetful hearer but an effectual doer, this man will be blessed in what he does" (Jas 1:25).

Christ's commandments are expressed clearly in the Sermon on the *Mount*, the counterpart of the Mosaic Law given on *Mount* Sinai. Fully apprised of the consequences of their actions (building on rock or sand), God's people now have a free will choice to make (i.e., obey or disobey). No one is "doomed" to sin and evil by God's foreknowledge/decree. Whatever option Man chooses, he will have to bear full responsibility for the outcome. This is not to say that grace and mercy will not be available to God's children. Mistakes, if made, may not be final, as abundantly shown by the Lord's dealings with his people in the Old Testament. "But you, O Lord, are a God merciful and gracious, slow to anger and abundant in lovingkindness and truth" (Ps 86:15).

---

10. Christ does not give the option to "come after him" and yet not "deny oneself." Man's choices are limited within the Lord's predetermined boundaries!

CHRIST OR SELF.

"If anyone comes to me and does not hate his own father and mother and wife and children and brothers and sisters, yes, and even his own life, he cannot be my disciple" (Luke 14:26). Christ gives his audience a free will choice between options. One can choose to be "all in" or one can choose to be "all out." "I know your deeds, that you are neither cold nor hot; I wish that you were cold or hot. So, because you are lukewarm, and neither hot nor cold, I will spit you out of my mouth" (Rev 3:15–16). The lukewarm, "halfway" approach, if stubbornly taken, would result in a worse outcome than the other two choices.

"He who has found his life shall lose it, and he who has lost his life for my sake shall find it" (Matt 10:39). The "all in" option (Christ first and foremost, "crucified with Christ," "take up one's cross daily," "lose one's life for his sake") will result in finding life. The "all out" option (me only, no Christ) will result in a "lost life." However, in this path, one could try to revel in the pleasures of this world without having to worry about God (e.g., Hugh Hefner). The "lukewarm" approach would prevent a full enjoyment of this realm (e.g., having to go to church on Sunday rather than sleeping in) without the benefit of an abundant life in the world to come ("I will spit you out of my mouth"). With the options and outcomes clearly defined, the people are thus well-informed and have complete freedom to decide. No one is held captive to serve God. The option to leave is always open. "As a result of this many of his disciples withdrew and were not walking with him anymore. So, Jesus said to the twelve, "You do not want to go away also, do you?" (John 6:66–67).

FIRST OR LAST.

Jesus understands that, as fallen human beings, we always want to be first. In his wisdom, he does not chastise us for desiring such a position.[11] He merely shows us how to attain our goal. "If anyone wants to be first,[12] he

11. Jesus affirmed that some people would sit in the honored positions on his right and on his left (Matt 20:23).

12. "If any man desire to be first; to have the pre-eminence and be in the chief place in the kingdom of the Messiah, the same shall be last of all, and servant of all." Gill's Exposition of the Entire Bible. "God is a God of order, not of confusion; there can be no order without a first as well as a last." Matthew Poole's Commentary. https://biblehub.com/commentaries/mark/9-35.htm

shall be last of all and servant of all" (Mark 9:35). Jesus gives his followers a free will choice. One can be first in this world and last in the next or one can be last in this world and first in the next. Up is down and down is up. First is last and last is first.[13]

Paul made his free will choice. "For though I am free from all men, I have made myself a slave to all" (1 Cor 9:19). Demas elected to quit. "For Demas, having loved this present world, has deserted me and gone to Thessalonica" (2 Tim 4:10). Ananias and Sapphira chose their paths and went to their deaths (Acts 5). Mark left Paul and suffered the consequences. "Paul kept insisting that they should not take him (Mark) along who had deserted them" (Acts 15:38). Mark later made the choice to return to the work and became "useful to me (Paul) for service" (2 Tim 4:11). Thus, men are given opportunities to repent as mistakes, if made, may not be final.

In summary, we have the free will to build on rock or sand, to seek Christ or self, to be first or last in this world. These options are available to us within the sovereign Lord's predetermined boundaries. In his mercy, we are also given a "sneak preview" of what would happen in each path (life or death, blessings or calamities). The choice is ours to make!

However, this is not to say that we are *always* given options. Cancers come uninvited and without the possibility of "opting out." Layoffs happen unexpectedly and without recourse. Innocent children are injured without warning in drunk driving accidents. Why does God allow these events in our lives? The answers may lie in the account of Peter's denials, and to that we will now turn.

---

13. This is not necessarily a matter of actual position. It is more of a matter of the heart and motives. For example, although he was an apostle of Christ, Paul considers himself "the worst of sinners," and "a servant to all."

Chapter 49

Peter's denials

WAS PETER FREE NOT to deny Christ? The answer had to be no since Christ prophesied that Peter would deny him (Luke 22:34). Why did Christ decree such a drastic step? Did Christ give Peter fair warnings before taking such a strong measure? What did Christ intend to accomplish with Peter?

After Jesus' transfiguration, the twelve disciples argued about who among them was the greatest. Jesus used the example of a child to show them that "he who is least among you, this is the one who is great" (Luke 9:48). Unfortunately, the disciples did not learn the lesson as James, John, and their mother went to Jesus to ask for the two top spots in the kingdom. "Command that in your kingdom these two sons of mine may sit, one on your right and one on your left" (Matt 20:21). This blatant approach to grab the "plum" appointments caused dissension among the twelve. "And hearing this, the ten became indignant at the two brothers" (Matt 20:24). Jesus had to admonish them, repeating what he had said before, "Whoever wishes to become great among you shall be your servant" (Matt 20:26). Jesus did not rebuke James and John for wanting the chief assignments. On the contrary, on hearing (and believing) their declaration of loyalty ("We are able" Matt 20:22), he granted them a great privilege, "My cup you shall drink" (i.e., share in Christ's suffering, 1 Pet 4:13). Although Jesus did not guarantee the brothers their exalted positions, the special favor of "sharing his cup" went a long way toward that goal. Very likely, had they asked, that prerogative would have been available to the other disciples.

Sadly, the teaching about servanthood was still not learned at the Last Supper. "And there arose also a dispute among them as to which one of them was regarded to be greatest" (Luke 22:24). Peter insisted that he was willing to lay down his life for Christ (and therefore was the greatest?). Jesus revealed that "Satan has demanded permission to sift you (plural, meaning all the disciples) like wheat" (Luke 22:31). And who was the one most at risk for succumbing to Satan's attack? Who was the "weakest link" among the apostles (not counting Judas since Satan had already entered him)? Who was the one who needed Jesus' prayer and protection the most? "But I have prayed for you (singular, meaning Peter), that *your faith may not fail*" (Luke 22:32). The one who thought he was the greatest was actually the weakest! "Pride goes before destruction, a haughty spirit before a fall" (Prov 16:18 NIV).

God allowed Satan to tempt Peter as a remedial *disciplinary* action for his *disciple*.[1] Thus, the Lord did not act capriciously, unfairly, and without reason. To cure him of his boastful pride, Christ decreed Peter's three denials during the Last Supper. "I say to you, Peter, *the rooster will not crow today* until you have denied three times that you know me" (Luke 22:34). Peter needed the strong medicine as he had not learned much about himself and his future task as an under-shepherd! In his mercy, Christ also assured Peter that after his foreordained fall, he would be restored to usefulness in the church. "And you, when once you have turned again, strengthen your brothers" (Luke 22:32).

After supper, Jesus and the eleven disciples "went out to the Mount of Olives. And Jesus said to them, you will all fall away, because it is written, 'I will strike down the shepherd, and the sheep shall be scattered' . . . But Peter said to him, 'Even though all may fall away, yet I will not.' And Jesus said to him, 'Truly I say to you, that this very night, before a rooster crows *twice*, you yourself will deny me three times'" (Mark 14:26–30). Obviously, Peter had learned nothing from Christ's previous declaration that he would deny his Lord three times. He still insisted that Christ was wrong in his assessment of him! Thus, the Lord had to apply further discipline, namely another set of three denials.[2]

The first prophecy was given during the Last Supper, foretelling three denials prior to *any* cock crowing (Luke 22:34 and John 13:38). The second prophecy was given on the way to the Mount of Olives, predicting another three denials "before a rooster crows *twice*" (Mark 14:30). Thus,

1. "Discipline comes from discipulus, the Latin word for pupil, which also provided the source of the word disciple." www.merriam-webster.com/dictionary/discipline. Thus, should we be surprised that Christ would discipline his followers?

2. Cheney, *The Life of Christ in Stereo,* 218–20.

the order of denials and cock crowing would be: three denials, a cock first crowed, three more denials, then the cock crowed a second time. Could we find six denials in the Scriptures?

Peter was at Annas's house (John 18:13). He was challenged by a slave-girl door-keeper and denied Christ (first denial, John 18:17). While he was "standing and warming himself" by a charcoal fire, Peter was questioned by some "slaves and officers" and denied Christ (second denial, John 18:18, 25). He was then confronted by a relative of Malchus (the servant whose ear was cut off by Peter) and denied Christ (third denial, John 18:27). "And immediately a cock crowed" (John 18:27). The first three denials happened in Annas's courtyard.[3] These events were only recorded in John.

Subsequently Jesus was taken to Caiaphas's house (Matt 26:57, Mark 14:53, Luke 22:54, and John 18:24). Peter followed and was "sitting" by a fire in Caiaphas's courtyard when he was accosted by a servant-girl and denied Christ (fourth denial, Matt 26:70, Mark 14:68, and Luke 22:57). He was then scrutinized by another servant-girl at the gateway and denied Christ (fifth denial, Matt 26:71-72, Mark 14:69-70, and Luke 22:58). Finally, after about an hour, he was challenged by some bystanders and denied Christ (sixth denial, Matt 26:73-74, Mark 14:70-71, and Luke 22:59-60). "And immediately, a cock crowed a second time" (Mark 14:72a). "And the Lord turned and looked at Peter" (Luke 22:61). Caiaphas's men were probably taking Jesus from the house out into the courtyard. "And Peter remembered how Jesus had made the remark to him, 'Before a cock crows twice, you will deny me three times'" (Mark 14:72b). "And he went outside and wept bitterly" (Luke 22:62).

As prophesied by Jesus, Peter repented and was restored. We can observe that exchange in John 21:15-17. "Jesus said to Simon Peter, 'Simon, son of John, do you love me more than these?'" (i.e., more than the other disciples).[4] Did Peter learn his lesson? Did he still believe that he was

---

3. John 18:19-24 related the confrontation inside Annas's house. Annas sent Jesus to Caiaphas only *after* the interrogation (John 18:24). The events in the courtyard were recounted in John 18:15-18 followed by John 18:25-27 as shown by the connecting statement, "Peter was standing and warming himself" appearing in *both* John 18:18 and John 18:25. John first related the events in the courtyard. He then described what happened inside the house. He resumed with further accounts in the courtyard. Thus, the three denials described by John were in Annas's courtyard. John neither recorded Peter's three denials at Caiaphas's house nor mentioned Jesus' inquest by Caiaphas.

4. Ellicott's Commentary for English Readers. http://biblehub.com/commentaries/john/21-15.htm

the greatest among the disciples, the one who loved Jesus the most? "He said to him, 'Yes, Lord; you know that I love you.'" Wisely, Peter removed the "more than these" from his answer. Three times, the Lord asked the question and three times Peter responded in the affirmative.[5]

The Lord then gave Peter a commission (repeated three times for emphasis) to care for his lambs and sheep, responsibility which Peter willingly accepted. The Lord's strong discipline rehabilitated Peter and cured his boastful pride, allowing him to start on his ministry to the church. Was he totally free of the tendency to compare himself with others? You be the judge! "Very truly I tell you (Peter), when you were younger you dressed yourself and went where you wanted; but when you are old you will stretch out your hands, and someone else will dress you and lead you where you do not want to go . . . When Peter saw him (John), he asked, 'Lord, what about him?' Jesus answered, 'If I want him to remain alive until I return, what is that to you?'" (John 21:18, 21–22 NIV).

The omniscient Lord knows when to apply discipline and when to forbear with our weaknesses. He decides whether to give us free will choices or to withhold options, lest we destroy ourselves. In his great wisdom, the sovereign Lord guides events of this fallen and evil world toward the fulfillment of his plans and promises to his people. "To the only wise God, through Jesus Christ, be the glory forever. Amen." (Rom 16:27).

"Evil" events (e.g., cancer, layoffs, car accidents) may happen in our lives by God's design (e.g., for the purpose of edification, discipline, deterrence, or rehabilitation). However, we can trust our heavenly Father that "all things work together for good to those who love God" (Rom 8:28) and that his plans are "for welfare and not for calamity to give you

---

5. Much has been made of the use of agape and phileo in the three questions and answers (agape/phileo, agape/phileo and phileo/phileo). "The change is not accidental; and once more we have evidence of the accuracy of the writer . . . Peter's preference for *philein* is doubly intelligible: (1) it is the less exalted word; he is sure of the natural affection which it expresses; he will say nothing about the higher love implied in *agapan*; (2) it is the warmer word; there is a calm discrimination implied in *agapan* which to him seems cold. In the third question Christ takes him at his own standard." Cambridge Bible for Schools and Colleges. http://biblehub.com/commentaries/john/21-15.htm. However, D. A. Carson commented: "Some expositions of these verses turn on the distribution of the two different verbs for "love" that appear . . . This will not do . . . The two verbs are used interchangeably in this Gospel. . . The Evangelist constantly uses minor variations for stylistic reasons of his own." Carson, *The Gospel According to John*, 676–77.

a future and a hope" (Jer 29:11). Can we affirm this principle in Paul's shipwreck?

Chapter 50

Paul's shipwreck

AFTER HIS ARREST IN Jerusalem, Paul was sent to Rome with some other prisoners to stand trial before Caesar. "When considerable time had passed, and the voyage was now dangerous, since even the fast was already over, Paul began to admonish them, and said to them, 'Men, I perceive that the voyage will certainly be with damage and great loss, not only of the cargo and the ship, but also of our lives'" (Acts 27:9–10). Considering that Paul had much sea experience (at least three shipwrecks), he could perceive that traveling in October[1] in these waters would be dangerous. "The tone is clearly that of a man who speaks more from the foresight gained by observation than from a direct supernatural prediction."[2] "But the centurion was more persuaded by the pilot and the captain of the ship than by what was being said by Paul" (Acts 27:11). So, they went, were caught in a harrowing storm, and had to jettison their cargo. God could have prevented them from sailing. However, he gave them the freedom to do what they wanted.

In their despair, Paul spoke up, "An angel of the God to whom I belong and whom I serve stood before me, saying, 'Do not be afraid, Paul; you must stand before Caesar; and behold, God has granted you all those who are sailing with you.'" (Acts 27:23–24). Later, when they neared Malta, "the sailors were trying to escape from the ship and had let down the ship's boat into the sea" (Acts 27:30). Recognizing their intention, "Paul said to the centurion and to the soldiers, 'Unless these men remain in the ship, you yourselves cannot be saved.'" (Acts 27:31).

1. http://www.generationword.com/notes/acts/acts_27_1–44.pdf

2. Ellicott's Commentary for English Readers. http://biblehub.com/commentaries/acts/27-10.htm

How could the Lord *guarantee* the lives of all on board when it appeared that the presence of the sailors on the ship would be *required* for such an outcome? Was God's decree conditional on how the soldiers acted? Did the Lord need Man's cooperation to fulfill his plan? The commentators are divided on the issue.[3] One said, "This does not show that the decree concerning the salvation of them was a conditional one, and that the condition was, that the mariners should stay in the ship."[4] However, another opined, "God, who has promised to save your lives, promises this on the condition that ye make use of every means he has put in your power to help yourselves."[5] A promise contingent on our often dismal performance would probably never be fulfilled. Considering Man's fallibility, things left in human hands might easily go awry and ruin God's designs. For example, would a NASA engineer rely on his five-year-old son to do even 1 percent of the complex calculations needed to bring astronauts back to earth? This is not to say that we should not do our best to carry out our task (e.g., evangelize a city). Unlike Paul in his shipwreck, we are not given any definite promise. Thus, we must work hard and trust the Lord with the results.

When the outcome was guaranteed, God often[6] decreed the means that would accomplish his purpose. For example, when the Lord promised Gideon victory over the Midianites, he also designated the manner (three hundred men rather than thirty-two thousand men) "lest Israel become boastful, saying, 'my own power has delivered me'" (Judg 7:2). God was well-aware that men had the tendency to usurp his glory by inflating their "contribution." When the Lord proclaimed that Jeroboam's altar in Bethel would be desecrated by human bones, he also ordained the process, through a king "born to the house of David, Josiah by name" (1 Kgs 13:2). When he decreed that "this whole land (Judah) shall be a desolation and a horror," he also appointed the agent. "I will send

3. http://biblehub.com/commentaries/acts/27–31.htm

4. Gill's Exposition of the Entire Bible. http://biblehub.com/commentaries/acts/27–31.htm

5. Adam Clarke Commentary. www.studylight.org/commentary/acts/27–31.html

6. God does not *always* decree the means to realize a certain outcome. For example, God wanted his temple built by Solomon and not by David (1 Chr 28). However, the means were left unspecified. David could have chosen to do nothing, something, or most everything (1 Chr 29) to prepare the way for Solomon to build the temple of the Lord.

to Nebuchadnezzar king of Babylon, my servant, and will bring them against this land" (Jer 25: 9).

In Paul's shipwreck, God decreed the outcome (saved lives for all). However, the means he planned to use were not mentioned. Was the actual scenario the *only* possible option within God's predetermined boundaries? After all, did he need the soldiers to prevent the sailors from escaping by cutting the ropes to the boat or could he do it himself (e.g., an "accidental" rupture of the ropes during the bad storm)? God's promise to save all on board was never contingent on Man's performance. Whether God specified the means to accomplish his purposes or not, he never *depended* on men to carry out his plans.

However, in God's love, he occasionally allows us to share in his work so that we may have sweet fellowship with him (that is why I would let my toddlers "help" me around the house when I could do the chores faster, better, and safer without them). If we do anything "for God," we have done nothing more than what we ought to have done. "So, you too, when you do all the things which are commanded you, say, 'We are unworthy slaves; we have done only that which we ought to have done.'" (Luke 17:10).

In the shipwreck, God gave men free will to choose among options within his predetermined boundaries (i.e., Paul must survive, Paul must go to Rome). Paul was free to advise caution against sailing late in the season. The pilot and the captain were free to disagree with Paul. The centurion was free to side with Paul or with the captain. Paul was free to pray and ask for the lives of his shipmates. The sailors were free to devise their escape plan. Paul was free to share his suspicions with the centurion. The centurion was free to believe or not believe Paul. The soldiers were free to decide what course of action to take.

For all this freedom, the Lord was still sovereign as he decreed some events to exalt his apostle in the eyes of everyone (and thus preserve his life). Paul's prediction came true when "a violent wind" was sent by God (Acts 27:14). His prayer for the lives of his shipmates was granted (Acts 27:24). The prophecy that they would "run aground on a certain island" was fulfilled (Malta Island, Acts 27:26, Acts 28:1). Paul's suspicion of the sailors was well-founded. His encouragement for all to eat and then jettison the rest of the provisions to lighten the ship was a good move as they were about to hit land and would not need the food. Even though "the soldiers' plan was to kill the prisoners, that none of them should swim away and escape,"[7] the Lord did *not* allow that option. "The centurion, wanting to bring Paul safely through, kept them (the soldiers) from their intention" (Acts 27:42–43). "All were brought safely to land" (Acts 27:44) confirming Paul's prophecy and God's omnipotence.[8]

In his wisdom, the Lord allows Man to make some free will choices within his predetermined boundaries (e.g., to sail or not). Nevertheless, he still guides the events to their foreordained conclusions (e.g., Paul arriving safely in Rome). Man's free will, though real, does not change the events already decreed by God. Thus, the Lord is sovereign, and Man has a measure of free will!

As in the Old Testament, the New Testament clearly shows that free will choices (alternative scenarios within God's predetermined boundaries, the heart of the Quantum Proposal) have always been in effect in God's economy. How should this newfound knowledge impact our lives?

---

7. "The stern code under which Roman soldiers live made them personally responsible for their prisoners. If one prisoner escaped, their lives were forfeit." Phillips, *Exploring Acts*, 513. Concerning Christ's tomb, "the Roman guards had also fled. Since the penalty in Rome for a guard leaving his position was death, we can assume they must have had a substantial reason for fleeing!" Rhodes, *Christ Before the Manger*, 223.

8. We can imagine other scenarios with the same end outcome of safety for Paul. The ship could have stayed at Fair Havens harbor. The soldiers and the prisoners could have disembarked and let the ship sail on without them. The loss of the ship was neither necessary nor required.

PART FIVE

Practical Applications

Chapter 51

How should we then live?

FREEDOM WITHIN GOD'S BOUNDARIES.

IN GOD'S SOVEREIGNTY, WE are free to make choices within God's predetermined boundaries. God's Word, as revealed by the Holy Spirit (since we no longer have prophets, high priests, or apostles to tell us God's will), points us to God's recommended paths in various circumstances of our lives.

For example, we are free to choose whom we want to marry. The Lord's choice for us is not to "be bound together with unbelievers" (2 Cor 6:14). However, we can decide otherwise. Consider these statistics (more anecdotal than rigorously scientific) from Oklahoma, Arkansas, and Kentucky between 1958 and 2010. "We learn that (at least from these three studies) our youth are increasingly marrying non-Christians (55 percent, 73 percent, 85 percent respectively). We also see that the vast majority of our youth who marry non-Christians leave the faith (72 percent, 80 percent, 75 percent respectively). Furthermore, we find that very few who marry non-Christians are ever able to convert their spouses (17 percent, 14 percent, 5 percent). And finally, we learn that these statistics bear out exactly what one would expect them to bear out."[1]

Rick Warren wrote in *The Purpose Driven Life*: "Character development always involves a choice, and temptation provides that opportunity."[2] Though we are free to choose among the options God graciously gives us, we must live with the consequences of ignoring God's word. After all, who knows what is best, the creator or the creature?

1. Higginbotham, "Unacceptable Statistics," lines 21–61.
2. Warren, *The Purpose Driven Life,* 202.

OBEDIENCE BRINGS BLESSINGS, DISOBEDIENCE BRINGS DISCIPLINE.

This principle is as clear in the New Testament as it is in the Old. "For those whom the Lord loves he disciplines, and he scourges every son whom he receives" (Heb 12:6). "Blessed rather are those who hear the word of God and obey it" (Luke 11:28 NIV). If anything, the standards of conduct have been raised in the New Testament, probably because we have the Holy Spirit in us.

For example, the command against physical adultery in the Old Testament has been expanded to include thought adultery in the New Testament. "Everyone who looks at a woman with lust for her has already committed adultery with her in his heart" (Matt 5:28). A 1988 survey of protestant ministers "by *Leadership* magazine found that 12 percent admitted to sexual intercourse outside of marriage, and that 23 percent had done something sexually inappropriate with someone other than their spouse. The researchers also interviewed nearly one thousand subscribers to *Christianity Today* who were not pastors. They found the numbers were nearly double: 45 percent indicated having done something sexually inappropriate and 23 percent having extramarital intercourse."[3] "When asked how often they (the protestant ministers) find themselves fantasizing about sex with someone other than their spouses, 6 percent said daily, 20 percent said weekly, another 35 percent said monthly or a few times a year, while 34 percent said almost never."[4]

The consequences of sexual immorality can be devastating to one's family and ministry. "Can a man take fire in his bosom and his clothes not be burned? Or can a man walk on hot coals and his feet not be scorched? So is the one who goes in to his neighbor's wife; whoever touches her will not go unpunished" (Prov 6:27–29). "Marriage is to be held in honor among all, and the marriage bed is to be undefiled; for fornicators and adulterers God will judge" (Heb 13:4). The newspapers and internet are replete with stories about Christian leaders caught in sexual immorality.[5] However, it does not have to be so. No one is "doomed" to sin and evil!

3. Anderson, "Adultery," lines 30–35.

4. The Editors of *Christianity Today*, "How Common is Pastoral Indiscretion?" http://www.christianitytoday.com/pastors/1988/winter/88l1012.html

5. www.washingtonpost.com/news/acts-of-faith/wp/2018/03/30/in-an-age-of-trump-and-stormy-daniels-evangelical-leaders-face-sex-scandals-of-their-own/?utm_term=.a23586455637

On the contrary, obedience to God's commands brings many blessings. For example, after a long and fruitful ministry, Elisabeth Elliot died in 2015 at the age of eighty-eight. Dr. R. C. Sproul, a lifetime advocate of biblical inerrancy, passed away in 2017 at the age of seventy-eight. After preaching the gospel to more than two hundred million people, Billy Graham went to be with the Lord in 2018 at the age of ninety-nine. "They will still yield fruit in old age; they shall be full of sap and very green" (Ps 92:14).

The Lord's mandate for his people is lofty indeed. "Therefore, you are to be perfect, as your heavenly Father is perfect" (Matt 5:48). Thus, the standard for making God-honoring free will choices is clear. Shall we build our house on the rock or on the sand?

THE MOTIVATION OF LOVE.

Even though it is true that obedience brings blessings and disobedience brings discipline, we should not have the desire for blessings (rewards) or the fear of discipline (punishment) as our sole motivator. "So, you too, when you do all the things which are commanded you, say, 'We are unworthy slaves; we have done only that which we ought to have done'" (Luke 17:10). "There is no fear in love; but perfect love casts out fear, because fear involves punishment, and the one who fears is not perfected in love" (1 John 4:18).

For example, the world's oldest Bible[6], the *Codex Sinaiticus*, was hand written on parchments by at least three scribes.[7] The final work had "over 1,460 pages, each of which measured approximately 41 cm tall and 36 cm wide . . . As is the case with most manuscripts of this antiquity, we do not know either the names of these scribes or the exact place in which they worked."[8] "The transcribing of Sacred Scripture is perhaps the highest form of work that is also prayer, for the monk not only reads the word of God, but allows his word to direct his hand."[9] This incredible labor of love, done in obscurity and anonymity over many long years, is a

6. Some claim that the Codex Vaticanus is older. http://www.oldest.org/religion/bibles/

7. http://www.codexsinaiticus.org/en/codex/production.aspx

8. http://www.bl.uk/onlinegallery/sacredtexts/codexsinai.html

9. http://www.rosarychurch.net/bible/making.html

powerful testimony of the selfless devotion of the scribes and their loving commitment to spread the gospel to the whole world.

Obedience for the sake of rewards is just self-seeking. Obedience for the fear of punishment is merely self-preservation. These are elementary concepts good for a tutor-child relationship. However, as mature Christians with the indwelling Holy Spirit, "we love, because he first loved us" (1 John 4:19), without any thought of reward or recognition.

"THY WILL BE DONE."

Free will choices within God's boundaries are best made with God's counsel (i.e., according to his Word and in prayer). However, once the Lord's advice has been sought, the options often narrow down to two (i.e., obey or disobey). Thus, it is important to ask the question "Am I willing to do whatever God said in his Word?" prior to coming to him for help. "Why do you call me, 'Lord, Lord,' and do not do what I say?" (Luke 6:46). "Therefore, to one who knows the right thing to do and does not do it, to him it is sin" (Jas 4:17).

Dietrich Bonhoeffer said: "It is God's love for us that he not only gives us his Word but also lends us his ear."[10] So, if we have our loving Father's full attention, "let us draw near with confidence to the throne of grace, so that we may receive mercy and find grace to help in time of need" (Heb 4:16). Let us not insist on our free will but rather say, "your will be done, on earth as it is in heaven" (Matt 6:10).

THE FIRST AND THE LAST.

Within God's predetermined boundaries, the last shall be first and the first last. As we make our free will choices, we need to remember that this fallen world is not our home and that we are only pilgrims and strangers here for a short while. Our toils, successes, and failures must be viewed in light of eternity. "For what does it profit a man to gain the whole world, and forfeit his soul? For what will a man give in exchange for his soul?" (Mark 8:36–37). Jim Elliot, one of the missionaries martyred by the Auca Indians, wisely remarked: "He is no fool who gives what he cannot keep to gain what he cannot lose."[11] Am I willing to be the servant of all, "be-

10. Bonhoeffer, *Life Together,* 97.

11. www.brainyquote.com/authors/jim_elliot

come all things to all men, so that I may by all means save some"? (1 Cor 9:22).

TRUST AND OBEY.

If after consulting the Lord's Word and much prayer, we realize that the advantages and disadvantages of the choices facing us are seemingly equal, then we are free to choose whichever one we deem best as they are all within God's boundaries for us. We do not need to agonize and try to determine which one is the "only preordained" option. After all, the Lord is not playing a guessing game with his children. He wants and expects his mature saints to make decisions, applying the advanced principles he has taught them through the Holy Spirit. For example, Peter was free to go anywhere after leaving the jail. The apostle decided to go first to Mark's house and then to "another place" (Acts 12). Furthermore, God can overrule our decisions if necessary. Paul wanted to go preach the gospel in Asia and Bithynia. However, Paul was overruled by the Holy Spirit who forbade him "to speak the word in Asia" and "did not permit them" to go into Bithynia (Acts 16:6–7).

Eric Liddell, the gold medalist of the 1924 Olympic four-hundred-meters race, had the choice of pursuing a track and field career or becoming a missionary. His story and his refusal to compete on Sunday were memorialized in the 1981 Oscar-winning film, *Chariots of Fire*. In 1925, Eric joined the London Missionary Society and went to Northern China. Did he regret the decision to leave the fame of athletics? "It's natural for a chap to think over all that sometimes but I'm glad I'm at the work I'm engaged in now . . . A fellow's life counts for far more at this than the other."[12] Eric died in 1945 as a prisoner in a Japanese internment camp in China. "Whoever loses his life for my sake and the gospel's will save it" (Mark 8:35). God is able to help his children choose the best path among the options given within his prescribed boundaries. We can trust and obey him!

MAKE DISCIPLES OF ALL NATIONS.

As Man is given free will to accept or reject the offer of salvation, evangelism is crucial for "how then will they call on him in whom they have

12. Burnton, "50 Stunning Olympic Moments," lines 130–32.

not believed? How will they believe in him whom they have not heard? And how will they hear without a preacher?" (Rom 10:14). However, God's work must be done God's way. The end never justifies the means. We should not use coercion, "scare tactics," or false promises to obtain converts. What would Jesus do? This is a question that we all need to prayerfully consider and come to some personal conclusions.

Prison Fellowship, an organization started by Charles Colson after his Watergate imprisonment, focuses on the needs of the much-neglected prison population and their families, both during and after incarceration (e.g., the reintegration of sixty-five million people with criminal records[13] into society). "It's also embedded in the American tradition to know we're a nation of second chances . . . We need to unleash that human potential, rather than treat them as less of a human being because of a debt they had to repay."[14] The love of Christ is shown to twenty-six thousand incarcerated men and women per month through the ministry's various programs. The Angel Tree initiative brings Christmas cheers to three hundred thousand children every year.[15] "Therefore, we are ambassadors for Christ, as though God were making an appeal through us; we beg you on behalf of Christ, be reconciled to God" (2 Cor 5:20).

PERSEVERANCE IN TRIALS.

In his wisdom, the sovereign Lord does use "evil" as a tool (in concert with love, mercy, and grace) in the lives of his children. God's purposes may include edification (e.g., Job), punishment (e.g., Israel), deterrence (e.g., Paul's thorn in the flesh), or rehabilitation (e.g., Peter). Regrettably, we cannot say that everything will "work together for good" for everyone. There is a qualifier in Romans 8:28, "to those who love God, to those who are called according to his purpose." For every Joseph (where things "work together for good"), there are many more Zedekiah (murdered children and gouged eyes), Jehoiakim (a donkey's burial), and Demas (desertion for the love of this world). Since Man is given free will by the

13. https://www.nelp.org/wp-content/uploads/2015/03/65_Million_Need_Not _Apply.pdf. Not all people with criminal convictions are sentenced to jail time. Some may receive fines or probation.

14. www.christianitytoday.com/news/2017/march/prison-fellowship-second-chance-month-criminal-justice-refo.html

15. www.prisonfellowship.org/about/

sovereign Lord, he can choose to submit to God's discipline or stubbornly resist God's chastisement "until there was no remedy" (2 Chr 36:16).

John Piper, the famous theologian and author of *Desiring God*, confessed his shortcomings and asked for a leave of absence from his congregation. "I see several species of pride in my soul that, while they may not rise to the level of disqualifying me for ministry, grieve me, and have taken a toll on my relationship with Noel (his wife) and others who are dear to me . . . Since I don't have just one deed to point to, I simply ask for a spirit of forgiveness; and I give you as much assurance as I can that I am not making peace, but war, with my own sins."[16] "If we judged ourselves rightly, we would not be judged" (1 Cor 11:31).[17] "A proper self-examination would save us from the divine judgment."[18] Furthermore, it is imperative not to abuse God's patience and long-suffering for God's judgments, once pronounced (as they are now in his Bible),[19] are irrevocable as God does not change his mind.

Since the Lord is never capricious in his use of evil and as he does everything for good reasons, we should be "quick to listen, slow to speak and slow to anger" (Jas 1:19). The sooner we learn our lessons, the sooner the trials will be over. "In this you greatly rejoice, even though now for a little while, if necessary, you have been distressed by various trials" (1 Pet 1:6). Trials allowed by God in the lives of his children are only "for a little while" and only "if necessary" for the purpose of "teaching, rebuking, correcting and training in righteousness" (2 Tim 3:16 NIV). Therefore, let us persevere "until we all attain to the unity of the faith, and of the knowledge of the Son of God, to a mature man, to the measure of the stature which belongs to the fullness of Christ" (Eph 4:13).

LIVING IN GOD'S PRESENCE.

"An ounce of prevention is worth a pound of cure" (Benjamin Franklin). Although evil cannot be totally avoided in this fallen world, we can limit the frequency or severity of temptation/evil by walking closely with

16. John Piper, "John Piper's Upcoming Leave," lines 11–18.

17. The context is the Lord's Supper but the principle is the same. If we judged ourselves and confessed our sins, we would be forgiven.

18. Vincent's Word Studies. http://biblehub.com/commentaries/1_corinthians/11–31.htm

19. Heb 13:4, 1 Thess 4:6, 1 Cor 11:29–32, Rev 3:15–18.

our Lord. If nothing else, we can lessen the need for his use of the "evil" tool to discipline, deter, or rehabilitate us.[20] Let us be quick to repent and return to a close relationship with him. "If we confess our sins, he is faithful and righteous to forgive us our sins and to cleanse us from all unrighteousness" (1 John 1:9). Let us continue to pray, "do not lead us into temptation but deliver us from evil" (Matt 6:13).

Brother Lawrence, in his classic book, *The Practice of the Presence of God,* said: "Our only business in this life is to please God, and that all besides is but folly and vanity . . . I reflect, on one hand, upon the great favors which God has done, and incessantly continues to do me; and on the other, upon the ill-use I have made of them . . . Let us generously renounce, for the love of him, all that is not himself; he deserves infinitely more. *Let us think of him perpetually.*"[21] By continually living in God's presence, we are protected from evil for "greater is he who is in you than he who is in the world" (1 John 4:4).

LOVE ONE ANOTHER.

While we need to "judge ourselves rightly" and even strictly (for we have the tendency to gloss over our own sins), concerning others, "do not go on passing judgment before the time, but wait until the Lord comes who will both bring to light the things hidden in the darkness and disclose the motives of men's hearts" (1 Cor 4:5). "So then each one of us will give an account of himself to God. Therefore, let us not judge one another anymore, but rather determine this—not to put an obstacle or a stumbling block in a brother's way" (Rom 14:12–13).

Norma had a difficult childhood as a ward of the state. Her father left when she was thirteen; her mother was an alcoholic; her cousin allegedly molested her. She was briefly married at the age of sixteen and had a child, later given for adoption. She became pregnant again and wanted an abortion. The resulting legal controversy ended up at the Supreme Court with the Roe versus Wade ruling. Norma McCorvey (aka Jane Roe) worked at an abortion clinic and lived as a lesbian with her long-time partner. However, in 1995, she was baptized by Flip Benham, an evangelical minister and the national director of Operation Rescue. In 2005, Norma asked the Supreme Court to reconsider its ruling. Unfortunately, the petition was

---

20. God may still use "evil" for our edification.

21. Brother Lawrence, "*The Practice of the Presence,*" 27–28.

denied. Norma joined the Catholic Church and continued to be active in pro-life activities until her death at the age of sixty-nine.[22]

Whether Norma was saved or not, whether she did or did not lose her salvation, these facts are known by God for "the Lord knows those who are his" (2 Tim 2:19). Paul said, "But to me it is a very small thing that I may be examined by you, or by any human court; in fact, I do not even examine myself. For I am conscious of nothing against myself, yet I am not by this acquitted; but the one who examines me is the Lord" (1 Cor 4:3–4). Thus, we should leave the judging to God.

Furthermore, since "we must all appear before the judgment seat of Christ, so that each one may be recompensed for his deeds in the body, according to what he has done, whether good or bad" (2 Cor 5:10), what standard do we want the Lord to use to judge us? A very lenient one or a harsh one? The measure God will use in our judgment in heaven is the same measure we use with others on this earth. "Do not judge, or you too will be judged. For in the same way you judge others, you will be judged, and with the measure you use, it will be measured to you" (Matt 7:1–2 NIV). So, how strict do we want to be with the people around us? While we are in this fallen world with its many heartaches and sufferings, let us follow our Lord's admonition, "As I have loved you, so you must love one another" (John 13:34 NIV).

THE GREATEST COMMANDMENT.

If we believe that we are mature Christians, "a guide to the blind, a light to those who are in darkness, a corrector of the foolish, a teacher of the immature," do we not teach ourselves? (Rom 2:19–21). Do we not read in the Scriptures, "Let not many of you become teachers, my brethren, knowing that as such we will incur a stricter judgment" (Jas 3:1)? Should we run roughshod over other people because we know "better"? "If anyone supposes that he knows anything, he has not yet known as he ought to know" (1 Cor 8:2). With the knowledge of God and of his will comes the responsibility of obedience. "And that slave who knew his master's will and did not get ready or act in accord with his will, will receive many

---

22. www.washingtonpost.com/national/norma-mccorvey-jane-roe-of-roe-v-wade -decision-legalizing-abortion-dies-at-69/2017/02/18/24b83108-396e-11e6-8f7c- d4c723a2becb_story.html?noredirect=on&utm_term=.8d4a8132d6fa

lashes, but the one who did not know it, and committed deeds worthy of a flogging, will receive but few" (Luke 12:47–48).

Thomas à Kempis wrote in his classic devotional, *The Imitation of Christ*: "As soon as you shall yield yourself to God with all your heart, and seek nothing for your own will and pleasure, but place yourself without reserve at his disposal, you shall find yourself united to him, and at peace. Nothing will afford you more joy and satisfaction than the perfect fulfilling of God's will."[23]

Should we not focus first and foremost on our personal walk and pray that we may "love the Lord your God with all your heart, and with all your soul, and with all your mind, and with all your strength" (Mark 12:30)? Is this not the *great and foremost* commandment?

IT IS NEVER TOO LATE!

As we have seen in the Old and New Testaments, mistakes (if made) may not be final. In his mercy, the compassionate Lord often gives his people future free will choices to mend their ways. As it is never too late, as long as one still has life and breath, God stands ready to welcome the prodigal son home no matter what he did (Luke 15:11–32). No one is "doomed" to remain in trespasses and sins.

In 1997, when he was seventy-eight years old, Billy Graham reflected on his long career. Did he have any regrets? "Every day I was absent from my family is gone forever. Although much of that travel was necessary, some of it was not."[24] Recognizing that it was never too late, he cut back on his ministry schedule. "On their 60th wedding anniversary in 2003, Ruth Graham said of their marriage: 'There was some adjusting during the first few years, but it has pretty well adjusted now.' Her husband took a more romantic view: 'We have a better relationship now,' he said. 'We look into each other's eyes and touch each other. It gets better as you get older.'"[25]

Freedom to choose among options is available to the children of God. "For you were called to freedom, brethren; only do not turn your freedom into an opportunity for the flesh, but through love serve one another" (Gal 5:13). "It was for freedom that Christ set us free; therefore,

---

23. Kempis, *The Imitation of Christ*, 348.

24. https://billygraham.org/story/notable-quotes-from-billy-graham/

25. ElHage, "Billy Graham's Legacy," lines 70–72.

keep standing firm and do not be subject again to a yoke of slavery" (Gal 5:1). We can see from these verses that God through Christ gives us freedom to "keep standing firm" and "through love serve one another." Or we can "turn our freedom into an opportunity for the flesh" and "be subject again to a yoke of slavery." In God's sovereignty and wisdom, we are given free will to decide our path within his predetermined boundaries. How should we then live?[26]

26. Schaeffer, *How Should We Then Live?*

Chapter 52

Conclusion

THE QUANTUM PROPOSAL OFFERS a credible solution to the paradox of God's sovereignty and Man's free will. The thesis is strongly supported by countless evidence from the Old and New Testaments and provides answers for the thorniest theological problems that have plagued the church over the centuries.

The Quantum Proposal acknowledges with Calvinism that the Lord foreordains every event. It extends God's decrees to include *non-mutually-exclusive* options within the Lord's predetermined boundaries.

The Quantum Proposal asserts with Arminianism that God's foreknowledge is all-inclusive. It broadens God's foreknowledge to embrace more than one path.

The Quantum Proposal affirms with Molinism that the Lord knows all possible scenarios. It expands God's creative activity to incorporate some alternative choices in this actualized world.

The Quantum Proposal agrees with Open Theism that Man has actual free will choices. However, it upholds God's unrestricted omnipotence, unlimited omniscience, and unchallenged sovereignty.

Is God the Lord of his creation? Assuredly! In his sovereignty, he grants Man a degree of free will within his predetermined boundaries to help Man grow to his greatest potential in this fallen world and develop a unique fellowship with the savior in the world to come. Man can live safely and fruitfully within his God-given "boundaries of freedom" by obeying his benevolent creator.

Does Man's free will to obey or disobey logically require the possibility of disobedience? Undoubtedly yes! Is the fall of Man God's decreed/

foreknown/recommended path? Emphatically no, for our God is a good and loving Lord who eschews sin and evil!

In his omniscience and wisdom, the Lord has prepared a means to redeem Adam's descendants, should Man insist on disobedience. The plan of salvation through our Lord Jesus allows the return of the sons of Adam and the daughters of Eve to a new heaven and a new earth where peace and righteousness will forever reign. Man has made a long and painful detour but will be fully restored to his rightful place in the eternal presence of the Lord.

What shall we do in our few remaining days on this earth? We can freely choose to live for ourselves and insist that our will be done. Or we can heed the Lord's desire for his people and earnestly pray, "Your will be done on earth as it is in heaven." In God's sovereignty, the free will choice is ours, choices we entertain as we consider a quantum leap proposal in the creator's matchless universe!

Appendix

Questions and Answers

HOW DO WE CONTACT THE AUTHOR FOR QUESTIONS OR COMMENTS?

You can contact the author at leethaimd@blogspot.com.

WHY USE THE TITLE THE "QUANTUM" PROPOSAL?

Light in Quantum Mechanics is used as an analogy of Man's free will choices within the sovereign Lord's predetermined boundaries. If God decrees/foreknows infallibly (in the past or timelessly) that Adam will take path two (i.e., disobey), then path two is fixed. If so, Adam has no choice (i.e., "free will"[1] choice). However, if two non-mutually-exclusive paths/choices are created, known by God, and are real[2] (as light is both a

1. "Libertarians typically believe that a free will that is incompatible with determin-ism is required for us to be truly morally responsible for our actions, so that genuine moral responsibility, as well as free will, is incompatible with determinism. Genuine free will, we believe, could not exist in a world that was *completely* determined by Fate or God, or the laws of physics or logic, or heredity and environment, psychological or social conditioning, and so on." Kane, "Libertarianism," 7. Libertarian free will is not universally accepted. See Clarke, "Libertarian Accounts." Also see Carlsson, "Notre Dame Philosophical Reviews."

2. "A dialetheia is a sentence A such that both it and its negation -A are true." Priest et al., line 1. The Quantum Proposal does not advocate that options A and not A are both true at the same time, in the same sense, and *for the same experiencer*. In Jeremiah 38:17–18, God gave Zedekiah a "sneak peek" of the future. Zedekiah-1 (the obedient Zedekiah) surrendered, saved his children from death, and the city from destruction. Zedekiah-2 (the disobedient Zedekiah) refused to surrender, his children were killed,

267

particle and a wave[3] in Quantum Mechanics),[4] then Adam has an actual free will choice between alternatives (e.g., he can choose to experience light as a wave or as a particle). He could have done otherwise than what he did. Since Adam made a free will choice to disobey, God rightfully held him responsible for his action.

ARE THERE PHILOSOPHICAL SOLUTIONS TO THE PROBLEM OF SOVEREIGNTY AND FREE WILL?

The philosophical solutions are summarized in the article "Foreknowledge and Free Will" in the *Stanford Encyclopedia of Philosophy*.[5]

The compatibilist solutions.

The Aristotelian solution "restricts the range of God's knowledge, so it has religious disadvantages in addition to its disadvantages in logic."[6]

The Boethian solution "does not solve the problem of theological fatalism by itself, but since the nature of the timeless realm is elusive, the intuition of the necessity of the timeless realm is probably weaker than the intuition of the necessity of the past. The necessity of the past is deeply embedded in our ordinary intuitions about time; there are no ordinary intuitions about the realm of timelessness."[7]

The Ockhamist solution argues that "God's past beliefs about the future are not strictly past because they are facts that are in part about the future . . . The problem is that God's past beliefs seem to be as good a candidate for something that is strictly past as almost anything we can think of, such as an explosion that occurred last week . . . It is hard to avoid the conclusion that the Ockhamist solution is ad hoc."[8]

The Molinist solution "is neither necessary nor sufficient to avoid theological fatalism by itself."[9]

and the city was burned. Both paths/scenarios were created by God within his predetermined boundaries and were available for Zedekiah to choose.

3. Gray, "Einstein Was Right!" line 1.

4. Laudisa and Rovelli, "Relational Quantum Mechanics."

5. Zagzebski, "Foreknowledge and Free Will."

6. Zagzebski, "Foreknowledge and Free Will," section 2.1

7. Zagzebski, "Foreknowledge and Free Will," section 2.2

8. Zagzebski, "Foreknowledge and Free Will," section 2.3

9. Zagzebski, "Foreknowledge and Free Will," section 2.4

The Frankfurtian solution (using a thought experiment of a special device implanted in a free agent's brain) "is counterfactually manipulative even if it is not actually manipulative. In contrast, infallible foreknowledge is not even counterfactually manipulative. There is no close possible world in which foreknowledge prevents the agent from acting freely."[10]

The incompatibilist solutions.

"The denial of libertarian freedom has always had many supporters . . . Philosophers who deny libertarian freedom may affirm a type of free will compatible with determinism, or they may instead simply accept the consequence that human beings lack free will."[11]

"The other incompatibilist position is to affirm libertarian free will along with the principle of alternative possibilities . . . and to deny the possibility of infallible foreknowledge. This position has recently become well-known in the view called 'open theism.'"[12]

DOES GOD FOREKNOW BECAUSE HE FOREORDAINS, OR DOES HE FOREORDAIN BECAUSE HE FOREKNOWS?

In the Quantum Proposal, God foreknows the scenarios within his pre-determined boundaries because he created them. He foreordains (and thus foreknows) all the events in each path. Thus, he can give people a "sneak peek" of the options prior to their free will choice (e.g., Zedekiah's "way of life" and "way of death").

WHY CAN'T GOD CREATE ADAM WITH FREE WILL AND NO CAPACITY TO SIN?

It is illogical to ask God to create Adam with the free will to obey or disobey and, at the same time, demand no possibility of disobedience (e.g., no sin entering the world).

Believers in heaven cannot disobey (i.e., sin). "Your will be done, on earth as it is in heaven" (Matt 6:10). Jesus never disobeys the Father, and neither will we in heaven as we will be united to him as the bride of

10. Zagzebski, "Foreknowledge and Free Will," section 2.5

11. Zagzebski, "Foreknowledge and Free Will," section 3

12. Zagzebski, "Foreknowledge and Free Will," section 3

Christ. "I do exactly as the Father commanded Me" (John 14:31). The scenario of Man having free will and yet being unable to sin (i.e., heaven) will be discussed in a subsequent book dealing with the problem of evil.

IN THE QUANTUM PROPOSAL, DOES GOD HAVE TWO OR MORE WILLS (E.G., EFFICIENT/PERMISSIVE)?

In the Quantum Proposal, God only has one will.[13] He wants all men to love (i.e., obey, John 14:21) him voluntarily. In his sovereignty, he (sometimes) gives Man limited choices within his predetermined boundaries. However, his will is for man to obey him and take the recommended path.

HOW CAN GOD "PROLONG" A PERSON'S LIFE WHEN HE ALREADY DECREED THE DAY OF HIS DEATH?

The Lord promised Solomon: "If you walk in my ways, keeping my statutes and commandments, as your father David walked, then I will prolong your days" (1 Kgs 3:14). However, Psalm 139:16 said: "Your eyes have seen my unformed substance; and in your book were all written the days that were ordained for me, when as yet there was not one of them." How could God "prolong" Solomon's life when the number of his preordained days was already written in God's book? In the Quantum Proposal, as there are alternative scenarios within God's predetermined boundaries, two (or more) possible outcomes could have been created by the Lord in eternity past. For example, option one could be the obedient path resulting in a "prolonged" life (e.g., one hundred years). Option two could be the disobedient path with a lifespan of eighty years. Solomon had the free will to select the option he desired. Both options included a decreed day of death.

---

13. "No distinction between God's will and God's permission! . . . why shall we say permission unless it is because God so wills?" Calvin, *Institutes,* 3.23.8.

Bibliography

Abasciano, Brian and Martin Glynn, "An Outline of the FACTS of Arminianism vs. the TULIP of Calvinism." evangelicalarminians.org/an-outline-of-the-facts-of-arminianism-vs-the-tulip-of-calvinism/

Adams, Marilyn McCord. *Horrendous Evils and the Goodness of God*. Ithaca: Cornell University Press, 1999.

Alcorn, Randy. *hand in Hand: The Beauty of God's Sovereignty and Meaningful Human Choice*. Colorado Springs: Multnomah, 2014.

Anderson, Kirby. "Adultery." https://bible.org/article/adultery#text6

Aquinas, Thomas. *Summa Theologica*. *https://www.ccel.org/ccel/aquinas/summa.FP_Q19_A7.html*

Arminius, James. *The Works of James Arminius*. Translated by James Nichols and William Nichols. Grand Rapids: Baker, 1991.

Augustine, *Of the Spirit and the Letter*. Translated by Peter Holmes. Chapter 34. www.logoslibrary.org/augustine/spirit/34.html

————. *On Free Choice of the Will*. Translated by Thomas Williams. Indianapolis: Hackett, 1993.

Bailey, Randall. "Elijah and Elisha: The Chariots and Horses of Israel in the Context of ANE Chariot Warfare." www.academia.edu/9114779/Elijah_and_Elisha_The_Chariots_and_Horses_of_Israel_in_the_Context_of_ANE_Warfare

Barlow, Jonathan. "Calvinism." http://www.reformed.org/calvinism/

Barrett, Matthew and Thomas J. Nettles, eds. *Whomever He Wills: A Surprising Display of Sovereign Mercy*. Cape Coral: Founders, 2012.

Barrick, William. "The Openness of God: Does Prayer Change God?" *The Master's Seminary Journal* 12/2 (2001) 149–66.

Barrier, Roger. "Did Judas Have a Choice, or Was He Predestined to Betray Jesus?" https://www.crosswalk.com/church/pastors-or-leadership/ask-roger/did-judas-have-a-choice-or-was-he-predestined-to-betray-jesus.html

Basinger, David and Randall Basinger, eds. *Predestination and Free Will: Four Views of Divine Sovereignty and Human Freedom*. Downers Grove: InterVarsity, 1986.

Beale, G. K. "An Exegetical and Theological Consideration of the Hardening of Pharaoh's Heart in Exodus 4–14 and Romans 9." *Trinity Journal* 5 (1984) 129–54.

Beilby, James and Paul Eddy, eds. *Divine Foreknowledge: Four Views*. Downers Grove: InterVarsity, 2001.

Ben-Yashar, Menahem. "Balak, Balaam, and the G_d of Israel." https://www1.biu.ac.il/indexE.php?id=14608&pt=1&pid=14607&level=0&cPath=43,14206,14375,14607,14608

Berkhof, Louis. *Systematic Theology*. Grand Rapids: Eerdmans, 1941.

Blank, Susan, et al. "Circumcision Policy Statement." *Pediatrics* 130/3 (2012) 585–86. http://pediatrics.aappublications.org/content/pediatrics/130/3/585.full.pdf

Bob, Steven. *Jonah and the Meaning of Our Lives.* Lincoln: University of Nebraska Press, 2016.

Bonhoeffer, Dietrich. *Life Together: The Classic Exploration of Christian in Community.* New York: Harper One, 2009.

Boyd, Gregory. "Ask an Open Theist." http://rachelheldevans.com/blog/ask-open-theist-greg-boyd-response

———. "Five Ways the Bible Supports Open Theism." http://reknew.org/2015/10/5-ways-the-bible-supports-open-theism/

———. *God of the Possible: A Biblical Introduction to the Open View of God.* Grand Rapids: Baker, 2000.

———. "Isn't God Changing His Mind an Anthropomorphism?" http://reknew.org/2008/01/isnt-god-changing-his-mind-an-anthropomorphism

Bullinger, E.W. *Figures of Speech Used in the Bible.* Grand Rapids: Baker, 1968.

Burnton, Simon. *50 Stunning Olympic Moments: No 8 Eric Liddell's 400 Meters Win, 1924.* https://www.theguardian.com/sport/2012/jan/04/50-stunning-olympic-moments-eric-liddell?newsfeed=true

Cahn, Steven. *A New Introduction to Philosophy.* Eugene: Wipf and Stock, 1971.

Calvin, John. *Commentary on Genesis. Vol. 1.* https://www.ccel.org/ccel/calvin/calcom01

———. *Concerning the Eternal Predestination of God.* Louisville: Westminster John Knox, 1997.

———. *Institutes of the Christian Religion.* Peabody: Hendrickson, 2008.

Carlsson, Erik. *Notre Dame Philosophical Reviews,* (2004). https://ndpr.nd.edu/news/libertarian-accounts-of-free-will/

Carson, D.A. *Divine Sovereignty and Human Responsibility: Biblical Perspective in Tension.* Eugene: Wipf & Stock, 2002.

———. *The Gospel According to John.* Grand Rapids: Eerdmans, 1991.

———. *How Long, O Lord: Reflections on Suffering and Evil.* 2nd ed. Grand Rapids: Baker, 2006.

Castellano, Dan J. "Revised Chronology of the Monarchies of Israel and Judah." http://www.arcaneknowledge.org/catholic/kings.htm

Chafer, Lewis. *Systematic Theology (4 volumes).* Grand Rapids: Kregel, 1993.

Cheney, Johnston. *The Life of Christ in Stereo.* Portland: Multnomah, 1969.

Christensen, Scott. *What about Free Will? Reconciling Our Choices with God's Sovereignty.* Phillipsburg: P&R, 2016.

Ciocchi, David. "Reconciling Divine Sovereignty and Human Freedom." *Journal of the Evangelical Theological Society* 37/3 (1994) 395–412.

Clarke, Randolph. *Libertarian Accounts of Free Will.* Oxford: Oxford University Press, 2003.

Cole, Graham. *Engaging with the Holy Spirit: Real Questions, Practical Answers.* Wheaton: Crossway, 2007.

Cottrell, Jack. "The Nature of the Divine Sovereignty." In *The Grace of God, the Will of Man: A Case for Arminianism,* edited by Clark Pinnock, 97–120. Grand Rapids: Zondervan, 1989.

———. "Sovereignty and Free Will," http://www.dabar.org/SemReview/sovfrwill.html

———. *What the Bible Says about God the Creator.* Joplin: College Press, 1983.

———. *What the Bible Says about God the Ruler*. Joplin: College Press, 1984.

———. *What the Bible Says about God the Redeemer*. Joplin: College Press, 1987.

Cox, Dorian Coover. "The Hardening of Pharaoh's Heart in Its Literary and Cultural Contexts." *Bibliotheca Sacra* 163 (2006) 292–311.

Craig, William Lane. "The Middle-Knowledge View." In *Divine Foreknowledge: Four Views*, edited by James Beilby and Paul Eddy, 119–43. Downers Grove: InterVarsity, 2001.

———. "A Molinist View." In *God and the Problem of Evil: Five Views*, edited by Chad Meister and James Dew, 37–55. Downers Grove: InterVarsity, 2017.

———. *The Only Wise God*. Grand Rapids: Baker, 1987.

Critchlow, James. *Looking Back for Jehoiachin: Yahweh's Cast-Out Signet*. Eugene: Wipf & Stock, 2012.

De Caussade, Jean-Pierre. *Abandonment to Divine Providence*. Floyd: Sublime, 2015.

Dembitz, Lewis, and Kaufmann Kohler. "Adoption." http://www.jewishencyclopedia.com/articles/852-adoption

De Molina, Luis. *On Divine Foreknowledge: Part IV of the Concordia*. Translated by Alfred J. Freddoso. Ithaca: Cornell University Press, 1988.

De Sales, Francis. *Introduction to the Devout Life*, edited by W. H. Hutchins. London: Rivingtons, 1882.

Diller, Kevin. "Are Sin and Evil Necessary for a Really Good World?" In *The Problem of Evil: Selected Readings*. 2nd ed. Edited by Michael Peterson, 390–409. Notre Dame: University of Notre Dame Press, 2017.

Dungan, D.R. *Hermeneutics: A Text-Book*. Delight: Gospel Light, 1888.

Edersheim, Alfred. *The Temple: Its Ministry and Services*. New York: Revell, 1881.

Edwards, Jonathan. *The Works of President Edwards Vol II*. New York: Leavitt & Allen, 1852.

ElHage, Alysse. "Billy Graham's Legacy Includes a Loving, Faithful Marriage." https://ifstudies.org/blog/billy-grahams-legacy-includes-a-loving-faithful-marriage

Epperson, Michael. "The Common Sense of Quantum Theory: Exploring the Internal Relational Structure of Self-Organization in Nature." In *Coding as Literacy*, edited by Vera Bühlmann, Ludger Hovestadt, and Vahid Moosavi, 214–35. Basel: Birkhäuser, 2015.

Erickson, Millard. *Christian Theology*. Grand Rapids: Baker, 1985.

Feinberg, John. "God Ordains All Things." In *Predestination and Free Will: Four Views of Divine Sovereignty and Human Freedom*, edited by David Basinger and Randall Basinger, 19–43. Downers Grove: InterVarsity, 1986.

———. *No One like Him: The Doctrine of God*. Wheaton: Crossway, 2006.

———. *The Many Faces of Evil: Theological Systems and the Problem of Evil*. Grand Rapids: Zondervan, 1994.

Fisher, John, Robert Kane, Derk Pereboom, and Manuel Vargas. *Four Views on Free Will*. Malden: Blackwell, 2007.

Foreman, Benjamin. "The Blood of Ahab: Reevaluating Ahab's Death and Elijah's Prophecy." *Journal of the Evangelical Theological Society* 58/2 (2015) 249–64.

Frame, John. *The Doctrine of God*. Phillipsburg: P&R, 2002.

Fruchtenbaum, Arnold G. "Doctrine of Israelology." In *Dictionary of Premillennial Theology: A Practical Guide to the People, Viewpoints, and History of Prophetic Studies*, edited by Mal Couch, 197–203. Grand Rapids: Kregel, 1996.

Gaebelein, Arno. "The Gospel of Matthew. Part 1." http://biblecentre.org/content. php?mode=7&item=94

Geisler, Norman. *Chosen but Free: A Balanced View of God's Sovereignty and Free Will.* 3rd ed. Minneapolis: Bethany, 2010.

———. "God Knows All Things." In *Predestination and Free Will: Four Views of Divine Sovereignty and Human Freedom,* edited by David Basinger and Randall Basinger, 63–84. Downers Grove: InterVarsity, 1986,

———. *Systematic Theology, Vol. 2.* Minneapolis: Bethany, 2003.

———, and Peter Bocchino, *Unshakable Foundations.* Bloomington: Bethany, 2001.

———, and Winfried Corduan. *Philosophy of Religion.* Eugene: Wipf & Stock, 1988.

Gray, Richard. "Einstein Was Right! Light is Captured as a Wave *and* a Particle at the Same Time in First Ever Photograph." http://www.dailymail.co.uk/sciencetech/art icle-2977849/Einstein-RIGHT-Light-captured-wave-particle-time-photograph. html

Grudem, Wayne. *Systematic Theology.* Grand Rapids: Zondervan, 1994.

Gundry, Stanley, and Dennis Jowers, eds. *Four Views on Divine Providence.* Grand Rapids: Zondervan, 2011.

——— and J. Matthew Pinson, eds. *Four Views on Eternal Security.* Grand Rapids: Zondervan, 2002.

Haji, Ishtiyaque, and Justin Caouette, eds. *Free Will and Moral Responsibility.* Newcastle upon Tyne: Cambridge Scholars Publishing, 2013.

Hallesby, O. *Prayer.* Minneapolis: Augsburg Fortress, 1994.

Harless, Hal. *How Firm a Foundation: The Dispensations in the Light of the Divine Covenants.* New York: Peter Lang, 2004.

Harton, George. "The Meaning of 2 Kings 3:27." *Grace Journal* 11(3) (1970) 34–40.

Hasker, William. "An Open Theist View." In *God and the Problem of Evil: Five Views,* edited by Chad Meister and James Dew, 57–76. Downers Grove: InterVarsity, 2017.

———. "Why Simple Foreknowledge Is Still Useless." *Journal of the Evangelical Theological Society* 52/3 (2009) 537–44.

Helm, Paul. "An Augustinian–Calvinist Response." In *Divine Foreknowledge: Four Views,* edited by James Beilby and Paul Eddy, 114–18. Downers Grove: InterVarsity, 2001.

Helseth, Paul. "Response to William Lane Craig." In *Four Views on Divine Providence,* edited by Stanley Gundry and Dennis Jowers, 101–13. Grand Rapids: Zondervan, 2011.

Higginbotham, Steve. "Unacceptable Statistics." http://preachinghelp.org/unacceptable-statistics

Hobbes, Thomas. *Of Liberty and Necessity: A Treatise.* Manchester: Heywood, 1839.

Hodge, Charles. *Systematic Theology (3 volumes).* Peabody: Hendrickson, 1999.

Hoehner, Harold. *Chronological Aspects of the Life of Christ.* Grand Rapids: Zondervan, 1978.

Horn, Siegfried. "The Babylonian Chronicle and the Ancient Calendar of the Kingdom of Judah." *Andrews University Seminary Studies* 5 (1967) 12–27. http:// digitalcommons.andrews.edu/cgi/viewcontent.cgi?article=1051&context=auss

Hume, David. *An Enquiry Concerning Human Understanding.* Withorn: Anodos, 2017.

Hunt, David. *Calvin's Dilemma: God's Sovereignty vs. Man's free will.* Bend: The Berean Call, 2015.

————. "The Simple-Foreknowledge View." In *Divine Foreknowledge: Four Views*, edited by James Beilby and Paul Eddy, 65–103. Downers Grove: InterVarsity, 2001.

Jackson, Kevin. "An Explanation of Simple Foreknowledge." https://wesleyanarminian. wordpress.com/2011/11/23/an-explanation-of-simple-foreknowledge/

Josephus, Flavius. *Antiquities of the Jews.* http://www.perseus.tufts.edu/hopper/ text?doc=J.%20AJ

Jowers, Dennis. "Open Theism: Its Nature, History, and Limitations." *Western Reformed Seminary Journal* 12/1 (2005) 1–9.

Kane, Robert. "Introduction: The Contours of Contemporary Free-Will Debates (Part 2)." In *The Oxford Handbook of Free Will.* 2nd ed. Edited by Robert Kane, 3–37. Oxford: Oxford University Press, 2011.

————. "Libertarianism," in *Four Views on Free Will*, 5–43. Malden: Blackwell, 2007.

Keathley, Kenneth. *Salvation and Sovereignty: A Molinist Approach.* Nashville: B&H, 2010.

Keller, Timothy. *Prayer, Experiencing Awe and Intimacy with God.* New York: Penguin, 2016.

Kempis, Thomas à. *The Imitation of Christ.* Sydney: ReadHowYouWant, 2006.

Key, Thomas, and Robert Allen. "The Levitical Dietary Laws in the Light of Modern Science." *Journal of the American Scientific Affiliation* 26 (1974) 61–64.

Kraus, C. Norman. *Jesus Christ Our Lord: Christology from a Disciple's Perspective.* Revised Edition. Eugene: Wipf & Stock, 2004.

Kreeft, Peter. *The Problem of Evil.* http://www.peterkreeft.com/topics/evil.htm

Laudisa, Federico, and Carlo Rovelli. "Relational Quantum Mechanics." *The Stanford Encyclopedia of Philosophy* (Summer 2013 Edition), Edward N. Zalta (ed.) https:// plato.stanford.edu/entries/qm-relational/

Lawrence, Brother. *The Practice of the Presence of God.* Nashville: Thomas Nelson, 1999.

Leibniz, Gottfried. *Leibniz Selections,* edited by Philip Wiener. New York: Charles Scribner's Sons, 1951.

Litwak, Kenneth. "The Use of Quotations from Isaiah 52:13–53:12 in the New Testament." *Journal of the Evangelical Theological Society* 26/4 (1983) 385–94.

Luther, Martin. "On the Bondage of the Will," in *Luther and Erasmus: Free Will and Salvation,* edited by E. Gordon Rupp and Philip S. Watson. Louisville: Westminster John Knox, 1969.

Lutzer, Erwin. *The Doctrines That Divide: A Fresh Look at the Doctrines That Separate Christians.* Grand Rapids: Kregel, 1998.

MacArthur, John. *The Gospel According to Jesus.* Revised edition. Grand Rapids, Zondervan, 1994.

Madison, Lucy. "Richard Mourdock: Even Pregnancy from Rape Something 'God Intended.'" www.cbsnews.com/news/richard-mourdock-even-pregnancy-from-rape-something-god-intended/

Maidman, Paul. *Nuzi Texts and Their Uses as Historical Evidence.* Atlanta: Society of Biblical Literature, 2010.

Mariottini, Claude. "The Seven Prophetesses of the Old Testament." https://claude mariottini.com/2013/12/16/the-seven-prophetesses-of-the-old-testament/

Meister, Chad and James Dew, eds. *God and the Problem of Evil: Five Views.* Downers Grove: InterVarsity, 2017.

Meyers, Carol, and Eric Meyers. *Zechariah 9–14.* New York: Doubleday, 1993.

Nogalski, James D. *The Book of the Twelve and Beyond: Collected Essays of James D. Nogalski.* Atlanta: Society of Biblical Literature, 2017.

O'Connor, Timothy. "Free Will." *The Stanford Encyclopedia of Philosophy* (Summer 2016 edition), Edward N. Malta, (ed.), https://plato.stanford.edu/archives/sum2016/entries/freewill/

Oden, Thomas. *Classic Christianity: A Systematic Theology.* New York: Harper, 2009.

Olson, Roger. *Arminian Theology: Myths and Realities.* Downers Grove: InterVarsity, 2006.

Oord, Thomas Jay. "The Essential Kenosis Response." In *God and the Problem of Evil,* edited by Chad Meister and James Dew. Downers Grove: InterVarsity, 2017.

Origen. *The Writings of Origen, vol 1.* London: Hamilton, 1869.

Packer, J. I. *Evangelism and the Sovereignty of God.* Downers Grove: InterVarsity, 1961.

Pentecost, J. D. *Things to Come: A Study in Biblical Eschatology.* Grand Rapids: Zondervan, 1965.

Peterson, Robert and Michael Williams. *Why I Am Not an Arminian.* Downers Grove: InterVarsity, 2004.

Phillips, John. *Exploring Acts: An Expository Commentary.* Grand Rapids: Kregel, 1986.

Pink, A. W. *The Sovereignty of God.* Blacksburg: Wilder, 2008.

Pinnock, Clark. "God Limits His Knowledge." In *Predestination and Free Will: Four Views of Divine Sovereignty and Human Freedom,* edited by David Basinger and Randall Basinger, 143–62. Downers Grove: InterVarsity, 1986.

———. *Most Moved Mover: A Theology of God's Openness.* Grand Rapids: Baker, 2001.

Pinson, J. Matthew, ed. *Four Views on Eternal Security.* Grand Rapids: Zondervan, 2002.

Piper, John. "The Agonizing Problem of the Assurance of Salvation." https://www.desiringgod.org/articles/the-agonizing-problem-of-the-assurance-of-salvation

———. "John Piper's Upcoming Leave." https://www.desiringgod.org/articles/john-pipers-upcoming-leave

Plantinga, Alvin. *God, Freedom and Evil.* Grand Rapids: Eerdmans, 1973.

———. "Supralapsarianism, or 'O Felix Culpa.'" In *The Problem of Evil: Selected Reading.* 2nd ed. Edited by Michael Peterson, 363–89. Notre Dame: University of Notre Dame Press, 2017.

Priest, Graham, Francesco Berto, and Zach Weber. "Dialetheism." *The Stanford Encyclopedia of Philosophy* (Fall 2018 Edition), Edward N. Zalta (ed.), forthcoming URL = <https://plato.stanford.edu/archives/fall2018/entries/dialetheism/>.

Prinsloo, G. T. M. "A Contextual and Intertextual Reading of Psalm 118." *Old Testament Essays* 16/2 (2003) 401–21.

Reed, Jonathan. *Archaeology and the Galilean Jesus: A Re-examination of the Evidence.* Harrisburg: Trinity, 2000.

Reichenbach, Bruce. *Divine Providence.* Eugene: Cascade, 2016.

———. "God Limits His Power." In *Predestination and Free Will: Four Views of Divine Sovereignty and Human Freedom,* edited by David Basinger and Randall Basinger, 101–24. Downers Grove: InterVarsity, 1986.

Rhodes, Ron. *Christ Before the Manger: The Life and Times of the Preincarnate Christ.* Eugene: Wipf and Stock, 2002.

Rice, Richard. *The Openness of God: The Relationship of Divine Foreknowledge and Human Free Will.* Minneapolis: Bethany, 1980.

Riddle, J. E. *A Manual of the Whole Scripture History and of the History of the Jews.* London: Longman, 1857.

Rogers, Austin. "Calvinism, Arminianism, and Open Theism." https://godsoloved.wordpress.com/2010/04/17/calvinism-arminianism-and-open-theism/

Ryrie, Charles. *Basic Theology*. Wheaton: Victor, 1986.

Sanders, John. *The God Who Risks: A Theology of Providence*. 2nd ed. Downers Grove: InterVarsity, 2007.

———. "The Key Ideas of Openness Theology." http://drjohnsanders.com/open-theism/

———. "Why Simple Foreknowledge Offers No More Providential Control than the Openness of God." *Faith and Philosophy* 14/1 (1997) 26–40.

Schaeffer, Francis. *How Should We Then Live? The Rise and Decline of Western Thought and Culture*. Wheaton: Crossway, 2005.

Simons, Geoff. *Iraq from Sumer to Saddam*. 2nd ed. London: MacMillan, 1996.

Spiegel, James. *The Benefits of Providence: A New Look at Divine Sovereignty*. Wheaton: Crossway, 2005.

Sproul, R. C. *Chosen by God*. Carol Stream: Tyndale, 1986.

———. "Double Predestination." http://www.ligonier.org/learn/articles/double-predestination/

———. *Now, That's a Good Question!* Carol Stream: Tyndale, 1996.

———. *Willing to Believe: The Controversy over Free Will*. Grand Rapids: Baker, 2002.

Standish, Colin, and Russell Standish. *The Evangelical Dilemma*. Rapidan: Hartland, 1994.

Stefanovic, Zdravko. *Daniel: Wisdom to the Wise. Commentary on the Book of Daniel*. Nampa: Pacific, 2007.

Strauss, Mark. *Four Portraits, One Jesus*. Grand Rapids: Zondervan, 2007.

Stump, Eleonore. "Review of Peter Van Inwagen, *God, Knowledge, and Mystery*." *Philosophical Review* 106 (1997) 464–67.

Tanner, J. Paul. "Is Daniel's Seventy-Weeks Prophecy Messianic? Part 1." *Bibliotheca Sacra*, 166 (2009) 181–200.

Thiessen, Henry. *Lectures in Systematic Theology*. Revised by Vernon Doerksen. Grand Rapids: Eerdmans, 1979.

Timpe, Kevin. "Free Will." *Internet Encyclopedia of Philosophy*. https://www.iep.utm.edu/freewill/

Tkach, Joseph. "Are Old Testament Laws Still Binding on Christians?" https://www.gci.org/law/otlaws

Toussaint, Stanley. "A Critique of the Preterist View of the Olivet Discourse." *Bibliotheca Sacra* 161 (2004) 469–90.

Trakakis, Nick. "The Evidential Problem of Evil." *The Internet Encyclopedia of Philosophy*, http://www.iep.utm.edu/evil-evi/

Voss, Peter. "The Nature of Free Will." optimal.org/voss/freewill.html

Walls, Jerry and Joseph Dongell. *Why I Am Not a Calvinist*. Downers Grove: InterVarsity, 2004.

Ware, Bruce. *God's Lesser Glory: The Diminished God of Open Theism*. Wheaton: Crossway, 2000.

Warren, Rick. *The Purpose Driven Life*. Grand Rapids: Zondervan, 2002.

Williams, Thaddeus. *Love, Freedom, and Evil: Does Authentic Love Require Free Will?* New York: Rodopi, 2011.

Winnail, Douglas S. "Bible Health Laws." *Tomorrow's World*, March-April 2004. https://www.tomorrowsworld.org/magazines/2004/march-april/bible-health-laws

Yancey, Philip. *Prayer, Does It Make Any Difference?* Grand Rapids: Zondervan, 2006.

Zagzebski, Linda. "Foreknowledge and Free Will." *The Stanford Encyclopedia of Philosophy* (Summer 2017 Edition), Edward N. Zalta (ed.), https://plato.stanford.edu/entries/free-will-foreknowledge/

Name and Subject Index

Scripture Index

GENESIS

2:7	139
2:9	15
2:17	139
2:24	140
3:1	139
3:3	140
3:4	139
3:5	139
3:6	139n1, 140, 141
3:14	140
3:17	103
3:21	141
4:7	60n7, 69
6:6–7	18n14
6:17	139
6:22	75
12	142
12:2	48
12:16	142
12:17	142
12:20	143
13:11	182
15	88n32
15:13–16	88n32
17:19	74
18	156, 157
18:6	156
18:10	156
18:25	25
19:8	157
19:24	104
20:2	143
20:5–6	143
20:7	143
20:12	142
20:17	143
22:17	120
24	157
24:67	156
28:20–21	115
32:10	115
39:9	76
41	101
48:5	150n1, 221n6
49	118, 119
49:10	159

EXODUS

1:10	88
1:11	88
1:16	89
2	157
2:15	145
3:11	145
3:13	145
3:20	89
4:1	145
4:10	145
4:13	145
4:14	145, 145n1
4:21	86
4:27	145
7:3	86
7:7	146
7:13	86
7:14	86